REA

Politics and Theory

This ground-breaking book is the first to take post-colonial theory out of its literary confines and apply it to the complexities and dynamics of post-colonial African politics. Pal Ahluwalia contends that post-colonial theory has marginalised a huge part of its constituency, namely Africa. Moreover, he argues that if post-colonial theory is to have any major and lasting effect within social and political theory, it needs to engage with matters overtly political.

Eurocentric theory has failed to understand post-colonial Africa: *Politics and Post-colonial Theory* traces how African identity has been constituted and reconstituted by examining movements such as negritude and the rise of nationalism and decolonisation. The book questions how helpful post-colonial analysis can be in understanding the complexities which define institutions such as the nation-state, civil society, human rights and citizenship. Finally, the book examines the relevance of globalisation to post-colonialism, as well as Africa, and looks at the ways in which Africa and Africans are now reconstituting their identity in order to meet the challenges of everyday life. It illustrates how Africa and Africans transform and inflect the institutions inherited as a result of colonialism.

Politics and Post-colonial Theory bravely breaks down disciplinary boundaries. Its radical vision will be essential reading for all those engaged in post-colonial studies, African studies, literary theory and in the political and social sciences in general.

Pal Ahluwalia teaches Politics at the University of Adelaide. He has written extensively on African politics and post-colonial theory. He recently co-authored *Edward Said: The Paradox of Identity*, also published by Routledge.

Politics and Post-colonial Theory

African inflections

Pal Ahluwalia

London and New York

First published 2001
by Routledge
11 New Fetter Lane, London EC4P 4EE

Simultaneously published in the USA and Canada
by Routledge
29 West 35th Street, New York, NY 10001

Routledge is an imprint of the Taylor & Francis Group

Typeset in Baskerville by Taylor & Francis Books Ltd
Printed and bound in Great Britain by TJ International Ltd,
Padstow, Cornwall

British Library Cataloguing in Publication Data
A catalogue record for this book is available from the British Library

Library of Congress Cataloging in Publication Data
Ahluwalia, D.P.S. (D. Pal S.)
Politics and post-colonial theory: African inflections/Pal Ahluwalia.
Includes bibliographical references and index.
1. Africa–Politics and government–1960– 2. Democratization–Africa.
3. Postcolonialism–Africa. 4. Postcolonialism. I. Title.

JQ1879.A15 A384   2000
320.96–dc21   00-062571

ISBN 0–415–23746–7 (hbk)
ISBN 0–415–24750–0 (pbk)

For Babaji, Bhai Sahib Bhai Mohinder Singh Ji
For giving me the opportunity to be part of his world

Contents

Acknowledgements   *ix*

Introduction   1
Post-colonialism, post-structuralism and postmodernism 1
Post-colonialism and Africa 8
Post-colonialism beyond literary studies 14
Scope and organisation 18

1 'Negritude and nativism': in search of identity   20
Senghor's negritude 23
Césaire's negritude 27
Critiques of negritude 30
Conclusion 32

2 Decolonisation and national liberation   34
Frantz Fanon: the oppressed consciousness of the colonised 39
Edward Said and resistance 43
Fanon and Said: a strategy towards liberation 49
Conclusion 50

3 Modernity and the problem of the nation-state   52
The crisis of the African state 53
African studies and the conceptualisation of the African state 55
Post-colonialism, modernity and the African state 66
Conclusion 71

4 Striving for democratisation: the complexities of civil
   society and human rights   73
   The rise of authoritarian rule 74
   African perspectives on 'good governance' 76
   The centrality of civil society 77
   Human rights in Africa 86
   The African Charter of Rights 92
   Conclusion 95

5 Citizenship, subjectivity and the crisis of modernity   97
   Citizen and subject: the argument 98
   Problems with the Mamdani thesis 102
   The complexities of citizenship and subjectivity 105
   Citizenship and subjectivity: post-colonial reflections 108
   Conclusion 112

6 Globalisation and post-colonialism: towards the
   reconstitution of identity   113
   Culture and globalisation 117
   Post-colonialism and globalisation 122
   Globalisation and inflections 124
   Conclusion 130

7 Afterword   132

   Notes   *136*
   Works cited   *142*
   Index   *158*

Acknowledgements

This book is an outgrowth of my engagement with post-colonial theory and my commitment to Africa. The book owes a great deal to the generosity of friends, family and institutions, whom I am grateful to acknowledge. Bill Ashcroft has provided me with sustained encouragement, warmth and intellectual support. I am deeply indebted to colleagues at the University of Adelaide and, in particular, Paul Nursey-Bray and Peter Burns whose constant support and faith in me has been invaluable. A large part of this book was written whilst I was on special studies leave, and I wish to thank Jeff Steeves of the University of Saskatchewan, who has always been much more than a mentor to me, for hosting my visit to Saskatoon. I am also extremely grateful to Mahmood Mamdani for his very useful comments on the chapter on citizenship. I am thankful to Abebe Zegeye and Julia Maxted, who invited me to South Africa where I gained much from lively discussion. Their friendship and support is greatly appreciated. I also wish to thank Parama Roy and the critical theory workshop at the University of California, Riverside, for inviting me and giving me much-needed feedback. As always, Sue Ahluwalia read, commented on and made this a much better book. Many thanks are extended to Chris McElhinney and Tina Esca in the Politics Office at the University of Adelaide, who, as always, provided phenomenal support. I am indebted to Craig Fowlie as well as Milon Nagi at Routledge for their ongoing support in this project. Thanks are extended also to the University of Adelaide ARC scheme as well as the ARCHSS teaching release fellowship which provided the institutional support necessary for this project.

Thanks and love are extended to my family in California and Oxford who have sustained me in more than a physical way on my numerous visits. Many thanks to my parents, Harcharan and Balbir, my brother and sister-in-law, Moni and Bhapo, and my uncle and aunt in Oxford, Satinder and Sawinder, whose love I can never repay. My deepest and loving acknowledgements are to my wife Sue, who is not only my best friend but my most ardent supporter, and my son Kultar, whose love sustains me in all my endeavours.

Introduction

The terms 'post-colonial', 'post-coloniality' and 'post-colonialism' evoke responses in both the metropole and the periphery. In both locations, there is much debate and discontent about the manner in which the term has entered the lexicon of colonial and post-colonial discourse. The debate ranges from whether 'post-colonial' should be hyphenated to the very legitimacy of the term as well as its currency in the academy.

Post-colonial theory is subject not only to critique and challenge from the outside but also from within. There is little agreement about its disciplinary boundaries or its political implications. Such debate and discontent may signal, for some, a crisis in post-colonial theory. On the contrary, as we begin the new millennium and the processes of globalisation intensify, it is important to view such developments in post-colonial theory positively, as part of its vibrancy at the very time when other 'post'-isms are being read increasingly as part of the dominant and hegemonic tradition of Western theory. This book is concerned with exploring the post-colonial predicaments which the nation-states of Africa have endured and continue to experience. It is, at its core, about understanding the dilemmas of modernisation and the manner in which African states negotiate their way through complexities that have grown out of the colonial experience.

Post-colonial theory has been characterised as being epistemologically indebted to both post-structuralism and postmodernism. Such a reading denigrates the authenticity of post-colonial theory and renders it subservient and theoretically vulnerable to charges levelled at post-structuralism and postmodernism. This book seeks to challenge such assumptions and assertions. It seeks to clarify and explain the need to differentiate between post-colonialism and other 'post' phenomena.

Post-colonialism, post-structuralism and postmodernism

Despite such protestations regarding post-colonialism, there is considerable agreement that Edward Said's pioneering work, in his now celebrated *Orientalism*, inaugurated the field of colonial discourse analysis which ultimately led to the development of post-colonial theory. Said's *Orientalism* is a theoretical marriage between the post-structuralism of Michael Foucault and Antonio Gramsci's Marxism (Ashcroft and Ahluwalia, 1999). Although Said has subsequently moved on theoretically and jettisoned Foucault's methodology, post-colonialism remains beleaguered by charges that it is a by-product of post-structuralism and postmodernism.

The debate surrounding the relationship between post-structuralism, post-modernism and post-colonialism is now highly developed. There are a host of critics, such as Linda Hutcheon, Arif Dirlik and Aijaz Ahmad, who have a tendency to conflate these 'post' -isms. This conflation is made possible because of the many concerns which are shared by the different 'posts' under considera-tion. As Linda Hutcheon has noted despite the differing definitions of the 'posts', what most theorists share is, 'their common oppositional grounding in – or, rather, against – what has been generalised and usually demonized into this thing called "modernity" ' (Hutcheon 1994: 205).

The common lamenting of modernity by these 'post' -isms arises from their position as critiques of the failure of the Enlightenment tradition 'to construct autonomous subjects who are capable of overcoming their alienation by reconciling their "authentic" subjectivity against that of the "other" through the master narratives of identity formation' (McLaren 1991: 8). These common concerns have meant also that the language of post-colonial theorists and those of both post-structuralism and postmodernism is similar. This leaves post-colonialism open to the charge that it is essentially a discourse of Third World intellectuals who operate from within their privileged position in the First World. Arif Dirlik goes so far as to claim that post-colonialism is 'a child of post-modernism' (Dirlik 1994: 348). Dirlik's critique rests on the subservience of post-colonialism to postmodernism and is in the same vein as Frederic Jameson's view of the relationship between postmodernism and developments within late capitalism. Dirlik argues that post-colonialism is a progeny of postmodernism and that this can be observed in the manner in which post-colonial critics acknowledge their debt to both postmodernist and post-structuralist thinking. This allows Dirlik to conclude that the most original contribution of post-colonial critics 'would seem to lie in their rephrasing of older problems in the study of the Third World in the language of post-structuralism' (*ibid.*: 352).

By conflating the 'post' -isms, Dirlik is able to argue that post-coloniality is appealing in the West primarily because post-coloniality 'disguises the power relations that shape a seemingly shapeless world and contributes to a conceptu-alization of that world that both consolidates and subverts possibilities of resistance' (*ibid.*: 356).

Aijaz Ahmad shares Dirlik's sentiments, declaring that the East 'seems to have become, yet again, a *career* – even for the "Oriental" this time, and within the "Occident" too' (Ahmad 1992: 94).[1] Ahmad argues that post-colonial theory merely re-inscribes the very forms of domination which it seeks to deconstruct. This is necessarily so, Ahmad argues, because post-colonial critics 'had themselves been influenced mainly by poststructuralism' (*ibid.*: 68). Ahmad's most trenchant criticism is made in a recent article in *Race and Class*, where he claims that post-colonialism is the progeny of postmodernism:

> the term 'postcolonial' also comes to us as the name of a *discourse* about the condition of 'postcoloniality', so that certain *kinds* of critics are 'postcolonial' and others not .... the rest of us, who do not accept this apocalyptic anti-Marxism, are not postcolonial at all ... so that only those intellectuals can be truly *postcolonial* who are also *postmodern*.
>
> (Ahmad 1995a: 10)

The commonly-held view which associates and conflates postmodernism and post-colonialism is sophisticated, particularly in the case of Linda Hutcheon. Hutcheon argues that there is a great deal of overlap in 'their concerns: formal, thematic, strategic' (Hutcheon 1989: 151). She sees similarities in the manner in which tropes such as irony are used as common discursive strategies. Hence, she argues:

> The post-*colonial* is therefore as implicated in that which it challenges as is the post*modern* .... the post-colonial has at its disposal various ways of subverting from within the dominant culture – such as irony, allegory, and self-reflexivity – that it shares with the complicitous critique of postmodernism ....
>
> (Hutcheon 1989: 170–1)

The postmodern connection is made all the more explicit in the case of Vijay Mishra and Bob Hodge, who argue that the major Australian post-colonial work, *The Empire Writes Back*, is really postmodern. For them, this version of post-colonialism is postmodern primarily because of the place of settler colonies within the post-colonial space. They argue that, 'the project of *EWB* is essentially postmodernism .... The central problematic arises out of the status of settler cultures, and their place in this unified field. The "justifying" discourse which allows this settler incorporation into post-colonialism is clearly postmodernism' (Mishra and Hodge 1993: 36).

For Anne McClintock, the relationship between the 'post' -isms is more of a marketing strategy, whereby post-colonialism appears to be riding on the postmodern bandwagon. She views the post-colonial turn as a disciplinary trend which legitimises Third World studies in the West, making them more palatable and less threatening than previous incarnations. She argues that the 'term borrows, moreover, on the dazzling marketing success of the term "post-modernism". As the organizing rubric of an emerging field of disciplinary studies and an archive of knowledge, the term "post-colonialism" makes possible the marketing of a whole new generation of panels, articles, books and courses' (McClintock 1992: 11). Robert Young also has a tendency to conflate the 'post' -isms, albeit while recognising that post-colonialism is not simply 'a marginal adjunct to more mainstream studies'. For Young, it is the politics of post-structuralism which 'forces the recognition that all knowledge may be variously contaminated, implicated in its very formal or "objective" structures' (Young 1990: 11).

It is important to note the position articulated by Ashcroft *et al.* (1995), who point out that the confusion is caused because a key aspect of postmodernism is the deconstruction of the logocentric meta-narratives of European culture, which is much like the post-colonial project of breaking down the binaries of imperial discourse. For them, the conflation between the post-colonialism and postmodernism arises because of their shared concerns, such as the 'decentring of discourse, the focus on the significance of language and writing in the construction of experience, the use of subversive strategies of mimicry, parody and irony' (*ibid.*: 117).

The linkages between post-colonialism and post-structuralism as well as postmodernism have a tendency to become blurred when the post-colonial is not tied to a specific geographical space but refers to marginalised groups in a particular society. The use of the post-colonial as an oppositional stance has the effect of shifting the focus from locations and institutions to individuals and subjectivities (Loomba 1998: 17). It is this shift which is seen to be complicit with the other 'post' phenomena. The term post-colonial then is one which needs to be used with careful consideration, taking into account the specific historical processes and the manner in which colonialism has affected a particular colony. For, nowhere was colonialism itself monolithic. It was carried out differentially, depending upon the particular circumstances prevailing in any given colony. In a similar way, post-colonialism cannot be seen to be an all-encompassing term. Rather, post-colonialism embodies the effects of colonialism, whilst recognising the specificity of each case in which it is deployed.

It is not my purpose here to enter into a debate to refute the various claims which the conflation between the 'post' -isms has produced in the various authors. Rather, it is necessary to illustrate that this is the manner in which post-colonialism has come to be accepted. And, yet, even the acceptability of the term post-colonial evokes criticism. Ella Shohat argues that such acceptability 'serves to keep at bay more sharply political terms such as "imperialism" or "geopolitics" ' (1993: 99). The implication of her argument is that post-colonial is a more palatable term, primarily because it does not have the obvious connotations of exploitation and dependency which have characterised relations between the metropole and the periphery. A great deal of difficulty is caused by the term post-colonial itself. This arises due to the confusion that post-colonial does not mean after colonialism. The 'post', nevertheless, is suggestive of something that comes after, and it is this that critics find problematic. It is this that forces Shohat to question 'when exactly, then, does the "postcolonial" begin?' (*ibid.*: 103).

The difficulty for Shohat is that the term has a tendency to universalise the experiences of all colonised peoples. The idea that the historical experiences of white settler colonies such as those in Canada, Australia and New Zealand can be equated with the harsh and bitter realities of a colonialism which was based upon economic exploitation and cultural denigration in India, Uganda and

Senegal is one that many critics find hard to swallow. And yet, within those white settler colonies are indigenous peoples who have suffered in much the same way as their Third World counterparts. In addition, for example, the white settlers in the 'Dominion' colonies of Canada, Australia and New Zealand themselves were considered as being culturally inferior. As Edward Said points out, the works of Australian writers such as Robert Hughes and Paul Carter 'reveal a vast history of speculation about and experience of Australia, a "white" colony like Ireland, in which we can locate Magwitch and Dickens not as mere coincidental references in that history, but as participants in it, through the novel and through a much older and wider experience between England and its overseas territories' (1993a: xvi).

The centrality of colonisation is one that Aijaz Ahmad finds problematic because 'periodising our history in the triadic terms pre-colonial, colonial and post-colonial ... privileges as primary the role of colonialism as the principle of structuration in that history, so that all that came before colonialism becomes its own prehistory and whatever comes after can only be lived as infinite aftermath' (1995b: 6–7). This problem is addressed also by Anne McClintock, who points out that at the time when the formal age of empire has ended 'colonialism returns at the moment of its disappearance' (1992: 2). Furthermore, McClintock is troubled by the implication that colonialism, and more importantly neo-colonialism, are no longer existent. But to take such a position is to view colonialism from a very narrow perspective. For Said, the colonised have expanded to include, regardless of geographical location, 'women, subjugated and oppressed classes, national minorities, and even marginalized or incorpo-rated academic subspecialties' (1989: 207).

R. Radhakrishnan asks the question 'why is it that the term "postcoloniality" has found such urgent currency in the First World but is in fact hardly ever used within the excolonized worlds of South Asia and Africa?' (1993: 750). His question is reminiscent of Dirlik's attack that post-colonialism is a legitimising discourse for Third World intellectuals located in the First World. For Dirlik, the answer is simple – it is due to the manner in which post-colonialism has adopted the central premises 'such as the repudiation of post-Enlightenment metanarra-tives [which] were enunciated first in post-structuralist thinking and the various postmodernisms it has informed' (1994: 336). However, what critics such as Dirlik fail to point out is the importance of the post-colonial critique of postmodernism, which centres on the latter's denial of subjectivity, an option not available to post-colonial cultures who have been marginalised and thus seek a space from where they can be heard.

A particularly helpful intervention in the debate over what is the post-colonial is that by Gyan Prakash. The current theoretical impasse that the Left finds itself in is a result of the debunking of dependency analysis, world-systems theory and deterministic Marxian analysis. It is in the aftermath of this theoretical impasse that post-colonialism emerges. It recognises that globalisation is a complex process which 'produces new global forms of unevenness, inequality, difference and discrimination' (Prakash 1996: 199). It is therefore a strategic response to contemporary globalisation. Stuart Hall has pointed out that the concept of the 'post-colonial' may be helpful in capturing the shift between 'the age of Empires to the post-independence or post-decolonisation moment. It may also help us … to identify what are the new relations and dispositions of power which are emerging in the new conjecture' (1996: 246). Prakash's conception of post-coloniality entails the breaking down of binaries around the oppositional stances to colonialism and challenges assertions that post-colonialism fails to deal with the challenges of global capitalism. For Prakash, post-coloniality

> signifies a critical realignment of colonial power and knowledge. It is to evoke the immanent nature of its reinscriptive position that elsewhere I have referred to postcoloniality as an aftermath, as an after – as a location formed in the fragile functioning of colonialism. Postcoloniality in this sense does not represent either the transcendence or the reversal of colonialism, and it sidesteps the language of beginnings and ends. Containing a link to the experience of colonialism, but not contained by it, postcoloniality can be thought of as a form of realignment that emerges in *media res* [sic], critically undoing and redrawing colonialism's contingent boundaries.
>
> (Prakash 1996: 188–9)

By conceiving post-colonialism along these lines, it is possible to differentiate between post-colonialism and postmodernism. The former is a counter-discourse which seeks to disrupt the 'cultural hegemony of the modern West with all its imperial structures of feeling and knowledge, whereas postmodernism is primarily a counter-discourse against modernism that emerges within modernism itself' (Xie 1996: 164). It is important to note also the antipathy which Edward Said has towards post-structuralism and postmodernism for not being affiliated to the world (Ashcroft and Ahluwalia, 1999). For Said, theory can be effective only when it is located firmly within the world. He attacks theory which fails to do so on the grounds that, for such theory

> there seems to be no contact with the world of events and societies, which modern history, intellectuals, and critics have in fact built. Instead, contemporary criticism is an institution for publicly affirming the values of our, that is, European, dominant elite culture, and for privately setting loose the unrestrained interpretation of a universe defined in advance as the endless misreading of a misinterpretation. The result has been the regulated, not to say calculated, irrelevance of criticism …
>
> (Said 1983: 25)

In her recent intervention, Leela Ghandi (1998) points out that post-colonialism has a dialectic relationship between Marxism and post-structuralism/postmodernism. It is necessarily so because of the articulation of contemporary post-colonial theory with past Marxist accounts and narratives. This dialectic relationship is a modification of the point that Adebayo Williams makes that, 'postcolonialism is the dialectical mirror-image of postmodernism' (1997: 824). For Ghandi, post-colonial theory is locked into addressing the needs of the Western academy, and, as such, that is its main constituency. She maintains that the task for post-colonialism is to, 'diversify its mode of address and learn to speak more adequately to the world which it speaks for. And, in turn, that it acquire the capacity to facilitate a democratic colloquium between the antagonistic inheritors of the colonial aftermath' (1998: x).

It is in this spirit that Samir Dayal (1996) has argued that post-colonialism needs to mark its distance from postmodernism. The notions of progress and rationality which underpin European modernity are precisely what the Third World needs to avoid. Dayal argues that it is imperative for those subjects politically and psychologically marginalised 'in the global cultural economy to emancipate himself or herself from that myth of progress by conceptualizing his or her culture in terms of happy rather than vicious repetition' (*ibid.*: 120).

Although there are distinct differences between the colonies, as well as within a particular colony, what is clear is that the processes of colonisation fundamentally have altered and affected their future course of history. It is not possible to recover some pristine, 'pure' pre-colonial culture, because colonialism has an irreversible rupturing effect. It has the effect of producing a different culture which is a product of amalgamation and evolution. Although certain critics see colonialism as a minor part of a long and complex history, what they fail to see is that the very course of history is altered by the colonial process. In this way, Ania Loomba argues that 'it is more helpful to think of post-colonialism not just as coming literally after colonialism and signalling its demise, but more flexibly as the contestation of colonial domination and the legacies of colonialism' (1998: 12).

In *Culture and Imperialism*, Edward Said points to the manner in which the world has come to be located firmly within the West's orbit. This can be discerned in the land it has occupied in the last two centuries: from 1800, when it controlled 35 per cent of the earth's surface, to 1914, when it held 85 per cent (1993a: 6). This explosion of European dominance and the age of empire, coupled with the massive movement of peoples since the advent of both the slave trade and indentured labour, as well as the mass migrations of the twentieth century, mean that post-colonial identities and locations are now highly intertwined, intermixed and complex. It is not surprising therefore that Gayatri Spivak proclaims that, 'We live in a post-colonial neo-colonialized world' (1990: 166). What Spivak appears to signal is that neo-colonialism is not the same as colonialism, and that the processes of neo-colonialism are not confined to nation-state boundaries.

The problem of European modernity is one with which post-colonial theory seeks to engage, particularly in terms of its emphasis on progress. This emphasis has necessitated that the engagement between Europe and its 'others' is predicated on violence. It is pertinent to question why such an engagement causes such angst. Is it because post-colonial theory seeks to break down the disciplinary boundaries which have defined relations between the First and the

Third World? The former, through its ideas of progress and superiority, has dictated terms on which the latter has had to operate in order to be considered legitimate. It is the task of post-colonialism to confront the existence of difference, to bring together theory from both sides of the imperial divide and to make it relevant to the conditions that exist for all those who endure the post-colonial condition, regardless of their geographical location. It is a task which Spivak captures in her essay, 'Poststructuralism, Marginality, Postcoloniality and Value' which is 'about the difference and the relationship between academic and "revolutionary" practices in the interest of social change' (1996: 219).

The radical and critical edge which post-colonial theory embodies is to a large extent due to its continual decentring from both within and without. This continual questioning of the very boundaries of post-colonialism is what energises the field of study. As Kalpana Seshadri-Crooks points out, 'it is this shapelessness, this refusal to stay still, to define itself, or defend itself, that makes postcolonial studies a particularly hospitable interstice from which to work out the paradoxes of history (the temporality of modernity) and the colony (imperialism and nationalism)' (1995: 67). It is this vibrancy of post-colonialism that helps inform the importance of a post-colonial perspective on Africa.

Post-colonialism and Africa

Kwame Anthony Appiah is one of the first to examine post-colonialism and Africa. For him, the 'post' in post-colonialism certainly is different from that in postmodernism. The post-colonial is the 'space clearing gesture' (1997: 432). This gesture can be discerned in his discussion of the two stages of African writing. The first stage can be encapsulated in novels which were part of the struggle for independence and were nationalist in orientation. The second stage is the post-colonial stage, where the nation is not celebrated but where novels are engaged in a process of delegitimation,

> rejecting the Western imperium ... but also rejecting the nationalist project of the postcolonial national bourgeoisie. And, so it seems to me, the basis for that project of delegitimation is very much not the postmodernist one: rather, it is grounded in an appeal to an ethical universal; indeed, it is based, as intellectual responses to oppression in Africa largely are based, in an appeal to a certain simple respect for human suffering, a fundamental revolt against the endless misery of the last thirty years.
>
> (Appiah 1997: 435)

It is against this background that Appiah tries to make sense of the post-coloniality of contemporary African culture which, he argues, has been commodified for consumption in the West. In this context, he asserts that:

> Postcoloniality is the condition of what we might ungenerously call a *compra-dor* intelligentsia: of a relatively small, Western-style, Western trained group

of writers and thinkers who mediate the trade in cultural commodities of world capitalism at the periphery. In the West they are known through the Africa they offer; their compatriots know them both through the West they present to Africa and through an Africa they have invented for the world, for each other, and for Africa.

(Appiah 1997: 432)

If, for Appiah, post-coloniality is about elites and their mediation in the trade of African cultural commodities, for Adebayo Williams a key problem with post-colonialism has been its failure to infuse 'an authentic and well sustained African input into the paradigm' (1997: 831). Given that post-colonial theory has argued vigorously against the idea of authenticity on the grounds that there are no pure cultures, that cultures continually make and remake themselves, it is difficult to ascertain what an 'authentic' African input might include. Nevertheless, Williams correctly points out that a large slice of the post-colonial constituency – Africa – has been rendered curiously silent in recent post-colonial formulations. He suggests that there could be three reasons for this omission. The first could be that African scholars are not capable intellectually to deal with the theoretical formulations of post-colonial debates. The second possibility is that the general economic crisis within African universities means that they are at a considerable disadvantage. The third reason could be that the specific colonial experience of Africa has meant that the African condition has been theorised in a different manner (*ibid.*: 831). Williams points out that the first two of his speculations are not sustainable, given that the crisis in tertiary education in Africa has 'created a diasporic intelligentsia' who have shown that they can hold their 'own in all the major institutions of learning in the Western world' (*ibid.*: 831). To this, it is important to add that, despite the economic and political tribulations faced by African scholars, they have continued none the less to persevere and to produce some of the most important works on Africa.

It is important, however, to reflect on the third possibility which Williams offers. For him, a different trajectory can be traced in the manner in which intellectual traditions in India and Africa developed. The implication of this suggestion is that post-colonialism is associated unequivocally with India. The intellectual tradition in India, he claims, grew out of the feudal aristocracy, whereas in the case of Africa the new emerging elite had no 'blood ties to the tribal chieftains' (*ibid.*: 831). The subaltern studies project is traced through such a trajectory, albeit that it is inflected with a 'nativised Marxism'. It is these differences which allow for the centrality of colonialism in the case of India and neo-colonialism in the case of Africa. He argues:

Thus, while the doctrine of postcolonialism is informed by a buoyant optimism that colonialism has, in the main, been supplanted, the credo of neo-colonialism is suffused with the profound pessimism that colonialism has merely been transformed into a new and potentially far more devastating form of colonisation. Postcolonialism is marked by a virtual decoupling of the original postcolonial critic from the parent nation-state. The irony does not end here. While the postcolonial state in the Indian subcontinent – at least in India – has created something new, a uniquely Indian political culture despite its foibles, the postcolonial state in Africa, has, by and large, suffered serious reverses, often leading to the phenomenon of failed states.

(Williams 1997: 833–4)

I have quoted Williams at length to illustrate his complete misreading of the contemporary debates within post-colonial studies. Not only is post-colonialism not Indian-centric, as he would have us believe, but it is a term which was inaugurated with the publication of, *The Empire Writes Back*, a volume produced by Australian academics (Ashcroft *et al.* 1989). It is important to reflect on the origins of post-colonialism from its Australian location. It is not surprising that these authors were Australian. Whilst Australia can be seen as a white settler colony with all the pretensions of a regional power, nevertheless, it has endured a colonial past. Its relationship with the South Pacific and its indigenous population has meant at times that it has usurped the role of coloniser. And yet, it is undeniably a post-colonial nation seeking to come to terms with its own identity. It is a country full of ambivalence as it seeks to identify its own culture. These cultural machinations, as well as the mass migrations of people from all parts of the world, have problematised Australia's status as a 'white' colony. In addition, its geographical location means that it is very much part of an African-Asian nexus. Thus, despite the obvious difficulties in conflating the experiences of any one colony with another, the writers of *The Empire Writes Back* were able to produce and inaugurate the term post-colonial primarily because of their location and the colonial experience which they share with other Commonwealth nations – experiences which have been portrayed in Commonwealth literature. It is a process that Said captures when he points out that, 'One of imperialism's achievements was to bring the world closer together and, although in the process the separation between European's and natives was an insidious and fundamentally unjust one, most of us should now regard the historical experience of empire as a common one' (1993a: xxiv).

Far from seeing post-colonialism as having supplanted colonialism, as Williams argues, it is clear that post-colonial theory recognises that colonialism is an ongoing process which necessarily factors in Nkrumah's important work on neo-colonialism. It is certainly part of Robert Young's call of responsibility when he argues that the 'burden of neocolonialism remains for all those who suffer its effects; and responsibility cannot be ignored by those who find themselves part of those societies which enforce it' (1991: 3). To talk of a unified Indian culture is to miss the point that cultures are not static but dynamic. Finally, it is important to point out that, while the Indian nation might appear as unified, it faces its own problems and challenges from diverse competing ethnicities which are demanding secession, as in the case of Punjab and Kashmir. These destabilising tendencies are the products of colonialism and have emerged in similar ways in both India and Africa.

Post-colonialism has to be seen necessarily as Western metaphysical violence underpinned by the processes of imperialism which continue even after the formal dissolution of empire. In the case of Africa this can be witnessed, for example, in the way in which the International Monetary Fund (IMF) and the World Bank continue to discipline the continent. This new form of discipline is one that US President Truman inaugurated in 1949, when he affirmed the civilising mission of colonialism under the rubric of development and proposed the West as a model for the entire world. He said:

> I believe that we should make available to peace-loving peoples the benefits of our store of technical knowledge in order to help them to realize their aspirations for a better life ... What we envisage is a program of development based on the concepts of democratic fair dealing ... Greater production is the key to prosperity and peace. And the key to greater production is a wider more vigorous application of modern scientific and technical knowledge.
>
> (Truman, cited in Escobar 1995: 3)

It is a mission which the United States has advocated diligently since that time. It is a process that has been pursued theoretically under the aegis of the modernisation school and its current neo-liberal manifestation, which is mediated by the IMF, the World Bank and donor countries through the discourse of good governance.[2]

If the dominant discourse is so pervasive, with the capacity to discipline and silence, it needs to be asked what role post-colonialism can play or offer. To the avalanche of practices characteristic of colonialism and neo-colonialism that dominate contemporary Africa, post-colonialism presents a challenge by reading history discursively. By reconfiguring and challenging dominant narratives, it is able to, 'write back to the empire' or in Said's terms make the 'voyage in' (1993a: 261). It is in this way that it is a particularly empowering discourse for those who have been marginalised.

While much has been made of the multiplicities of identities, a conceptualisation in which post-colonialism has played a key role, it is pertinent to remember that for most African and Third World countries such identities have always been prominent. They are the legacy of colonial rule which operated through a policy of 'divide and rule'. For most Third World peoples, multiple identities are a reality, and they have learnt to negotiate these as part of the practice of their everyday lives. As part of the decolonisation process, it was necessary to forge a unified identity and undergo the process of nation-building. However, the calls for nationalism, which characterised Appiah's first stage of African writers, who were fixated on notions of the nation, are, as the second stage demonstrated, no longer necessary or tenable. Rather than taking notions such as hybridity to Africa, it must be recognised that the very ideas of creolisation and hybridity are part of African history, at least since the time of the slave trade. Thus, although post-colonial theory is seen to be very much a discourse which in the metropole has emanated from diasporic intellectuals, it is important to remember that this is possible only because of the shared experiences and ravages of colonialism which have come to define contemporary global relations. Post-colonialism therefore has to be viewed as part of an on-going strategy which arises out of the impasse and disillusionment caused by the failure of earlier theoretical formulations and paradigms, such as dependency. This does not mean that post-colonialism rejects or suffers amnesia when it comes to earlier works which sought to come to terms with the inherent problems of Third World societies. Rather, it draws its critical energy and vitalisation from those works, with the important caveat that it does not wish to be entrapped within the confines of those discourses and head down paths similar to those that have led to the current theoretical impasse. Finally, it must be emphasised that the question of identity is one that links African studies and post-colonial studies.

The problematising of the notion of a single monolithic identity has meant that post-colonialism is marking its difference by focusing on the marginalised and dispossessed. However, its concern with multiple identities, hybridity and subjectivity as well as epistemological questions has meant that it has been portrayed as being unable to deal with the practice of everyday life and the manner in which it affects the lives of Third World peoples. Post-colonialism is characterised as out of touch and mired in abstraction with its concerns of representation, knowledge and discourse. This attack, however, is made by a very narrow reading of the field and with a focus on Said, Bhabha and Spivak and their form of colonial discourse analysis. While they have made a huge contribution to post-colonial studies, the field is developing and evolving rapidly with an emphasis on the relationship between modernity, globalisation and the local. The focus is on the interactions between the local and global and the manner in which the global is inflected by the local in order to empower them to move forward (Ashcroft 1997; Clifford 1997; Loomba 1998; Prakash 1995, 1996).

In a recent intervention, titled *Globalism, Post-Colonialism and African Studies*, Bill Ashcroft (1997) suggests that there are three ways in which African writing is, or might be, represented and analysed. These three ways are themselves metonymic of the ambivalent place of Africa in the world: a new internationalism, which appears to absorb Africa into a global, transnational cultural and economic reality; a 'discourse of Africa', which continually finds itself drawn to an essentialist view of African identity and cultural practices; and post-colonial discourse, which attempts to investigate the range of responses and subject positions which African societies have produced and responded to, and which engage with colonialism. Ashcroft suggests that post-colonialism – which has sometimes been constituted as itself a new hegemony or centre, inimical to the goals of African liberation – may present a more sensitive and transformative analysis of African cultural practice. It is important to examine his argument more closely.

Ashcroft questions the usefulness of the concept of 'Africa'. The idea of 'Africa' is one that comes from Europe. He equates Africa, as Said equates the Orient, with Europe's other. This idea, he suggests, 'precedes and justifies colonialism, and this idea persists to the present' (*ibid.*: 11). The significance of this is that it is the representations of Africa which lie behind the West's hegemonic role. It is this representation which ascribes to Africa the notion of the 'Dark Continent'. In this way, Africa exists as an invention not only in the very scramble for Africa, but as an invention of the West's imagination (Ahluwalia 1996a; Ashcroft 1997: 12; Kanneh 1998; Mudimbe 1988, 1994).

Ashcroft argues that this idea of Africa is one that continues to dominate and haunt all discussion of Africa. This claim is particularly pertinent for African studies, which has objectified its subject, dealing with it in a detached manner. However, he argues, 'what we generally fail to examine, indeed appear unable to examine, is the discourse within which we are located, the discourse within which our talk about something called Africa circulates entirely within the imagination of Europe' (1997: 13). Critically, the 'we' here includes African intellectuals. It is this power of representation which effectively contains African subjects. The important question, or sets of questions, which he poses are, how can Africanists and African subjects break down the tyranny of the discourse which constructs such representations? The difficulties entailed in this process can be traced to the manner in which colonial binaries, such as black/white and inferior/superior, are deployed. Ashcroft points out that at different times projects such as negritude and nationalism have sought to dismantle such binaries, but that they ultimately have succumbed and established new binaries.

In order to escape from this quagmire, Ashcroft advocates the adoption of post-colonialism. But post-colonialism is not another grand theory of the sort that Arif Dirlik, Aijaz Ahmad and a number of other Marxist critics have been seeking. Rather, post-colonialism is a way in which

> the African subject re-imagines itself by confirming the very porous borders of Africa as a discourse of geography, history, culture, nation and identity. It looks beyond Africa to see that African cultures share something crucial with many other cultures around the world; they share a history of colonial contact, with its inevitable material effects, its conflicts, its complicities and oppositions, its filiations and affiliations. They share these things regardless of the radical specificity and differences between local cultures themselves.
> (Ashcroft 1997: 23–4)

This re-imagination of Africa along the lines advocated by post-colonialism would allow new strategies of resistance and change at the local level, whilst not losing sight of the disempowering effects of contemporary imperial practices. As Ashcroft puts it, 'we need to recognise that change occurs at the level of the local, at the level of the struggle of representation, and that political and cultural change occurs first in the minds of those who imagine a different kind of world' (1997: 25). Homi Bhabha points out the manner in which the post-colonial perspective differs from earlier theoretical formulations, such as dependency and the sociology of underdevelopment. It is a perspective which does not seek to historicise the post-colonial world by establishing a binary opposition between the First and the Third worlds. Rather, it 'resists the attempt at holistic forms of social explanation. It forces a recognition of the more complex cultural and political boundaries that exist on the cusp of these often opposed political spheres' (1994: 173).

In the case of Africa, the term post-colonial does not mean 'after independence'. Rather, it is a concept which takes into account the historical realities of the European imperial incursions into the continent from the fifteenth century onwards. These incursions manifested themselves in the transatlantic slave trade. The violent conquest of the continent in the nineteenth and twentieth centuries, in what may be described as the 'scramble for Africa', formally lasted until the decolonisation processes were complete. These processes began in the 1950s and culminated in the 1990s with the liberation of South Africa. Nevertheless, the enduring legacy of colonialism continues to be characterised by its neo-colonial practices. In an attempt to define the 'post-colonial' in the African context, D. A. Masolo points out that, in the case of a family of six members who may live together under the tyranny of a dominant person of authority, each of these members experiences that authority in particular ways. What Masolo is pointing to, in such an analogy, is that the colonial experience is by no means monolithic. The problem which he is identifying is the difficulty which many post-colonial writers and theorists have when articulating the emancipatory potential of post-colonialism – that is, the essentialisation of identity. Masolo perceptively points to this twofold problem:

> first, that all formerly colonized persons ought to have one view of the impact of colonialism behind which they ought to unite to overthrow it; second, that the overthrow of colonialism be replaced with another, liberated and assumedly authentic identity. So strong is the pull toward the objectivity of this identity that most of those who speak of Africa from this emancipatory perspective think of it only as a solid rock which has withstood all the storms of history except colonialism. Because of the deeply political gist of the colonial/postcolonial discourse, we have come to think of our identities as natural rather than imagined and politically driven.
>
> (Masolo 1997: 285)

Masolo correctly identifies the problem with the notion of fixed identities which are ascribed and internalised. This is aligned with the way in which post-colonial theory illustrates the constructedness and contingency of identities. As noted earlier, in the African context, multiple identities are part of the very fabric of society. In short, African identities are complex and diverse and rooted in the post-colonial experience.

Post-colonialism beyond literary studies

Post-colonial theory has come to be synonymous with the disciplinary areas of literary and cultural theory, both of which are located within the rubric of

English or Literature departments in the Western academy. Critics such as Ahmad argue that colonial discourse analysis as well as post-colonial theory fail to engage with other disciplines which have similar concerns. Despite the interdisciplinary nature of, for example, Edward Said's work, post-colonial theory has failed to transcend disciplinary boundaries. By and large, much recent work continues to emanate from within Literature and English departments. The historian Russell Jacoby, however, questions the interdisciplinarity of post-colonialism:

> As they move out from traditional literature into political economy, sociology, history, and anthropology, do the postcolonial theorists master these fields or just poke about? Are they serious students of colonial history and culture or do they just pepper their writings with references to Gramsci and hegemony?
>
> (Jacoby, cited in Moore-Gilbert 1997: 14)

While Jacoby appears to be raising important methodological questions, it is important, nevertheless, to take stock of a point, made by Peter Childs and Patrick Williams, that 'post-colonial work has always had a measure of interdisciplinarity, and that the best of it is sensitive to debates in areas such as sociology and political economy in a way few of those areas could emulate' (1997: 17).

David Scott has argued recently that a major weakness in post-colonialism is its failure to deal with the political. Scott examines the criticisms levelled by Dirlik that post-colonialism, in rejecting master narratives, makes Eurocentrism its central organising task (Dirlik 1994: 334). The implication of this rejection of Enlightenment rationality is the 'rejection of the progressivist Marxist narrative that founds modern history in the unity of capital' (Scott 1996: 7). It is this rejection of the Marxist narrative and the failure to make the critique of capitalism the foundational principle of post-colonialism that Dirlik finds unacceptable. However, as Scott points out, such a portrayal of post-colonialism is fraught with difficulty, given the focus on the transformation of capitalism which is part of post-colonial theory. However, what is central to Scott's argument is not a defence of post-colonialism along such lines but rather the teasing out of the implicit relationship which has existed between post-colonialism and 'actually existing socialism'. He suggests that, because both colonialism and neo-colonialism were defined in relation to the globalisation of capitalism, post-colonialism has functioned in the ideological opposition between capitalism and socialism which has characterised the political terrain in this century (*ibid.*: 10). Scott argues that:

> if it is true that an anticapitalism and an antiliberalism have often circulated through postcolonial criticism, it is as true that the implications of those for a theory of politics have been little more than gestural. And one of the conditions that has enabled this deferral of the question of the political is that our

political futures were assumed to be covered by the moral authority of (some version of) socialism. It is this that can no longer be taken for granted.

(Scott 1996: 10)

Scott notes that the promise of the 1960s and 1970s, when socialism was in vogue in such disparate Third World locations as Tanzania, Jamaica and Sri Lanka, gave way to its decline in the 1980s under the strictures of World Bank structural adjustment programmes. In addition, the collapse of the Soviet empire has meant that such countries no longer have the political cover which the Soviet Union provided during the Cold War. This has been exacerbated by the triumphalism of liberalism, which presents itself as the only credible option for the future. The point that Scott makes is that, in the changed configuration of global relations, both old positions and theoretical formulations are inadequate to meet the challenges of the future. In this context, 'it becomes imperative for postcolonial criticism to begin to fold into its practice a criticism that distances itself from the Enlightenment project of both Marxism and liberalism and that constructs a problematised relation to the claims and the categories of our political modernity' (Scott 1996: 15).

The argument which Scott makes is particularly pertinent for Africa and African studies. African socialism was pursued with vigour, and its best known exponent was Julius Nyerere of Tanzania. African studies on the left were enamoured with the Tanzanian experiment and used it as the model to be emulated, celebrating its ideas of community, self-determination, anti-imperialism and pan-Africanism. Its appeal was so widespread, that African leaders in the newly-independent nations found it necessary to proclaim an allegiance to socialism even when they were avowedly pursuing a capitalist strategy. For example, in the case of Kenya, this was done in the name of African socialism as defined by Tom Mboya's Sessional Paper Number Ten (Ahluwalia 1996a). However, the 1990s ushered in a new era which witnessed the call for democratic reform. Even the most ardent defender of the one-party African socialist state, Julius Nyerere, repudiated his earlier position. Nyerere, in a public speech in February 1990, challenged the ruling party's legitimacy, arguing that it had lost touch with the people. In 1991 Nyerere resigned from his position as Chair of the ruling party and advocated that Tanzania should move towards a competitive political system (Baregu 1995: 3). Hence, in Africa as elsewhere, the failure of the socialist project and the triumphalism of liberalism means that post-colonialism needs to examine closely modern liberal democracy. This does not mean that post-colonialists turn a blind eye to its obvious weaknesses, such as its focus on individualism and rationality, but that we engage with its achievements. As Scott argues, 'Postcolonial criticism needs a different account of our political modernity, a different account of the political dead ends at which we have unquestionably arrived' (1996: 21). Scott suggests that such an engagement can be undertaken constructively by an engagement with the Enlightenment project.

Although much of Scott's argument is necessary for post-colonialism, it is difficult to share his optimism of defining post-colonial futures within the

Enlightenment project. After all, much of the contemporary African condition is attributable to the ill effects of such a project when it was transported to Africa under the aegis of colonialism. As Eze asks, 'could the same European modernity and Enlightenment that promoted "precious ideals like the dignity of persons" and "democracy" also be so intimately and inextricably implicated in slavery and the colonial projects?' (1997: 12). Nevertheless, it is important to heed the call for the engagement with the political.

It is pertinent to question what such an engagement with the political entails. It would be far too crude and reductive to suggest that post-colonial studies emanating largely from their literary locus are non-political. This confusion and tension appears to arise out of the charge that post-colonialism remains detached – limited at best to works of the imagination – with a focus on texts and discourses rather than any serious engagement with the 'real' world. It is this tension which is exploited constantly by critics in order to represent post-colonialism merely as a discourse of diasporic intellectuals who are capable only of theorising from a distance rather than being engaged at the coal-face. It is a problem, of course, which has been at the heart of Edward Said's project. It is through the notion of 'worldliness' that Said seeks to overcome the quagmire of contemporary literary theory, which appears to be far removed and not grounded in social experience. Worldliness, for Said, is about the materiality of the text's origin. It is the recognition that the text does not exist outside the world but that it is a part of the world which it addresses. It is equally important that the critic recognise his or her engagement with the world, and so, for Said, the worldliness of the critic is just as important as the worldliness of the text.[3] This sense of worldliness pervades his work and is poignantly evident in his overtly political work on Palestine. It is this notion of worldliness that post-colonial theory needs to embrace in order to engage with its constituency, the post-colonial world.

It is to this task that this book is addressed. However, it approaches its task through the notion of African inflections. What is meant by inflections here is similar to the notion of contact zones that Mary Louise Pratt (1992) has identified. This process of cultural interaction between different cultures, or transculturation, can best be understood by invoking her notion of 'contact zones', which she defines as the 'space in which peoples geographically and historically separated come into contact with each other and establish ongoing relations, usually involving conditions of coercion, radical inequality, and intractable conflict' (Pratt 1992: 6). Pratt points out that a contact perspective is one that, 'treats the relations among colonizers and colonized ... not in terms of separateness or apartheid, but in terms of copresence, interaction, interlocking understandings and practices, often within radically asymmetrical relations of power' (*ibid*.: 7). The concept of transculturation is one that is used also by Françoise Lionnet, who points out that the prefix 'trans-' 'suggests the act of traversing, of going through existing cultural territories' (1995: 13). The use of transculturation is that it helps to break down binaries such as metropolitan/colonial, developed/underdeveloped and civilized/primitive.

By deploying the perspective of inflections through the lens of post-colonialism, it is possible to see how African societies have constituted and reconstituted themselves by an engagement with modernity. In each of the chapters that follow, it is the notion of African inflections which points out the way in which Africa has confronted its colonial legacy whilst at the same time it defines its post-colonial future. To this end, post-colonialism seeks to move beyond the confines of literary criticism and to engage with the political for that is where its future lies.

Scope and organisation

This book is divided into six chapters. The first begins by highlighting the centrality of identity and its relationship to post-colonialism. It examines the negritude movement and the manner in which this movement constructs identity. It is argued that the negritude movement has served as an easy target for post-colonialism to suggest that such a reversion or construction of identity leads to a reaffirmation of the very binary structure which the negritude movement sought to challenge. Whilst this is certainly the case, the negritude movement needs to be viewed in the context of its contribution in forging an African identity that was vital to the decolonisation process. It is also important to recognise that the movement was not monolithic, and that there were important differences between its two main founding fathers, Léopold Sédar Senghor and Aimé Césaire.

The second chapter examines decolonisation and national liberation. It traces the manner in which the decolonisation process occurred in Africa. However, it points out that, whilst formal decolonisation may have occurred, the more difficult task of decolonising the mind remains elusive. It challenges the assertion that decolonisation processes are linked to geographical locations and suggests that they are firmly grounded in the imagination. This chapter traces the importance of two major post-colonial theorists, Frantz Fanon and Edward Said, examining their strategies for liberation and resistance.

The third chapter, titled, 'Modernity and the Problem of the Nation-State', argues that the post-colonial state is a product of colonialism. It examines the manner in which the questions of modernity are intertwined with the post-colonial state and the way in which the state has adopted the goals of rationality, progress, modernisation and development. This chapter further examines recent Africanist literature on the state and posits a post-colonial perspective, taking into account the specificity of the African case. It demonstrates how African states have endured the colonial legacy and the manner in which this legacy has been inflected in the post-colonial state.

The fourth chapter examines the contemporary transitions towards democratisation. It analyses the debates about civil society, tracing their epistemological roots. The faith in civil society which is evident in much Africanist literature is addressed. It is suggested that the role of the state needs to be examined separately in both the economic and political sphere before proclaiming the demise of the African state. It is in this context that post-colonial theory is helpful, suggesting that a polity be examined in totality from the rupturing moment of colonisation. In this way, too, the issue of human rights in Africa is examined. This chapter shows how African countries have taken human-rights discourse and inflected this discourse in particular ways.

In Chapter 5 there is a close reading of Mahmood Mamdani's book, *Citizen and Subject* (1996a). It examines his argument that, as a result of colonisation and its continuing legacy, there remains a distinction between citizens and subjects in the nation-states of Africa. This chapter critically engages with Mamdani's book, reflecting on this core thesis. Deploying a post-colonial perspective, however, it argues that such a simple binary is ineffective. Post-colonial theory brings questions of subjectivity to the foreground. It illustrates the complexities of post-colonial identity, particularly at a time of intense globalisation. This chapter argues that we need to view post-colonial identities as complex formulations in which we are *all* citizen/subjects.

Chapter 6 examines globalisation debates and post-colonialism in Africa. It points out that Africa has been marginalised in globalisation discourses. Nevertheless, globalisation remains important to the future of the continent. Further, such discourses surrounding globalisation are an important means of empowering people by linking the local with the global. The chapter also examines the transformative potential of globalisation and suggests that it might be an important way for post-colonial identity to be reconstituted in effective and efficient ways. Finally, the Afterword brings together the major themes of the book, pointing out the modernisation imperatives which have produced post-colonial predicaments for Africa and the manner in which Africa has and can negotiate these predicaments through the trope of inflections.

1 'Negritude and nativism'

In search of identity

Is it not a painful thing that, if I want to go to a court of justice, I must employ the English language as a medium, that when I become a barrister, I may not speak my mother-tongue and that someone else should have to translate to me in my own language? Is not this absolutely absurd? Is it not a sign of slavery? Am I to blame the English for it or myself? It is we, the English-knowing Indians, that have enslaved India. The curse of the nation will rest not upon the English but upon us.

Mahatma Gandhi

Must the educated black from abroad come back to recolonise us? Must he walk about with his mouth open, startled by the beauty of African women, by the black man's 'heightened sensitivity'? It's all so embarrassing.

Ezekiel Mphahlele

It is not culture which binds the peoples who are of partially African origin now scattered throughout the world, but an identity of passions. We share a hatred for the alienation forced upon us by Europeans during the process of colonization and empire, and we are bound by our common suffering more than our pigmentation.

Ralph Ellison

For centuries, Europe has affirmed its identity in relation to 'others' based on 'fears, fantasies and demons' which have inhabited 'the Western mind from Herodotus to Pliny, and from St Augustine to Columbus' (Sardar *et al.* 1993: 1). The European 'discovery' of Africa in the fifteenth century, as well as Columbus's 'discovery' of the Americas, meant that these new geographical spaces, and in particular their inhabitants, had to be re-inscribed in European discourse. As Michel de Certeau has noted:

In history, which leads from the subject of mysticism in the sixteenth century to the subject of economics, primitive man lies between the two. As a cultural (or even epistemological) figure, he prepares the second by inverting the first, and by the end of the seventeenth century, he is erased, replaced by the native, the colonized, or by the mentally deficient.

(de Certeau 1982: 227)

The negritude movement of the 1930s was full of contradictions and ambivalence. It was by no means a movement that could be regarded simply as
relativist, and one which merely reaffirmed the racial binaries which it sought to
dismantle. On the contrary, it was an important moment in the long and arduous
struggle for decolonisation. Indeed, it was a formative moment for the African,
who had been denigrated over centuries and represented as child-like and unable
to be a member of the 'civilised world'.[1] It was essential to the process which
sought to break down the tyranny of the web of representations which had been
forged over centuries. This chapter examines the conditions which gave rise to
the negritude movement and seeks to trace its evolution in the thought of its
founding fathers, Léopold Sédar Senghor and Aimé Césaire. It illustrates the
centrality of identity and the role it plays within post-colonial discourse.

The 'curse of the nation' which Gandhi writes about in his dilemma with
regard to the English language is one that was also faced by Africans who had
endured the wrath of slavery.[2] These slaves, displaced from Africa and
transported to the New World, were forced to adopt the language of the
European oppressor, be it English, French, Spanish, Dutch, Portuguese, and/or
undergo a process of creolisation.[3] This forced contact between different peoples
resulted inevitably in hybridity and transformed existing cultures. It was this
amalgamation of influences which became part of the culture of the 'recaptives'
– those slaves who had been captured and in turn freed by the European naval
blockade as well as freed slaves who had returned to settle in Africa. These
returning slaves had been converted to Christianity through the missionary zeal
of the nineteenth century and, cherishing their freedom, looked to Europe, and
in particular Britain, as the bastion of values that needed to be established within
Africa. The values and political culture of Europe were inscribed deeply in their
imagination. It was through these 'new' Africans that European ideas were
transplanted on to the African continent (Davidson 1992: 26).

The arrival of 'new' Africans coincided with the intensive efforts of the
abolition movement in the late eighteenth century, when Africa was reconceptu-
alised as a market rather than as a mere source of labour for the New World.
This re-imagining led to the 'scramble for Africa' and culminated in its
colonisation, producing in its wake 'new legitimating ideologies: the civilizing
mission, scientific racism, and technology-based paradigms of progress and
development' (Pratt 1992: 74). Nevertheless, abolition provided these Africans
with a new-found optimism through which they saw the European incursion into
the interior of the continent as sincere and humanitarian. Edward Blyden
(1832–1912), originally from the Danish island of St Thomas, who settled in
West Africa, was an exemplary 'new' African who was convinced that, 'only the
Negro will be able to explain the Negro to the rest of mankind' (1888: 263). He
argued for the resettlement of American blacks as the best means of spreading
'civilization' in Africa. He wrote:

> There are fifteen thousand civilized and Christianized Africans striving to
> accomplish the twofold work of establishing and maintaining an independent

nationality, and of introducing the Gospel among untold millions of evan-
gelized and barbarous men.

(Blyden 1862: 19)

Although Mudimbe has detailed the romanticisms and inconsistencies in
Blyden's work, he points out that his 'political vision is probably the first proposal
by a black man to elaborate the benefits of an independent, modern political
structure of the continent' (1988: 118).

It is not surprising, therefore, that the founding father of the negritude
movement, Léopold Senghor, celebrated Blyden as the movement's 'foremost
precursor'. Although Senghor writes that he and his contemporaries had not
read Blyden when they began to formulate the concept of negritude, nevertheless clear resonances are evident in their work. As Irele notes, it was Senghor
who refined Blyden's 'conceptions of the African mind, to analyse its manner of
responding to the world, and to enunciate an African mode of experience' (Irele
1971: 41).

Because negritude has come under considerable attack for its reaffirmation of
racial binaries, its critical role as a predecessor to decolonisation has received
cursory attention. At best, particularly in the former British colonies, it is seen as
a cultural movement which had little to do with the 'real' political struggle
which led to independence. A significant amnesia therefore appears to have
crept into recent literary and critical theory, where the negritude movement is
seen more as an embarrassment than as occupying a central position in the
process of decolonising the mind that was an integral part of the struggle for
independence.

Negritude as a movement emerged in Paris in the early 1930s, amongst
African and West Indian students under the leadership of Léopold Sédar
Senghor from Senegal, Aimé Césaire, a Martiniquian, and the Guyanese Léon
Damas. The three established a newspaper, L'Etudiant noir (The Black Student), in
which they voiced their problems, stressing commonalties amongst all black
people around the world. Negritude needs to be contextualised against the
general background of colonisation and the manner in which the African's very
being was denigrated. As Irele has observed, this was 'not simply a rationalisa-
tion of white domination but ... a direct and crushing attack upon his
subjectivity' (1971: 26). It is perhaps not surprising that negritude took shape in
Paris, given the French system of colonisation. French colonies were seen as an
extension of France, and their subjects were considered citizens. In theory, this
form of colonialism was based on assimilation, but, in reality, the rights of
citizenship were extended to only the white French settlers in the colonies. When
these African and West Indian students arrived in Paris, they found that,
contrary to the theory of assimilation, they were isolated because of their colour.
In France, they discovered that they were not 'French'. This realisation led them
to undertake a journey to rediscover their past, their black roots and African
heritage. Through negritude the colonised sought to reverse the representations
ascribed to them, to turn those negative identities into positive images.

An important paradox of negritude was that the very people who were urging a return to authenticity and renewal were themselves thoroughly imbued with the values of the coloniser. It was their alienation in both cultures, their sense of not belonging in either their own culture or that of the colonisers, that became problematic. It was their 'preoccupation with the black experience' which 'developed into a passionate exaltation of the black race, associated with a romantic myth of Africa' (Irele 1981: 91). The negritude writers not only celebrated Africa by paying tribute to the 'African love of life, the African joy of love and the African dream of death' (Dathorne 1981: 59) but also challenged the colonisers in a way that they had never before been challenged. Césaire described negritude as 'the simple recognition of the fact of being black and the acceptance of this fact, of our destiny as black people, of our history and our culture' (cited in Irele 1981: 87).

Although the term negritude was first coined by Aimé Césaire in *L'Etudiant noir*, its development was the result of a partnership between Césaire and Senghor. Senghor describes the manner in which they developed the term:

> In what circumstances did Aimé Césaire and I launch the word negritude between 1933 and 1935? At that time, along with several other black students we were plunged into a panic-stricken despair. The horizon was blocked. No reform was in sight and the colonizers were justifying our political and economic dependence by the theory of the *tabula rasa*....In order to establish an effective revolution, our revolution, we had first to divest ourselves of our borrowed attire – that of assimilation – and assert our being, that is to say our negritude.
>
> (Senghor, cited in Bâ 1973: 12)

L'Etudiant noir folded after a few issues, and, although it was succeeded by several other publications in which the ideas of negritude were elaborated, it was not until the establishment of *Présence Africaine* that the movement had a permanent voice to propagate its ideas. Nevertheless, the movement's success in its formative days needs to be attributed to its favourable reception amongst the French intelligentsia. This was helped in part by the American Black Renaissance movement of the 1920s, the impact of which was being felt in Paris, particularly in music and entertainment.[4] This acceptance was in no small way the result of Senghor being able to persuade Jean-Paul Sartre to write a preface to an anthology of Black writers which he had edited. Sartre's essay, titled 'Orphée noir', not only gave the negritude movement a boost but at the same time embroiled it in controversy which persists until today.

Senghor's negritude

Negritude from its inception needs to be viewed as a notion which had a strong element of resistance. Senghor claimed that the very act of negating the representations of the black person was liberating. Negritude was at its core about returning to black people a humanity that had been denied to them by centuries of denigration and brutalisation which reached its apex through the colonial process. Senghor's writings were an affirmation that black people were humans, contrary to the manner in which their identity had been problematised within European discourse.[5]

A key aspect of Senghor's negritude, for which he and the entire movement has been criticised severely, is the affirmation of racial images celebrating merely blackness. That is, any negative trait that had been attributed to a black person is celebrated as a positive element. For Senghor, negritude is the 'sum total of African cultural values'. His proclamations of a unique black psychophysiology can be discerned in statements such as 'emotion is black as reason is Greek' (Reed and Wake 1965: 30) and in a speech at Oxford, in which he proclaimed:

> 'I think, therefore I am', wrote Descartes, the European *par excellence*. 'I feel, I dance the other' the Negro-African would say. He does not need to think, but to live the other by dancing him.
>
> (Senghor, quoted in Irele 1981: 77)

Abiola Irele sees emotion as the key notion in Senghor's theory 'which he virtually erects into a function of knowledge and attributes to the African as a cardinal principle of his racial disposition' (1996: 18). Senghor has responded to such criticisms, claiming that he has been read out of context, that it was not his intention to suggest that black people were not rational, but, on the contrary, that reason was common to all individuals. Rather, he sought to emphasise the 'very real differences in personality and temperament that influence the way in which the occidental and the black African relate to the external world' (Bâ 1973: 76).

Sylvia Washington Bâ has suggested a useful and convenient way to characterise negritude by making a distinction between historical negritude and essential negritude. The former is a recognition of being black in a white world, while the latter is 'a far more controversial concept, since the idea of a black African personality, a black specificity, is based on the explosive notion of race' (1973: 160). The distinction between historical and essential negritude is an adaptation of Sartre's subjective and objective negritude. Essential negritude is what Sartre claimed in 'Orphée noir' as 'neither a state nor a definite ensemble of vices and virtues, of intellectual and moral qualities, but a certain affective attitude toward the world' (Sartre, cited in Bâ 1973: 166). For Sartre, however, negritude was a contingent phenomenon which would disappear eventually after the resolution of black–white conflict and result in the creation of human society without racism.

Sartre's primary task in this essay was to demonstrate how negritude was analogous to Marxist theory. For black people, it was important to recognise that race was the key factor in their oppression. Sartre wrote:

> A Jew, white among whites, can deny that he is a Jew can declare himself a man among men. The Negro cannot deny that he is a Negro nor claim for

himself that abstract colorless humanity: he is black. Therefore he is driven toward authenticity: insulted, enslaved, he stands up, he picks up the word 'nigger' that they had thrown at him like a stone, he asserts his rights as black, facing the white man with pride. The final unity that will draw all oppressed people together in the same combat must be preceded by what I call the moment of separation or of negativity: this antiracist racism is the only road that can lead to the abolition of racial differences.

(Sartre, cited in Arnold 1981: 17)

Negritude was to be seen to be synonymous with the proletariat and as having the same potential for social change. But, for Sartre, this was a temporary phenomenon: after the revolution, French racism would disappear, as would its antithesis, negritude, because in the new society race would have no place. This part of Sartre's essay has been criticised for denying the negritude writers their basic premise. As Janet Vaillant notes, for Sartre 'it is only after he has ceased to live unreflectively and totally within the world of objective Negritude that he feels the need to express his subjective Negritude' (Vaillant 1990: 250).

Frantz Fanon in his *Black Skin, White Masks* also accuses Sartre of blocking the source of negritude. He writes that at the very moment when he was 'trying to grasp my own being, Sartre, who remained The Other, gave me a name and thus shattered my last illusion' (1986: 137). This illusion of being able to find yourself by reclaiming your past African heritage, of being black, was shattered, and Fanon writes: 'Not yet white, no longer wholly black, I was damned. Jean-Paul Sartre had forgotten that the Negro suffers in his body quite differently from the white man' (*ibid.*: 138). Fanon's relationship to negritude can at best be described as ambivalent (Parry 1994). He was conscious of the essentialised nature of identity which was being advanced by negritude, but at the same time recognised its necessary positive effects. He recognised the need for the affirmation of black identity. In this context negritude was not only necessary but infeasible. It was necessary because it effected 'a shift between black–white relations', offering the black person a source of pride, while at the same time a white person 'recognises in the Negro qualities that he now experiences himself as lacking, such as closeness to nature, spontaneity, simplicity' (Kruks 1996: 130). In this process, there is finally a sense of recognition. It is through this affirmation of identity that the black person at last gains recognition.

Whilst recognising negritude's importance and rebuking Sartre, ultimately Fanon adopts a stance akin to Sartre. Fanon documents the alienation entailed in not belonging in either culture and sees that the only way out is, 'to reject the two terms that are equally unacceptable, and through one human being, to reach out for the universal' (1986: 197). He criticises negritude's search for a black identity in some distant African past as irrelevant, because it is not possible to achieve freedom without looking toward the future. In short, Fanon recognised that it was important to celebrate and affirm one's black identity, but that in itself was not enough to change the course of history – a task to which he was fundamentally committed in the struggle for Algeria.

Fanon's position on negritude is much like Gayatri Chakravorty Spivak's notion of 'strategic essentialism', in which essentialist forms of native identity are seen to be important in order to transcend the assimilationist phase of colonialism so as to develop a decolonised national culture.[6] In other words, it is an important phase in the process of decolonising the mind. This 'strategic essentialism' is certainly one which Chinua Achebe recognised when he wrote:

> You have all heard of the African personality; of African democracy, of the African way to socialism, of negritude, and so on. They are all props we have fashioned at different times to help us get on our feet again. Once we are up we shall not need any of them any more. But for the moment it is in the nature of things that we may need to counter racism with what Jean-Paul Sartre has called an anti-racist racism, to announce not just that we are as good as the next man but that we are better.
>
> (Achebe, cited in Moore-Gilbert 1997: 179)

In articulating a philosophy of negritude, Senghor was preoccupied with trying to understand his position as a black man in an essentially white-dominated world. When viewed from such a perspective, negritude becomes 'an expression of one's emotional state, a total commitment to *living* one's blackness in the world' (Senghor, cited in Bâ 1973: 172). It is to this negritude that Wole Soyinka reacted by questioning whether a tiger needs to claim its tigritude. But, for Senghor, negritude became all-encompassing once he entered politics, eventually becoming President of Senegal. Markovitz has characterised the development of negritude in three phases. The first is the period, beginning in the 1930s and lasting up to World War II, when the movement was essentially about discovering personal identity. The second is the period from the end of the war to 1960, when Senegal gained independence; this was a time when negritude had to become relevant and part of the process of forging a national identity. The third is the period after independence, when negritude 'grew into an ideology for unity, economic development and cultural growth' (Markovitz 1969: 49). However, Senghor never denounced colonialism as Césaire did. Rather, for him, colonialism also constituted the history of Africa. His notion of negritude eventually evolved to the point of forging a dynamic symbiosis of European technology and African culturalism. This symbiosis was a consistent theme for Senghor, and one that was evident in the 1940s when he advocated the creation of a Franco-African union. For him, this was a natural process, given that all civilizations are the result of 'cross-breeding'. For Césaire, colonialism was not a symbiotic process at all. On the contrary, he rhetorically questioned whether colonialism placed civilizations in contact, and emphatically answered that it was a process which only entailed domination and submission (1972: 21).

Senghor's views of negritude were appropriated directly in the political realm through his version of African socialism. This was an amalgamation of the values of negritude and aspects of European socialism. For Senghor, African socialism was reliant on African tradition combined with Western technology and scientific methods of planning. It was compatible with African traditions because of Africa's communitarian roots. By proclaiming such an ideology, he was able to use it as a rallying call for freedom. He made the connection between negritude and African socialism explicit: 'We wish then to liberate ourselves politically precisely in order to express our Negritude, that is to say our real black values' (Senghor, cited in Vaillant 1990: 270). While this was an effective policy for gaining independence, it ultimately failed to live up to the expectations of the Senegalese population. As a political ideology, negritude was unable to deal with the realities of people who sought solutions to their poverty and underdevelopment.

Césaire's negritude

Although Césaire and Senghor conceived the concept of negritude together, over time they have developed it in different ways. By the time Césaire wrote *Discourse on Colonialism*, it is possible to discern a significant change. In this work Césaire is far more concerned with examining colonialism, rather than with celebrating a unified and dignified black identity. It is here that he attacks the civilising mission of colonialism with all its pretensions of progress and development, noting instead its ravaging effects. Nevertheless, the two men maintained an important friendship. In a speech in 1976, on the occasion of Senghor's visit to Martinique, Césaire said:

> For forty years, we have lived in parallel ... leaving each other, as life went, but nonetheless never truly separating. Was this surprising? After all, our adolescences were entirely blended. We read the same books, often the same copy, shared the same dreams, loved the same poets. We were torn by the same anguish and, above all, were weighed down by the same problems ... our youth was not banal ... It was marked by the tormenting question, who am I? For us, it was not a question of metaphysics, but of a life to live, an ethic to create, and communities to save. We tried to answer that question. In the end, our answer was Negritude.
>
> (Césaire, cited in Vaillant 1990: 90)

For Césaire, Senghor was Africa, his link to his roots – as he put it, 'in meeting Senghor, I met Africa' (Vaillant 1990: 91). This was all the more important given the ways in which the 'African' was represented as 'barbarian' by French West Indians, who certainly did not consider themselves to be black. It was in Paris that this myth was shattered with the realisation that it did not matter where you were from, if you were not white, you were black. In his celebrated 1939 work *Cahier d'un retour au pays natal* (*Notebook of a Return to the Native Land*), Césaire attempts to come to terms with the history of black denigration and degradation. He does so by his imagined return to his homeland, a process which entails acceptance of the past, both its positives and its negatives.[7] However, in a 1986 lecture, Maryse Condé questions the meaning of such a return, 'To be Antillean, in the end, I'm not always sure exactly what that means! Must a writer have a native land? ... Could the writer not be a perpetual nomad, constantly wandering in search of other people' (cited in Lionnet 1995: 71). Condé finds the idea that all blacks are similar problematic. She argues that negritude caused a great deal of suffering for West Indians as well as African Americans, particularly after they discovered that Africa was not the ideal home for which they had been searching. She argues that without 'Négritude we would not have experienced the degree of disillusionment that we did. The issue of "likeness" or "similarity" is erroneous even in the Antilles' (Condé 1994: 60). Condé was rearticulating the critique and anger of the Haitian poet René Depestre that negritude was not a progressive idea and that it had become a new form of alienation which promoted the interests of neo-colonialism. It is a position which Ran Greenstein has reiterated, pointing out that it is not possible to reconstruct pre-colonial discourses of Africa because it was unlikely that indigenous people conceptualised themselves in terms of the continent as a whole. In that sense, 'Pan-Africanism, Negritude and Black Consciousness have all emerged in the aftermath of the colonial encounter, and not just in their written forms, although they have drawn on and sought to mobilize pre-colonial discourses' (1995; 227).

Abiola Irele has commented recently that it is not only in Anglophone countries that negritude has come under attack; it was met with considerable hostility in the French-speaking world. Irele notes that Senghor's theory was seen to be complicit with imperialism and that, 'the question of African identity required ... a different approach which could not play into the hands of imperialism, which offered no form of compromise with its theory or practice (1996: 21). It is in this context that the work of Stanislas Adotevi (1972) is important, because he not only criticises thoroughly the biological implications of Senghor's work but also sees its transformation into a political ideology as highly problematic, for it is no more than a form of acquiescence to colonial ideology by an African elite. This view, no doubt, is informed by the policies which Senghor pursued as President of Senegal.

It is important therefore to recognise that the concept of negritude developed differently in both Senghor and Césaire. The latter's concept of negritude was a 'sociocultural ideology without a firm theoretical base', and therefore 'has been at the mercy of shifting political conditions' (Arnold 1981: 15). It is ultimately this difference which led to a divergence of views between Senghor and Césaire as to the meaning of negritude. Nevertheless, they had much in common, particularly in what they read. One of the most influential intellectual exercises was their joint reading of the ethnographer Frobenius. This reading no doubt impacted on their views regarding race, and in the case of Senghor is central to his argument that negritude was determined biologically – an argument that has been debunked. Frobenius was an important catalyst for the founding fathers of negritude, engendering enthusiasm for Africa and giving them a basis for questioning the subject-centred rationality of European modernity. It is this reliance on Western anthropology that has led Paulin Hountondji to argue that there existed between the negritude writers and colonial anthropology a certain complicity, with the 'former using the latter in support of their cultural claims, the latter using the former to buttress their pluralistic theses' (1996: 159). While Senghor adhered to such a formulation, Césaire, in an interview in 1969, made it clear that he wished to maintain a distance from such a negritude. He said: 'I do not in the slightest believe in biological permanence, but I believe in culture: it is historical, there is nothing biological about it' (cited in Arnold 1981: 37). Césaire further distanced himself from Senghor's negritude, arguing that Senghor had 'tended rather to construct negritude as an essentialism, as though there were a black essence, a black soul, … but I never accepted this point of view' (*ibid.*: 44).

Ezekiel Mphahlele, one of the most ardent critics of negritude, also makes a distinction between Césaire and Senghor. What impresses Mphahlele is that Césaire uses negritude as a weapon against power. In contrast, 'neither Senghor nor his African peers nor his imitators really understood the essence and workings of white power – political and economic' (1974: 93). In this regard, Depestre makes the point that there is more than one negritude, and therefore it is important to examine various phases and historical circumstances that lead to its unifying tendencies.

Like Senghor, Césaire ultimately turned to politics, and for a while became a Marxist. His Marxism was the result of his analysis of Martinique and the realities of poverty. While he joined the French Communist party, he finally gave up in exasperation when it became clear that they had little interest in dealing with the economic and political liberation of black people – refusing, in particular, to support the Algerian revolution. On that occasion, he made his views clear, arguing that Marxism should have been used to serve the historical needs of black people, as opposed to black people serving Marxism. He argued:

> I hope I have said enough to make it clear that I am abandoning neither Marxism nor communism but only the use which some people have made of them, which I deplore. I wish to see Marxism and communism serving the black peoples, not the black peoples serving Marxism and communism … every doctrine is worthless unless it is rethought by and for us and adapted to our needs.
>
> (Césaire, cited in San Juan 1998: 251)

Césaire's writing most avowedly influenced by Marxism is the *Discourse on Colonialism* in which he equates colonialism with racism. In this text, he considers how colonialism not only dehumanises and objectifies the colonised but also affects the coloniser. This was a position which Frantz Fanon was to reiterate in his analysis of colonialism, claiming that, 'Marxist analysis should always be slightly stretched every time we have to do with the colonial problem' (1967: 32). But, as Arnold points out, the most important influences on Césaire remained the same since the inception of the movement – that is Frobenius, Spengler and Nietzsche. In 1979, when questioned about this, Césaire replied: 'I have remained faithful to certain ideas … without being beholden to any school, I choose within world culture what can help me' (Arnold 1981: 281).

Critiques of negritude

Negritude has come under perhaps the most vitriolic attack from the South African writer Ezekiel Mphahlele, on the grounds that it portrays the African much like the Europeans who he criticises for perpetuating the myth of the noble savage. Mphahlele (1974) rejects, in particular, Senghor's philosophy as a basis for African literature, on the grounds that all African writers do not write in the same way. Fanon also rejects a negritude which grounds itself on a historical black heritage because 'the emphasis placed by the African "bourgeois" writer on conserving traditional values eventually causes his literature to become less representative of African life, not more, because African society is caught up in a process of irreversible change' (cited in Spelth 1985: 31).[8] In short, as Koffi Anyinefa notes, 'the writers of Negritude locked (Black) African identity into a racial essentialism, which presents itself in opposition to a Western discourse on Africa, yet partakes of the dualistic structure and the same discourse it seeks to negate' (1996: 64).

What Mphahlele finds particularly disturbing is the exoticism which is replicated by negritude. However, for him, whilst this may well be useful in the Francophone context, it is not so in the case of South Africa:

> I personally cannot think of the future of my people in South Africa as something in which the white man does not feature. Whether he likes it or not, our destinies are inseparable. I have seen too much that is good in western culture – for example, its music, literature and theatre – to want to repudiate it.
>
> (Mphahlele 1974: 67)

For Mphahlele, cultural renewal and revival is no longer possible, for a new culture has emerged, and a longing to return to the past is ineffectual at the very time that the focus should be on the colonial subject. In short, Mphahlele sees negritude in its traditional manifestation as too simplistic, as unable to meet the challenges of the African continent. Negritude, he argues, 'needs to confront modern Africa with a sense of revolution' (1974: 84). In this regard, he articulates a position very similar to Fanon, for whom the purpose of literature was to act as a conduit for direct action. For both of them, 'when the blood ran in Sharpeville and Algeria, an academic pilgrimage back to their Negro origins was less indispensable than efficiency in the fight and in the field of protest' (Wauthier 1978: 179).

One of the most scathing attacks on negritude has been mounted by Ayi Kwei Armah, who wrote that Senghor's negritude as an artistic statement was symptomatic of his inferiority complex and slave mentality. Armah describes it as 'the flight from the classical Cartesian big white father France into the warm, dark, sensuous embrace of Africa, into the receiving uterus of despised Africa' (Armah 1967: 19). This attack on negritude is one that Armah has maintained consistently. But it is not only Armah who has condemned negritude. Other writers from the former British colonies, such as Wole Soyinka, Lewis Nkosi and

Mphahlele, have all been equally dismissive. Nobel prize-winning author Soyinka, in his *Myth, Literature and the African World*, criticises negritude for merely reinforcing the ideas of white supremacy which it sought to challenge. He notes:

> Négritude, having laid the cornerstone on a European intellectual tradition, however bravely it tried to reverse its concepts (leaving its tenets untouched), was a foundling deserving to be drawn into, nay, even considered a case for, benign adoption by European ideological interests.
>
> (Soyinka 1976: 134)

This assertion of Soyinka's is all the more surprising when one finds that the work of these writers is itself replete with major elements that characterised negritude. As Ogede has observed, these writers have tried to 're-assert and revive the cultural values, identity and dignity of Africans, and to glorify the ancestral achievements and beauty of Africa, through usages, images, references and symbols that are taken from African traditional life' (1993: 792). Ogede challenges the assertions of Ashcroft *et al.* (1989) that negritude did not feature prominently in the thought of Anglophone colonies. On the contrary, he demonstrates how Anglophone writers, despite their aversion, replicate much of what was central to negritude.

Latterly negritude has been attacked also for its representation of women. In particular, the images of 'Mother Africa' and an idealised African womanhood have been challenged. For example, Omofolabo Ajayi points out that:

> Although Senghor's objective is to vindicate Africa's compassion and its people-centred cultures, his work unmistakably echoes the colonialist's denigration of African civilization to justify colonizing and exploiting the people and their resources. It is within this haze of schism and assimilation that Negritude constructs its image of an idealized woman and the arche-typal Mother of Africa.
>
> (Ajayi 1997: 38–9)

Ayaji's work is part of a relatively recent feminist critique of negritude which seeks to expose the difficulties in the ideals espoused by a negritude politics of liberation which 'delivers a pungent criticism of the undemocratic ideals the mother symbolism embodies' (*ibid.* 48).

Edward Said has recently made a particularly incisive critique of negritude by portraying it as part of a general trend in reclaiming one's past, naming such a process 'nativism'. Nativism, for Said, is the enterprise which involves reassessing the relationship between the coloniser and the colonised. This reassessment results in the quest for delving into one's past, and is a 'narrative or actuality that stands free from worldly time itself' (1993a: 275). By deploying a contrapuntal reading, Said illustrates how William Butler Yeats, the great Irish poet, has much in common with the poets of the colonised world. He views Yeats as an 'exacerbated example of the *nativist* phenomenon which flourished elsewhere (e.g. *négritude*) as a result of the colonial encounter' (*ibid.* 275). For Said, it is important to move beyond the confines of such local identities that claim, for example, that only the Irish are Irish or the Africans Africans.[9] He sees nativism as constraining and as not the only option for resistance. Instead, he advocates a politics of liberation which owes much to Fanon. But Said also sees the potential to supersede nativism in Césaire's *Cahier d'un retour au pays natal*; when the poet proclaims that 'no race has a monopoly on beauty, on intelligence, on strength, and there is room for everyone at the convocation of conquest' (cited in Said 1993: 279). Thus, Said claims that one moves beyond the limitations of race (and, by implication, nationality).

Conclusion

The historical interactions of the slave trade, direct colonialism and neo-colonialism have determined the manner in which Africa has been dealt with in European discourse. The concept of negritude has developed since its inauguration to include a multiplicity of meanings as diverse as African personality, black renewal and Pan-Africanism. It had much in common with other movements of the struggle for liberation when it was crucial to break down the representations of the colonisers, when it was essential to reconstitute subjectivity. These divergent African experiences and modes of resistance are by no means monolithic, but they nevertheless bind the history of the African diaspora with that of the peoples of Africa. The experiences of Nkrumah, Nyerere, Mandela, Du Bois, Equiano, Blyden, Senghor and Césaire are locked into a common history in their opposition to a 'West' that has sought to denigrate them collectively. But they are all also engaged in the individual struggle against the oppressive nature of colonialism. It is in this context, that Benita Parry (1994) has warned against the all-too-easy dismissal of nativism on the basis of essentialism and, on the contrary, has uttered the rallying call of 'Two Cheers for nativism'. Parry is cognisant of the positive effects that negritude offers, above all else that it has important possibilities for anti-colonial resistance.

It is perplexing why the idea of a common African heritage arouses such passion, when, in contrast, Europeans (be they German, French or Italian, etc.) can claim a common Greek philosophical heritage without detracting from their individuality. As Drachler argues, 'serious inquiry does not hesitate to trace the mainstreams of the European heritage to their sources, nor to seek the common cultural ground on which Western men stand' (Drachler 1964: 168). While it is important to be careful not to replicate the essentialist positions advocated by the negritude writers, it would be far too reductive to simply dismiss and discredit the entire movement, as has been the case in much recent post-colonial writing. It was an important part of the development of a black awareness and consciousness which eventually paved the way for the liberation of Africa. It was necessary for black people to assert their blackness 'not only because of white racism that had dominated western culture for more than three thousand years, but also because of the racism and the fascism ravaging Europe in the 1930s' (Mezu 1973: 94). As Irele has argued:

> Negritude can be considered as not only the end point in the growth of psychological self-sufficiency on the part of the black man, but also as the decisive stage in the intellectual elaboration of modern African identity and consciousness. It represents, in a word, the coming to maturity of the modern African vision.
>
> (Irele 1971: 42)

Just before resigning from the Presidency in Senegal, Senghor noted that it was unlikely that he would see the Senegal he had dreamed about and that it was not easy to reconcile modernity with negritude. He wrote that when 'I open the window and see the sun rising over Gorée, over the island of slavery, I say to myself, all the same, since the end of the slave trade, we have made progress' (cited in Vaillant 1990: 344). The negative representations of Africa and blackness are deeply embedded within the European imagination, but, as Chinua Achebe has noted, 'African identity is in the making. There isn't a final identity that is African. But at the same time, there is an identity coming into existence. And it has a certain context and meaning' (cited in Appiah 1992: 173). It is within this continuing process of identity-formation that the negritude movement needs to be placed. It was an important moment in the long and arduous journey towards decolonisation.

2 Decolonisation and national liberation

When the missionaries came, they had the Bible and we had the land. They said 'Let us pray!' They taught us to close our eyes to pray, and when we opened them again, we had the Bible and they had the land.

Archbishop Desmond Tutu

By the time Belgium took over the Congo from Leopold, most of the major European states had followed their subjects into overseas territories to settle and administer them. They all rationalized ... that they were bringing light into darkness.

S.C. Burchell

The process of decolonisation which witnessed the breaking up of European empires was just as rapid as the colonisation of the continent. Between them, the major European powers in the scramble for Africa – Britain, France, Germany, Belgium, Portugal and Italy – carved out more than fifty territories which eventually became independent nation-states. Britain and France were the two most important European colonial powers in Africa. Together, after World War I, when German colonies were entrusted to them under a League of Nations mandate, they controlled more than seventy per cent of the continent. While decolonisation has become an accepted and important part of the lexicon concerned with the dismantling of empire, it is a term which has not been popular amongst the former colonies. Instead, the idea of liberation struggle is one that more aptly captures the fight for independence (Gifford and Louis 1982; Hargreaves 1979). It is this notion of struggle which indicates that the process of decolonisation is not one to be viewed as having occurred in a narrow time span. Until recently, decolonisation has been conceptualised as part of the history of the colonial power in question, with a focus on what led to the disbanding of empire. Scant attention has been paid to the continuing and enduring effects of colonialism, which cannot be viewed simply as an aftermath of the decolonisation process. Rather, the process merely began with colonisation itself – the colonisers in all cases faced resistance, and in most instances colonial rule was effected only through violence – but it did not end with the achievement of formal independence (Ranger 1985; Said 1993a). This chapter examines the decolonisation process in Africa from such a perspective, taking into account Amilcar Cabral's observation that, 'so long as imperialism is in existence, an independent African state must be a liberation movement in power, or it will not be independent' (1979: 116). It argues that decolonisation was by no means monolithic, and it recognises that the process of colonialism did not end with formal independence but that the structures and effects of colonialism continue to endure. To that end, it engages with the work of two post-colonial thinkers, Frantz Fanon and Edward Said, who have both theorised decolonisation as a process that persists and have offered insightful and compelling strategies and perspectives for liberation and resistance.

The decolonisation process in Africa was by no means uniform. Each country's struggle was unique, characterised by the particular colonising power. In all cases, the colonisers eventually instituted a system of indirect rule which, in theory, was to be a system whereby indigenous people were permitted to be governed under a system of customary law and practice.[1] It was the diversity of systems of rule which had been adopted in different colonies that determined the particular manner in which decolonisation occurred. Nevertheless, in 1947 the end of colonial rule in India served as an exemplar and intensified the struggle for freedom in Africa. The roots of the decolonisation process in India can be traced not only to the imposition of colonial rule and the Indian mutiny of 1857 but more importantly to Thomas Macaulay's infamous 'education minute' which denigrated Indian forms of learning and knowledge. The effect of the education minute, however, was the proliferation of Western-style education amongst the middle classes. In his essay, 'Of Mimicry and Man', Homi Bhabha illustrates the manner in which mimicry became an important strategy of colonial power and knowledge. But for Bhabha, mimicry is not a simple aping of the imperial master. Rather, it characterises the ambivalent relationship between both the coloniser and the colonised. This is necessarily so, because when the imperial master encourages its colonial subject to 'mimic', the resultant product is never exactly the same. As Bhabha points out, 'mimicry represents an *ironic* compromise', one which means that 'colonial mimicry is the desire for a reformed Other, *as a subject of a difference that is almost the same, but not quite*' (1994: 86). Mimicry for the colonised is about becoming like the coloniser whilst remaining different. But mimicry has a menacing side – it has the potential to become mockery and parody. As Bhabha notes, 'mimicry is at once resemblance and menace' (*ibid.*: 86).

Bhabha's adaptation of the notion of mimicry has its origins in both Lacan and Fanon. In the epigraph to his essay on mimicry, he cites Lacan, who sees mimicry as being analogous to camouflage as 'practised in human warfare' (*ibid.*: 85). It is in this way that the idea of menace and mimicry coexist, where the '*menace* of mimicry is its *double* vision which in disclosing the ambivalence of colonial discourse also disrupts its authority' (*ibid.*: 88). Bhabha cites Macaulay's 1835 'Minute on Indian Education' as integral to the colonial process of mimicry that gives rise to the 'mimic man':

> We must at present do our best to form a class who may be interpreters
> between us and the millions whom we govern; a class of persons, Indian in
> blood and colour, but English in taste, in opinions, in morals, in intellect.
>
> (Quoted in Bhabha 1994: 87)

A sense of the double, of mimicry and menace, is created by Macaulay's
vision. The mediating Indian who mimics the imperial master no longer remains
the model colonial subject, because the product of mimicry is ultimately beyond
the control of the colonial master – the 'mimic man' has the potential to become
an insurgent subject. As Bhabha notes, 'the ambivalence of colonial authority
repeatedly turns from mimicry – a difference that is almost nothing but not quite
– to menace – a difference that is almost total but not quite' (Bhabha 1994: 91).
It was in this context that Indian nationalism developed, bringing together
disparate peoples from different regions in order to fight a common enemy, the
British. The nationalist movement was by no means unified and almost from the
start fractured along religious and caste lines.

Perhaps the most important Indian nationalist, who came to embody the
nation itself, was the founding father, Mahatma Gandhi.[2] Gandhi was not unlike
the leaders of the negritude movement. While the French policy of assimilation
brought Africans such as Senghor to the metropole, Gandhi arrived in London
as a result of the British education policy. He came to study law and, like the
Africans in the negritude movement, 'wanted to identify with the British, even
down to choosing the right tailor and taking dancing lessons' (Chamberlain
1985: 17). Gandhi's trajectory was not significantly different from those of his
counterparts in the negritude movement. He moved to South Africa in 1893 and
established a newspaper, *Indian Opinion*, in 1904. An early theme became the
importance of breaking down the representations ascribed to the Asians and
Africans who were subjected to extreme levels of discrimination. It was here that
the essence of his philosophy of civil disobedience and non-violence was
developed.

While African nationalists turned to India for inspiration in order to spur
decolonisation, the colonising powers operated their African colonies on an
altogether different time scale. For them, it was not conceivable that African
countries would achieve their independence within a short time. However, it was
education for Africans in the metropole, from both French and British colonies,
which was an important mechanism not only for allowing them to gain
legitimacy at the centre but also for forging alliances which led ultimately to calls
for Pan-Africanism.[3] James Coleman asserted that the nationalist movements in
Africa were 'activated by the Western ideas of democracy … and self-
determination' (Coleman 1954: 407). He was partly correct in this assertion, but
only in so far as the resistance to colonisation gained legitimacy in Western terms
by adopting the language which the colonisers could understand.

The decolonisation of Africa began in 1957, in the British colony of Ghana,
where there existed a largely-decentralised system and where there was little in
the way of a settler presence. The Ghanaian experience was not meant to serve

as a precursor for the entire decolonisation process. However, Ghana set the pace and touched the imagination of all sub-Saharan African peoples; once Ghana was granted freedom, it became difficult to stem the tide. Ghana gained independence under the leadership of Kwame Nkrumah, who proclaimed that Africans should 'seek the political kingdom and that then all would be added'. In the case of Ghana, however, the hopes and dreams of the nation were dashed, as Nkrumah was unable to meet the rising expectations of the population. His response to the crisis was one which came to be replicated in most African countries – a turn towards authoritarianism and the adoption of the one-party state. Despite the Ghanaian problems, in February 1960 the British Prime Minister Harold Macmillan made his famous 'winds of change' speech which led to the rapid dismantling of the European empires. He noted:

> Ever since the break up of the Roman Empire one of the constant facts of political life in Europe has been the emergence of independent nations ... Fifteen years ago this movement spread through Asia ... Today the same thing is happening in Africa ... The wind of change is blowing through this continent ...
>
> (Macmillan, cited in Madgwick *et al.* 1982: 286)

To a large extent, this concession was the product of the protracted liberation war in Kenya, where a strong settler presence meant that the decolonisation process was characterised inevitably by violence (Ogot and Ochieng 1995). This pattern of violence was repeated in all colonies where a strong white settler presence existed, such as Algeria, Zimbabwe and South Africa.

Although violence was common during the decolonisation process in both British and French settler colonies, there remained important differences. These were a result of the manner in which French colonies were conceived – as an extension of France overseas. It was the assimilation policy which determined the relations between the coloniser and colonised. As Michael Crowder notes

> the French, when confronted with people they considered barbarians, be-lieved it their mission to convert them into Frenchmen. This implied a fundamental acceptance of their potential human equality, but a total dismissal of African culture as of any value. Africans were considered to be people without any history, without any civilization worthy of name, constantly at war with one another, fortunate to have been put in touch with the fruits of French civilization.
>
> (Crowder, as cited in Khapoya 1998: 120)

For France, the 'civilising mission' of colonialism became more of a reality through the view that its overseas colonies had to be subjected to the same laws and values as in France. Although in theory this policy of equality was promoted, in reality it was only applied to the white French settlers. Not until 1914 was the first black African elected to represent Senegal under the system which granted some colonies with representation in Paris (Chamberlain 1985: 56). In 1946 France reorganised its colonies into the French Union, with a number of colonies designated 'Associated States'. Under this configuration, the distinction between citizens and subjects in the Union was to be abolished; despite the rhetoric, though, the distinction remained until 1958, when Charles de Gaulle returned to power. Under de Gaulle, the Union was replaced by the French Community. However, the Community did not last long, as the 'winds of change' affected the French colonies, and a rapid process of decolonisation ensued.

The process of attaining independence, which began in the late 1950s, rapidly engulfed both British and French colonies, and by the mid 1960s most had attained freedom. But it was not until the 1970s that the Portuguese empire came to an end – Zimbabwe gained independence later in the decade, and in the 1990s South Africa finally succumbed to majority rule under the aegis of the African National Congress and Nelson Mandela. Although for the bulk of Africa the formal liberation struggle ended in the 1960s, the task of nation-building has been anything but liberating. This can be attributed to a large extent to the forms of governance bequeathed to the colonies in the dying moments of formal colonialism. The multi-party system of rule which was then inaugurated in all the colonies had little to do with the authoritarian forms of governance which had pervaded the colonial enterprise. As Basil Davidson points out, the 'transfer of power' was foremost a 'transfer of crisis' (1992: 190). In short, democratic rule was not a legacy of the European empires in Africa. Hence, it was not long before the victory of independence turned to patterns of domination and authoritarianism which replicated colonial rule (Ahluwalia 1996a). It was in this context that Nkrumah (1965) noted that colonialism had given way to neo-colonialism. Nkrumah's intervention signalled that decolonisation was a much wider concept than the mere transfer of power or the gaining of political power. It was a process that entailed social, economic and cultural, as well as political, liberation, and therefore was a phenomenon with many dimensions.

Although the decolonisation of political institutions which these nations inherited was rapid, critically it was the failure to decolonise the mind that ensured that, 'Africans continued to work on colonial assumptions, making cultural, emotional and intellectual decolonization difficult for the heirs of empire' (Birmingham 1995: 7). Ashis Nandy has written about how colonialism colonises the mind and unleashes cultural forces within colonised societies, thereby forever altering their priorities. He argues that it is important to conceptualise 'the concept of the modern West from a geographical and temporal entity to a psychological category. The West is now everywhere, within the West and outside, in structures and in minds' (1983: xi). It was precisely this need to decolonise the mind which Fanon had recognised as being central to liberation – a process that transcends the end of colonial occupation.[4]

Frantz Fanon: the oppressed consciousness of the colonised

Frantz Fanon recognised the centrality of the need to decolonise the mind, a task which he envisaged as far more difficult than the mere removal of the coloniser. It was Marx, in his 1853 essay 'The Future Results of British Rule in India', who envisaged the role of colonialism in the Indian context as that of a double mission: 'one destructive, the other regenerating – the annihilation of old Asiatic society, and the laying of material foundations of Western society in Asia' (1977: 322). What worried Fanon was the insidious nature of the colonising culture, which could so easily become part of the culture of the very people that it dominated.

Fanon had been born in Martinique on 20 June 1925, but at seventeen, while Martinique was under Nazi control, he fled the island and joined the Allied forces fighting against Germany in North Africa and Europe. The War had a profound effect on his identity. He had grown up in Martinique thinking that he was French, but during the War he experienced a great deal of racism, not only in the French Army but also from the French population. When he returned to Martinique as a decorated war veteran, Bulhan notes, he 'brought with him not only memories regarding the horrors of war, but also serious doubts about his identity as a Frenchman' (1985: 28). This identity had to be painfully reconstituted into that of a black West Indian when he moved to Paris to study, taking advantage of the scholarships that were available to war veterans.[5] After studying psychiatry in France, he went to Algeria, where he eventually joined the Algerian freedom fighters in their struggle for independence from French colonisation. In Algeria, he adopted a new black identity, which itself remained problematic – for, to the Algerian revolutionaries, Fanon 'remained a European interloper' (Gates 1991: 468).[6]

Robyn Dane has argued that, in order to understand Fanon's project, it is necessary to critically examine his *Black Skins, White Masks* and *The Wretched of the Earth*. She argues that, 'the former tells how colonization looks from inside the skull; the latter tells how it should theoretically look, albeit not completely, after the world ceases to be insane, *viz.* after the foreigners are expelled' (Dane 1994: 76). The central problematic that Fanon seeks to deal with in his work is that of, 'releasing possibilities of human existence and history imprisoned by the colonization of experience and the racialization of consciousness' (Sekyi-Otu 1996: 17). In *Black Skins, White Masks*, Fanon characterises the colonised as having deeply ingrained within their souls an inferiority complex which arises out of the death of their cultural origins (Fanon 1986). He carefully documents the manner in which colonialism distorts the colonial subject's psyche. He provocatively proclaims that the 'black man is not a man', that colonisation dehumanises and objectifies the colonised, rendering them incapable of being human.[7] He captures the profound alienation which is caused by the very processes of colonialism, which essentially objectify the colonised subject:

I was responsible at the same time for my body, for my race, for my ancestors. I subjected myself to an objective examination, I discovered my blackness, my ethnic characteristics, and I was battered down by tom-toms,
cannibalism, intellectual deficiency, fetishism, raunch defects, slave-ships and
above all else, above all: 'Sho' good eatin' ' .... I was hated, despised, detested,
not only by the neighbour across the street or my cousin on my mother's side,
but by an entire race.

(Fanon 1986: 112, 118)

For Fanon, the process of decolonisation entailed not only that, 'the last shall
be first and the first last' but also the 'putting into practice of this sentence'
(1967: 37). The colonial structure, he urged, needed to be dismantled by violence
in order that the colonised could regain a sense of self-hood. This was a
cathartic exercise which revitalised the colonised, thereby forging a new identity
not only for an individual but also for the collective society. This is possible only
through rejection of the coloniser's culture. In that sense, decolonisation could
not be anything but a success, because it represented a complete antithesis of the
colonial framework. It was a success because it reversed the colonial system of
rule that compartmentalised the worlds of the coloniser and the colonised, with
each seen to be operating in completely separate spheres. Here, a system of
binary opposites operated, such as French/Arab, white/black, developed/
underdeveloped.[8] This differentiation Fanon captured when he described the
spatiality of the colonial urban site:

The zone where the natives live is not complementary to the zone inhabited by
the settlers. The two zones are opposed, but not in the service of a higher unity
... they both follow the principle of reciprocal exclusivity. No conciliation is
possible, for the two terms, one is superfluous. The settlers' town is a strongly
built town, all made of stone and steel ... a well-fed town, an easy-going town;
its belly is always full of good things. The settlers' town is a town of white people, of foreigners.

The town belonging to the colonized people, or at least the native town, the
Negro village, the medina, the reservation, is a place of ill fame, peopled by
men of evil repute. They are born there, it matters little where or how; they die
there, it matters not where, nor how. It is a world without spaciousness ... a
hungry town starved of bread, of meat, of shoes, of coal, of light ... a town of
niggers and dirty Arabs.

(Fanon 1967: 39)

Abdul Janmohamed captures the paradoxes of colonialism in which the 'native'
is, on the one hand, completely denigrated, and, on the other, is absolutely
necessary to maintaining the superiority of the settler. The colonial system, he
points out, 'simultaneously wills the annihilation and the multiplication of the
natives' (1983: 4). A necessary part of colonialism is that the colonisers problematise
the culture and the very being of the colonised, and the latter come to accept the

'supremacy of the white man's values' (Fanon 1967: 43). During the period of decolonisation, it is this very acceptance that is repudiated. But, for Fanon, it does not follow that there is the possibility of a simple return to some essentialised pre-colonial culture. As Neil Lazarus convincingly points out, it is not that pre-colonial culture is seen to be 'primitive' but that it is destroyed by colonialism. It is because of this destruction that colonialism can be confronted only on its 'own terrain', on the 'basis of the struggle for national liberation' (1999: 87). And yet, in his discussion of Christopher Miller's *Theories of Africans* (1990), Lazarus suggests that Fanon may be susceptible to criticism. He argues that, 'the plain fact is that, throughout Africa and elsewhere in the colonial world, precolonial social, cultural, and ideological forms survived the colonial era meaningfully. Indeed, they continue to survive meaning-fully today, in the "postcolonial" present' (1999: 89). There is little argument that elements of pre-colonial cultural and social forms persist, but the importance of Fanon's argument for post-colonialism is that there is no *pure* pre-colonial culture which survives; rather, colonialism transforms the culture not only of the colonised but also of the coloniser.

The colonisation of the mind is manifested in the manner in which a people's history is denied, and they are made to feel inferior and incapable of challenging the colonial order. In this way the national identity of a people is denigrated and made non-functional. The colonised are rendered not only economically dependent but also psychologically dependent, thus making them subjects of the colonial power. Fanon notes that colonialism consciously sought 'to drive into the natives' heads the idea that if the settlers were to leave, they would at once fall back into barbarism, degradation and bestiality' (1967: 169). It is through decolonisation that the colonised country begins to construct a history. This can be conceived only as a result of the war of liberation, whereby the colonised nation is able 'to rediscover its own genius, to reassume its history and assert its sovereignty' (1970: 94).

In order to reclaim the history of the colonised, it is not enough that the colonial power be defeated. A new consciousness that is part of the national culture is required. It is in this context, that Fanon distances himself from the negritude movement. For him, there is no returning to an old culture. Rather, a national culture arises out of the struggle in the fight against colonialism. This national culture 'is the whole body of efforts made by a people in the sphere of thought to describe, justify and praise the action through which that people has created itself and keeps itself in existence' (1967: 188). This process of forging a national culture is ongoing and in many cases predates the struggle itself. Fanon observes that: 'Everything works together to awaken the native's sensibility and to make unreal and unacceptable the contemplative attitude, or the acceptance of defeat. ... His world comes to lose its accursed character' (*ibid.*: 196).

For Fanon, the revolutionary struggle is paramount. It is through such a struggle that a new consciousness as well as a new society are restructured. This new consciousness can arise only by destabilising the colonial order and, through the struggle, 'there is not only the disappearance of colonialism but also the disappear-ance of the colonised man' (*ibid.*: 197). Central to the forging of a new consciousness is the need for political education. It is not only the army and the party cadres who need to undergo a programme of political education, but the entire population. Fanon points to the centrality of educating the masses, for it is they who are integral to the process of transformation:

> To educate the masses politically ... is to try, relentlessly and passionately, to teach the masses that everything depends on them; that if we stagnate it is their responsibility, and that if we go forward it is due to them too, that there is no such thing as a demiurge ... but that the demiurge is the people themselves and the magic hands are finally only the hands of the people.
>
> (Fanon 1967: 157)

It is through this process of education that the cultural domination of the colonial power can be eradicated and a new national culture established into which the mass of the people can be integrated. It is the restructuring of consciousness that becomes central to the decolonisation process. Fanon demonstrates that it is not enough to merely attain decolonisation but that it is important to decolonise the mind. He argues that it 'is not possible to take one's distance with respect to colonialism without at the same time taking it with respect to the idea that the colonised holds of himself through the filter of colonialist culture' (1970: 114).

In recent times, a reconceptualisation of Fanon has emerged in which Fanon is seen as a global theorist who can be understood by problematising his identity.[9] Gates has noted this trend, commenting that this fascination is a result of the convergence of 'the problematic of colonialism with that of subject-formation. As a psychoanalyst of culture, as a champion of the wretched of the earth, he is an almost irresistible figure for a criticism that sees itself as both oppositional and postmodern' (1991: 458).[10] For Fanon, decolonisation is not enough. It is liberation that he strives for, and a liberation that not only frees black people but also white people, thereby showing the 'white man that he was the perpetrator and the victim of a delusion' (1976: 225). As Sekyi-Otu has noted, Fanon's message can be starkly stated as:

> the moral credibility of the fight against the white man, the legitimacy of the postcolonial age, the justice of transactions among its citizenry and of the forms of governance under which they live – all this rests on the degree to which the independence of persons is honoured.
>
> (Sekyi-Otu 1996: 237)

It is Fanon's vision of liberation which has a profound influence on Edward Said. Said undertakes a contrapuntal re-reading of Fanon in order to carry forward Fanon's project of liberation, pointing out that his work was aimed at forcing the metropole to rethink its history in the light of the decolonisation process.

Edward Said and resistance

Edward Said's (1993a) reflections, nearly fifteen years after the publication of *Orientalism*, are an important backdrop to an understanding of his strategy for resistance. As Said notes, he has borne the brunt of an attack that suggests that his work has not lived up to the promise of offering resistance, primarily because of the manner in which he conceives agency. However, such a conclusion is possible only as a result of a particular reading of Said, which views him as misappropriating Foucault. Although Said has a clear debt to Foucault, there are important points of departure. More than anything else, Said is unhappy with what he sees as a lack of political commitment within post-structuralist discourse. He accuses Foucault of eliminating the 'central dialectic of opposed forces that still underlies modern society', which means that he is unable to have the 'perspective of an engaged political worker for whom the fascinated description of exercised power is never a substitute for trying to change power relations within society' (1983: 221).

For Said, Foucault's conception of power leaves no room for resistance. He characterises it as a 'Spinozist conception [which] has drawn a circle around itself, constituting a unique territory in which Foucault has imprisoned himself and others with him' (*ibid.*: 245). Said's project, on the contrary, is not to be trapped; it is one in which he sees the potential to resist and recreate. This is implicit in *Orientalism*, which stresses the relationship between power and knowledge. For Said, the power of the Orientalists lay in their 'knowing' the Orient, which in itself constituted power and yet also was an exercise in power. Hence, for Said, resistance is twofold: to know the Orient outside the discourse of Orientalism, and to represent and present this knowledge to the Orientalists – to write back to them.[11]

However, what Said is writing back is not an authentic story of the Orient, which only an Oriental has the capacity to tell, but rather the fallacy of authentication, for there is no 'real' Orient since, '"the Orient" is itself a constituted entity, and the notion that there are geographical spaces with indigenous, radically "different" inhabitants who can be defined on the basis of some religion, culture, or racial essence proper to that geographical space is equally a highly debatable idea' (1979: 322). Hence, it is important to note that Said's non-coercive knowledge is one that runs counter to the deployment of discourse analysis within *Orientalism*. Despite his obvious debt to Foucault methodologically, he maintains distance and allows for authorial creativity.[12]

This Saidian strategy of resistance is premised upon intellectuals who exercise their critical consciousness. The task of such a critical consciousness is to 'occupy itself within the intrinsic conditions on which knowledge is made possible' (1983: 182). For Said, the location of critical consciousness lies in challenging both the hegemonic nature of dominant culture as well as 'the sovereignty of the systematic method' (1978: 673). By adopting such a perspective, Said argues it is possible for the critic to deal with a text in two ways – by describing not only what is in the text but also what is invisible. Here, Said clearly is advocating a Foucauldian strategy of textuality. He writes: 'my sense of the contemporary critical consciousness is that having initially detached itself from the dominant culture, having thereafter adopted a situated and responsible adversary position for itself, this consciousness begins its meaningful cognitive activity in attempting to account for, and rationally to discover and know, the force of statements in texts' (*ibid.*: 713). It is the development of this critical consciousness that is central to Said's strategy of resistance.

While the question of resistance is not made explicit in his earlier work, in *Culture and Imperialism* resistance becomes a central theme. In a dialectical relationship, Said argues that resistance against empire was ever pervasive with the advent of imperialism. He points out that the advent of colonisation always resulted in resistance. Said's claim here could well be read as an exemplar of Foucault's formulation that, 'where there is power there is resistance'. And yet, it is here that Said wishes to part company with Foucault. For Said, this is the playfulness of Foucault, the lack of political commitment. He argues that, 'resistance cannot equally be an adversarial alternative to power and a dependent function of it, except in some metaphysical, ultimately trivial sense' (1983: 246).

Said's strategy for resistance encapsulates a twofold process. It can be likened to the two phases of decolonisation which he discusses in *Culture and Imperialism*. The first is the recovery of 'geographical territory', while the second is the 'changing of cultural territory' (1993a: 252). Hence, primary resistance, which involves 'fighting against outside intrusion', is succeeded by secondary resistance, which entails ideological or cultural reconstitution. Resistance then becomes a process 'in the rediscovery and repatriation of what had been suppressed in the natives' past by the processes of imperialism' (*ibid.*: 253). The significance and emphasis of the prefix 're' here is 'the partial tragedy of resistance, that it must to a certain degree work to recover forms already established or at least influenced or infiltrated by the culture of empire' (*ibid.*: 253).

There are two motifs in this culture of resistance which Said explores by comparing the relationship between the self and the other. In the first motif, he juxtaposes Conrad's *Heart of Darkness* with Ngugi Wa Thiong'o's *The River Between* and Tayb Salih's *Season of Migration to the North*. This juxtaposition allows Said to conclude that Third World writers have been deeply affected by the colonial enterprise and that they are part of a process in which the 'formerly silent native speaks and acts on territory reclaimed as part of a general movement of resistance, from the colonialist' (*ibid.*: 256).

The second motif can be discerned in the reinterpretation of Shakespeare's *The Tempest* by writers in the Third World. The importance of this motif lies also in the manner in which texts within the European canon have been subjected to new readings. Said points out that:

> In a totally new way in Western culture, the interventions of non-European artists and scholars cannot be dismissed or silenced, and these interventions are not only an integral part of a political movement, but, in many ways the move-

ment's successfully guiding imagination, intellectual and figurative energy reseeing and rethinking the terrain common to whites and nonwhites.

(Said 1993: 256)

Here, Said notes how a post-imperial identity has been ascribed to Caliban. This inscription, for Said, is framed in terms of the problem 'how does a culture seeking to become independent of imperialism imagine its own past?' (*ibid.*: 258). Said sees three alternative solutions to the problem. The first is to become a willing servant of imperialism, a 'native informant'. The second is to be aware and accept the past without allowing it to prevent future developments. The third is what leads to nativism, and that arises out of the shedding of the colonial self in search for the essential pre-colonial self (*ibid.*: 258). While Said celebrates an anti-imperialist nationalism that emerges out of a configuration in which the self identifies with a subject people, he warns, as Fanon did, that 'nationalist consciousness can very easily lead to a frozen rigidity' which has the potential to degenerate into 'chauvinism and xenophobia' (*ibid.*: 258). In order to avoid this, it is best to have some sort of amalgamation of the three alternatives allowing Caliban to see his 'own history as an aspect of the history of *all* subjugated men and women, and comprehends the complex truth of his own social and historical situation' (*ibid.*: 258).

By effecting such an amalgamation, Said is conscious of not minimising the importance of such incipient nationalism, which allows people to see 'themselves as prisoners in their own land' (*ibid.*: 258). He argues that there are three topics that characterise decolonising cultural resistance, and they are interrelated. First, the restoration of community, of the nation itself, is necessary. He points to both Benedict Anderson's and Hannah Arendt's formulations which seek to explain the rise of such nationalism by the use of imagined solidarities. Second, resistance as an alternative method of reading history is critical. Here, resistance is viewed as writing back to the Occident in an attempt to break down the very discourse which constructs the self and the Other. This writing back, as Said notes, is the project of the Australian volume, *The Empire Writes Back* and Salman Rushdie's *Midnight's Children*. However, what is critical in this writing back is the breaking down of barriers which exist between different cultures. This process is encapsulated in Said's characterisation, the 'voyage in'. As he states, 'The conscious effort to enter into the discourse of Europe and the West, to mix with it, transform it, to make it acknowledge marginalized or suppressed or forgotten histories .... I call this effort the *voyage in*' (*ibid.*: 261).

The third topic is a movement away from separatist nationalism towards human community and human liberation. The interrelationship of these three topics becomes clear when viewed as a progressive formulation. The first topic seeks to assert a cultural resistance and in this process makes the Other strong. The second topic draws on this strength of the Other to break down the self and the Other. This culminates in the third topic, by bringing the self and the Other together. This formulation is consistent with Said's assertions of cultural hybridity and multiple identities. He argues that there is:

a consistent intellectual trend within the nationalist consensus that is vitally critical, that refuses the short-term blandishments of separatist and triumphalist slogans in favour of the larger, more generous human realities of community among cultures, peoples, and societies. This community is the real human liberation portended by the resistance to imperialism.

(Said 1993: 262)

For Said, this is not a simple rejection of nationalism, because, in the tradition of C.L.R. James, Fanon and Cabral, 'nationalist resistance to imperialism was always critical of itself' (*ibid.*: 264). What Said rejects is the manner in which such nationalism develops into nativism, as in the case of Négritude.

For Said, it is imperative to transcend such simplistic formulations even while recognising their role in the early stages of identity formation. This can be achieved by 'discovering a world *not* constructed out of warring essences' (*ibid.*: 277). In addition, such transcendence is possible if one recognises that people have multiple identities which allow them to think beyond their local identities:

I do not think that the anti-imperialist challenge represented by Fanon and Césaire or others like them has by any means been met: neither have we taken them seriously as models or representations of human effort in the contemporary world. In fact Fanon and Césaire … jab directly at the question of identity and of identitarian thought, that secret sharer of present anthropological reflection on 'otherness' and 'difference'. What Fanon and Césaire required of their own partisans, even during the heat of struggle, was to abandon fixed ideas of settled identity and culturally authorized definition. Become different, they said, in order that your fate as colonized peoples can *be* different.

(Said 1989: 224–5)

The focus, then, is not on a racialised notion of culture but on a decolonised culture where race is no longer a key element: a decolonised culture where consciousness and conscious activity will be liberated. For Said, an alternative, non-coercive knowledge which counters the dominant narrative becomes essential. It is this need for a counter-narrative which motivates him.

Said's voyage in begins by searching for possible sites of resistance. Despite the pervasiveness and hegemonic nature of dominant discourse, there is capacity to resist because, 'no matter how apparently complete the dominance of an ideology or social system, there are always going to be parts of the social experience that it does not cover and control' (1993a: 289). Under a Foucauldian formulation of power (which he in part endorses), such capacity to resist is problematic. Yet the ability to resist, to recreate oneself as a post-colonial, anti-imperialist subject is central for Said. This recreation of the self needs to be contextualised in terms of Sartre's influence on Said. Sartre's advocacy of an existentialist philosophy of freedom is one that Said heeds. For it is the construction of identity that constitutes freedom, because human beings are what they make of themselves, even if they are subjects of repressive discourses.

Mustapha Marrouchi has pointed out that, 'logic and the logic of identity are founded, for Said, on the opposition of inside and outside which inaugurates all binary opposition' (1991: 70). And yet Said objects to the homology between pairings such as us/them, inside/out. At the same time, he faces the problem that identity is constituted through a process of othering. As he argues, 'All cultures spin out a dialectic of self and other, the subject "I" who is native, authentic, at home, and the object "it" or "you", who is foreign, perhaps threatening, different, out there' (1986: 40). Identity is crucial to Said because the identity of a people determines the manner in which they organise knowledge. This is made clear in his argument that all humans view their differences as matters of interpretation: 'To have said that there was a characteristic French or British attitude in the nineteenth century is to have said – however vaguely – that there was a characteristic French or British way of dealing with reality' (1992: 143).

For Said, the workings of identity issues are clearly at the heart of his project. To him, identity is not static; rather, it is something that, 'each age and society re-creates ... over historical, social, intellectual and political process that takes place as a contest involving individuals and institutions' (1995: 332). Hence, the notion that any culture could be explained in terms of itself, without any reference to the outside, is an anathema to him. He rejects the notion that insiders have a privileged position from which to address these questions (1985: 15). It is these insights into identity that point towards Said's notions of resistance, which in turn allows us to appreciate how it is that he comes to argue that, despite the discourse of Orientalism, intellectuals from the colonies are able to 'write back'. The 'voyage in' for these intellectuals begins by:

> dealing frontally with the metropolitan culture, using the techniques, discourses, weapons of scholarship and criticism once reserved exclusively for the European. Their work is, on its merits, only apparently dependent (and by no means parasitic) on mainstream Western discourses; the result of its originality and creativity has been the transformation of the very terrain of the disciplines.
>
> (Said 1993a: 293)

By operating inside the discourse of Orientalism, these intellectuals negate the Orientalist constructions which have been ascribed to them. It is through this process of negation that they are able to become selves, as opposed to assuming the identity of mere others which they inherit. This is precisely the voyage that Fanon made when he wrote about the experience of colonisation from a French perspective, from 'within a French space hitherto inviolable and now invaded and re-examined critically by a dissenting native' (1993a: 295). The 'voyage in' negates the logocentric process by rendering it obsolete. For Said, this entails reading 'texts from the metropolitan centre and from the peripheries contrapuntally, according neither the privilege of "objectivity" to "our side" nor the encumbrance of "subjectivity" to "theirs"' (312).

The notion that texts are not finished objects is an important one that reflects the influence of Giambattista Vico on Said. The conception that texts are a result of a historical and dynamic process, that texts have contexts, is of particular significance. For Said, this rests on '*what is* and *what can be made to be* in Vico's work' (1976: 821, emphasis in original). What is important about a text, then, is not only what is there but what can be put there. The 'voyage in' allows for the development of texts that break down the tyranny of the dominant discourse. But to be able to do this is to recognise the relationship between the dominator and the dominated. This is essential because 'the great imperial experience of the past two hundred years is global and universal; it has implicated every corner of the globe, the colonizer and the colonized together' (1993a: 313).

Said's emphasis on the impact of the colonial experience on both the colonised and the colonisers has important ramifications for his strategy of resistance. It is here that he borrows directly from Fanon's discussion of the 'pitfalls of nationalist consciousness'. And it is here that Said's reading of Fanon is crucial. He states: 'If I have so often cited Fanon, it is because more dramatically and decisively than anyone, I believe, he expresses the immense cultural shift from the terrain of nationalist independence to the theoretical domain of liberation' (*ibid.*: 323–4).

For Fanon, it is important not only to recreate national identity and consciousness in the process of decolonisation but also to go beyond and create a social consciousness at the moment of liberation. Social consciousness becomes all the more important because, without it, decolonisation merely becomes the replacement of one form of domination by another. In *Culture and Imperialism* Said speculates that Fanon has been influenced by reading Lukacs' *History and Class Consciousness*. This conjecture allows Said to read violence in Fanon as 'the synthesis that overcomes the reification of white man as subject, Black man as object' (*ibid.*: 326). For Fanon, Said argues, violence is the 'cleansing force' that allows for 'epistemological revolution', which is like a Lukacsian act of mental will that overcomes the fragmentation and reification of the self and the Other. The need for such violence arises when the native decides that 'colonization must end'. For Fanon:

> The violence of the colonial regime and the counter-violence of the native balance each other and respond to each other in an extraordinary reciprocal homogeneity … The settler's work is to make dreams of liberty impossible for the native. The native's work is to imagine all possible methods for destroying the settler. On the logical plane, the Manicheanism of the settler produces a Manicheanism of the natives, to the theory of the 'absolute evil of the native' the theory of the 'absolute evil of the settler' replies.
>
> (Fanon, quoted in Said 1993a: 327)

This quotation has two important implications for Said's hypothesis of Lukacs' influence on Fanon. First, this influence meant that Fanon reified the subject and the object. Second, Fanon came to see violence as an act of mental will which overcomes this reification. Said argues that Fanon's is not a simplistic nationalism that arises out of the cleansing force of violence. Rather, Fanon recognises that 'orthodox nationalism followed along the same track hewn out by imperialism, which while it appeared to be conceding authority to the nationalist bourgeoisie was really extending its hegemony'. This allows Said to argue that, in Fanon, the emphasis on armed struggle is tactical and that he wanted 'somehow to bind the European as well as the native together in a new non-adversarial community of awareness and anti-imperialism' (1993a: 330–1). That, for Fanon, all colonial revolutions were to free blacks as well as whites and therefore 'show the white man that he is at once the perpetrator and the victim of a delusion' (1967: 225). It is in this context that Dane has argued that Fanon's 'mightiest act was not advocating violent "catharsis", it was legitimizing native rage against the absolute power of imperialism' (1994: 79).

This Lukacsian influence can be identified also within Said. For him, the act of will which overcomes this reification is the 'writing back' to cultural imperialism. Through this process, a new system of 'mobile relationships must replace the hierarchies inherited from imperialism' (Said 1993a: 330). Thus, the essence of liberation and emancipation is a consciousness and recognition of a universal self, which is a unification of the self and the Other. Such a conclusion is possible because Said views Fanon as not merely a theoretician of resistance and decolonisation but also one of liberation. A Saidian strategy of resistance is the ability to make the 'voyage in', to write back to imperialism. This is possible because of the potential for humans to negate their experiences, to imagine another world, a better world in which the colonisers and the colonised work towards liberation.

Fanon and Said: a strategy towards liberation

The massive problems which the nationalist leaders inherited at independence and the inability to forge a national identity have tempered the euphoria of independence. The Herculean task of development and the imperatives to modernise have meant that most African leaders, unable to meet the rising expectations of their populations, have retreated into authoritarian modes of rule. The malaise that appears to pervade Africa has been paralleled within African studies. The task for African studies lies in coming to terms with what is appropriate for the African condition – for too long Africa has endured a Eurocentric conceptualisation of theory. This is where Fanon and Said are instructive. They urge Africanists to place the continent within its socio-economic, historical and cultural perspective while recognising that the amorphous nature of imperialism has entailed a globalisation which has penetrated virtually every part of the continent. They have focused attention on the problem of decolonisation. Decolonisation, Said explains in an interview with Michael Sprinker, is viewed not merely in the narrow sense of gaining independence from a colonial power but also 'in the whole drama or spectacle of neocolonialism and dependency, the IMF, the debt trap, etc. ... It's the continuation of the colonization process which has not been contained by the moment of decolonization' (Sprinker 1992: 236).

Further, they see a dialectic relationship between independence and liberation. Said makes his debt to Fanon clear and points out that, 'One ought to be able to make more precise the interpretations of various political and intellectual communities where the issue is not independence but liberation, a completely different thing. What Fanon calls the conversion, the transformation, of national consciousness, hasn't yet taken place. It's an unfinished project, and that's where I think my work has begun' (Sprinker 1992: 236).

Conclusion

A common perception which has become predominant in both the metropole as well as the periphery is that colonialism entailed progress and modernisation. However, to simply accept such a truism uncritically is problematic. While colonialism brought with it new modernising imperatives, it was not possible to sustain colonial rule without tapping into traditional modes of power. Thus the colonial power, from the beginning, was caught in a double-bind. On the one hand, it sought to denigrate and erase the culture of the colonised, and yet it recognised that in order to sustain its rule it needed to retain elements of that very culture. It was the interaction of the coloniser and the colonised, however, which fundamentally transformed the cultures of both of them. As Jan Nederveen Pieterse and Bhiku Parekh note, 'The decolonization of imagination involves both the colonizers and the colonized. The decolonization of the *Western* imagination means re-viewing Western horizons in the light of the collusion with empire and colonialism, and with the ongoing asymmetries of global power' (1995: 3). Decolonisation has come to symbolise much more than the mere dismantling of colonial rule. The term colonialism itself signifies modes of domination regardless of geographical space. Hence, even in the metropole, it is common to speak about 'metaphorical "colonisations" having to do with region, class, race and gender' (Shohat and Stam 1985: 53).

Decolonisation also cannot be equated with 'after colonialism'. The term is suggestive of a temporal break with colonialism, but decolonisation is a dynamic, ongoing process which affects both the culture of the colonised and the colonisers. It is a process that Frantz Fanon recognised as essential to liberation and one that Edward Said has developed by articulating a theory of resistance. As the world increasingly becomes interconnected with a heightened sense of globalisation, the processes of decolonisation are no longer restricted to the geographical entities, the colonies. Rather, they are integral to the imagination. These imaginary constraints constructed by colonialism in order to police and maintain a system of oppressive rule are being challenged and the tyranny of structures dismantled. The task for Africa lies in confronting these colonial structures and recognising that there is no possibility of returning to a romantic essentialised pre-colonial past. Rather, there is an urgent need to confront the present in order to face the future. This can only be accomplished by dealing with colonialism and recognising the ensuing cultural hybridity which emanated and continues to emerge. As Chinweizu and Mechukwu note:

> on the one hand, our culture has to destroy all encrustations of colonial mentality, and on the other hand, has to map out new foundations for an African modernity. This cultural task demands a deliberate and calculated process of syncretism: one which, above all, emphasizes valuable continuities with our pre-colonial culture, welcomes vitalizing contributions from other cultures, and exercises inventive genius in making a healthy and distinguished synthesis from them all.
>
> (Chinweizu and Mechukwu 1985: 239)

3 Modernity and the problem of the nation-state

Colonies do not cease to be colonies simply because they are independent.

Benjamin Disraeli

Within the modern world which has come into being, changes have taken place as the effect of dominant political power by which new possibilities are constructed and old ones destroyed. The changes do not reflect a simple expansion of the range of individual choice, but the creation of conditions in which only new (i.e. modern) choices can be made. The reason for this is that changes involve the re-formation of subjectivities and the re-organization of social spaces in which subjects act and are acted upon. The modern state – imperial, colonial, post-colonial – has been crucial to these processes of construction/destruction.

Talal Asad

An important facet of post-colonial theory has been its engagement with nationalism and anti-colonial resistance. This concern arises from the decolonisation processes which witnessed the rise of nationalism in the colonies paving the way towards independence. Despite its focus on nationalism, post-colonial theory has failed to engage fully with the state. Aijaz Ahmad (1992, 1995a) points out that post-colonial theory is portrayed as having a certain amnesia in the way it deals with work done in the past, especially by the Dependency school and Marxist scholars whose work included an account of the state. In a recent piece, Ahmad revisits the work of Hamza Alavi (1972) and his notion of the 'Overdeveloped Post-Colonial State' as an example of the necessity to ground post-colonial theory.[1] These concerns find resonance within critiques of cultural studies which point out that, as a discipline, it has emerged out of the theoretical turmoil of Marxism as well as the general malaise of the economy that plagued the Western world after the OPEC oil crisis and the resultant escalating levels of inflation and unemployment. These criticisms raise serious questions about cultural studies as a particular project of the left. In part, Ahmad's concerns have been echoed by Jon Beasley-Murray, who argues that a fundamental problem with cultural studies – and, by implication, with post-colonialism – is the substitution of culture for state in its analyses. This substitution occurs because of the manner in which the concept of hegemony is theorised and the inability of cultural studies to recognise that the cultural 'may itself operate as a screen, a fetishized substitute, in the political logic of populist command' (Beasley-Murray 1998: 190–1).[2] In an attempt to discern whether the project of the left has a future, he argues that, while cultural studies is perhaps one of the best avenues via which to pursue critical theory, it nevertheless, 'has something like a compulsion to repeat the populist tendency of substituting culture for the state in its analysis' (*ibid.*: 190). Similarly, David Lloyd and Paul Thomas have pointed out that contemporary cultural studies 'has largely taken the concept of culture for granted and failed fully to critique the intrinsic relation of culture to the idea of the state' (1998: 8).

Although the relationship between culture and the state is explored implicitly in post-colonial studies through the trope of resistance and anti-colonial nationalism, it is nevertheless, important for post-colonial theory to take heed of the criticisms levelled at cultural studies and to begin to identify and establish this relationship explicitly. This chapter seeks to interrogate the manner in which modernity has spurned certain post-colonial predicaments, particularly for the nation-state in Africa. It considers the way in which African states negotiate these post-colonial dilemmas by inflecting them in specific ways. This is considered against the backdrop of the literature on the state amassed by African studies. This analysis suggests that colonisation must be foregrounded in order to understand the machinations of the post-colonial state.

The crisis of the African state

Despite sub-Saharan Africa pursuing what could be broadly referred to as either a capitalist or socialist development strategy, the economic crises which have plagued this region since the 1970s have led some analysts to theorise the phenomenon of 'collapsed states'. The notion of the collapsed state hinges on the argument that states collapse when they can no longer perform the basic functions required to politically sustain a community of people. Zartman points out that this entails the inability of the state to perform three crucial functions. First, it is unable to enact laws and maintain order. Second, as a symbol of identity, the state is no longer able to maintain legitimacy. Finally, it is unable to conduct public affairs. In short, then, it loses the right and ability to rule (1995: 5).

While some have proclaimed the demise or collapse of the state in Africa, Richard Sandbrook distinguishes between fictitious and healthy states. The former exist in a minimal sense, in that other governments recognise their territorial sovereignty, whilst the latter are 'highly structured and capable of devising and implementing diverse policies' (1985: 35). Regardless of the manner in which the state is characterised – collapsed, healthy or fictitious – the idea that the state is unable to perform its role is rooted firmly in what Colin Leys has labelled the 'African Tragedy' (Leys 1994, 1996).[3] The dimensions of the African tragedy can be captured most accurately as a failure of development. This failure of development means that Africa is seen as a perversion, an abnormality, and is reminiscent of the colonising mission which sought to modernise the continent (Crush 1995; Escobar 1995). The inability of the African state to deliver 'development' has meant that it is no longer permitted to engage in activities which a state normally would perform. Rather, these functions have been usurped, and the African state today is entrapped within a discourse of power whereby foreign institutions and agencies map out its future. In this new configuration, it is the World Bank, the IMF and a host of non-governmental organisations (NGOs) which determine and dictate fundamental policy. They are, in many respects, the new 'colonial administrators'.[4]

In 1981 the World Bank published its report *Accelerated Development in Sub-Saharan Africa*. The Berg report, as it was subsequently known, set the dimensions of the African crises and documented the lack of an effective infrastructure and the extent of economic mismanagement. The report placed blame squarely on the inadequate domestic policies of African governments. It was the African state that was singled out as being inappropriate to the task of development, due to the perception that it was highly interventionist. The African state was accused of gross mismanagement, implementing faulty economic and social policies, and of being protectionist. In response, over successive periods the World Bank and the IMF launched (and continue to run) Structural Adjustment Programmes (SAPs) which entail economic shock therapy in which local currency is devalued, state barriers are removed, budgets cut, the state sector trimmed and a programme of economic liberalisation introduced. The most significant effect of the Berg report was the conclusion that the African state was an inadequate agent of development, and that the state had to be 'rolled back' (World Bank 1981). The ideological underpinnings of this strategy are evident – they were aimed at returning Africa to some semblance of 'normalcy'.[5]

The rolling back of the state was meant to facilitate the 'natural' workings of the economy in order to make African economies viable in the global system. SAPs were seen as important tools to assist Africa and were justified on the grounds that the African state required funds because of a temporary deviation from which it had to adjust (Lawrence 1986: 84). The 'natural' workings to which African states were being returned were that of the neo-classical economic system in which the market prevailed. In the aftermath of the Cold War, African states were unable to play one superpower against another. Consequently, they rapidly found themselves increasingly dependent upon these multilateral institutions. In the past these institutions had insisted on the need to impose conditions to ensure that recipient countries met their debt obligations, but another dimension was also brought to bear upon African governments. It was now possible to advocate a certain ideology, and this was reflected in a new concern with governance. This agenda was exemplified in an influential 1989 World Bank document which argued that, 'underlying the litany of Africa's development problems is a crisis of governance' (World Bank 1989: 60). This meant the imposition of conditions aimed at promoting liberal democratic government.[6]

The imposition of SAPs and the political conditionalities designed to effect good governance have eroded state sovereignty in Africa. [7] In order to continue to receive essential foreign assistance, African governments have had to cede domestic political arrangements and policy options to international agencies and governments (Plank 1993; Rush and Szeftel 1994). It is not only Africa that has suffered a loss of state sovereignty in this era of globalisation and late capitalism. Nevertheless, the effects of such international pressures have exacerbated the precarious position of African states, given their historical condition of having only recently attained independence. It is not surprising that this erosion has led Yash Tandon to claim that:

> African governments are getting reduced to purely policing functions of the state. In so far as they are involved in welfare activities, these are also, in essence, merely extensions of the policing functions. The population cannot be allowed to starve to the point of revolt and disorder.
>
> (Tandon 1996: 1101)

However, it is not only from above that the African state is being pressured. It is subjected also to new pressures from below, as a host of NGOs, both foreign and local, seek to fill the void created by the rolling back of the state. It is not surprising that NGOs have become prominent at the very time that the African state has been forced to retreat. They are part of an agenda that seeks to minimise state involvement and liberalise the economy. NGOs have been characterised as being more efficient agents of development that can replace the top-down, state-led approach to development.[8] The NGO sector, in short, complements the neo-liberal agenda. A crucial consequence of the emergence of the NGO sector is that considerable funds from external aid donors have been diverted to NGOs and away from the state, which is seen as highly bureaucratic and corrupt. This inevitably has weakened the capacity of the African state, further compounding its problems and has led ultimately to a crisis of legitimacy.

As SAPs are implemented with rigour, NGOs move to cushion the effects of the social dislocation that results when the state is no longer able to provide even the most basic services. As the NGO sector gains prominence, it has rapidly emerged as a political actor, advocating democracy and the need to forge a viable civil society. The emphasis on citizen participation has meant that NGOs are at the forefront of development from below and part of a movement that seeks to empower local populations. As Ian Gary observes, 'NGOs, in their perceived ability to deliver "development", foster participation, promote civil society, and lessen the social cost of adjustment on "vulnerable groups"' fit in perfectly 'with the agenda to weaken the African state' (1996: 163).

African studies and the conceptualisation of the African state

Claude Ake has characterised the colonial state as having two principal features, absolutism and arbitrariness, which framed the domain of colonial politics. The colonial state was absolute in its power, and it applied such power at will. The state inherited at independence was no different – it was totalistic in scope and retained the statist economy of the colonial era. He notes that:

> at independence the form and function of the state in Africa did not change much for most countries in Africa. State power remained essentially the same: immense, arbitrary, often violent, always threatening ... politics remained a zero-sum game; power was sought by all means and maintained by all means. Colonial rule left most of Africa a legacy of intense and lawless political competition amidst an ideological void and a rising tide of disenchantment with the expectation of a better life.
>
> (Ake 1996: 6)

The effect of such an inheritance was that the African state rapidly degenerated and became a simulacrum of the colonial state in which absolute power was vested. It is in this context that the one-party state emerged and became the dominant mode of governance.

The one-party state

A great number of arguments have been postulated about the authenticity of the African one-party state.[9] In the period immediately after independence, African leaders rapidly adopted this form of governance on the grounds that it was 'African' and an essential part of traditional pre-colonial society. They claimed that traditional African society rested on a politics of consensus, rather than competition, and hence the one-party state was compatible with African political values. It was seen also as a method of preventing 'tribalism' – that is of avoiding a situation whereby political parties were formed along predominantly ethnic lines. The one-party state, it was argued, transcended narrow political agendas and was imperative for the 'national interest'. The one-party state was seen as vital to forging a national identity that could hold together the various ethnic identities which had coalesced in the struggle for independence, but which it was feared could fracture into sectional interests. The one-party state was also seen as an important mechanism for promoting development. However, regardless of these theoretical arguments, the reality was that one-party states did not foster a politics of consensus, nor did they forge national unity. Rather, they degenerated into extreme forms of authoritarianism designed to perpetuate the incumbent's rule. Christian Potholm captures the mode of operation of the one-party state in Ghana:

> Nkrumah took an essentially pluralistic society with a long history of individual freedom and personal achievement and attempted to rule it by increasingly arbitrary methods. He gradually outlawed all formal opposition, stifled dissent, and, by surrounding himself with a group of sycophants and expatriate white advisers, cut himself off from his people and ignored their

increasing alienation from his regime. He did not attempt much political mobilization after independence and generally disregarded the need to engage the people of Ghana politically. As a result, the CPP, formerly a true mass party, gradually withered away.

(Potholm 1979: 52–3)

This pattern of politics was not unique in Ghana, it was replicated in virtually all newly-independent states on the continent. Hence, it was not surprising that in 1989 there were only four countries in sub-Saharan Africa which had multi-party political systems.

African socialism

As the nationalist leaders gained power and sought to transform the conditions endured by their people under colonialism, they rapidly learnt that the colonial state had drained their economies. In response to the reality of inadequate resources to meet the rising expectations of the population, African governments sought alternatives. In 1967 President Julius Nyerere of Tanzania encapsulated the problems of the development strategy which had been inherited at independence and which was being pursued. He noted that a major consequence was that:

this was leading towards attitudes of social inequality … The country was beginning to develop an economic and social élite whose prime concern was profit for themselves and their families, and not the needs of the majority for better living standards.

(Nyerere 1973b: 277)

In order to attain the 'fruits of independence', African leaders began to experiment with, or combined, socialist doctrine with African traditional values. The product of this amalgamation resulted in African socialism. The term African socialism, however, was broad enough to be defined in a variety of ways and was open to interpretation. For example, African countries as disparate as Kenya, Uganda, Sudan, Benin, Senegal, Ethiopia, Zimbabwe and Tanzania proclaimed their own versions of African socialism which was coupled with the adoption of the single party rule. However, it was Julius Nyerere who expounded the idea most clearly and who applied it most vigorously in Tanzania. His views can be discerned clearly by examining the Arusha Declaration of 1967 which mapped out his African socialism strategy.

The Arusha Declaration

The Arusha Declaration was adopted by the Tanzania African National Union (TANU) national executive committee at its meeting at Arusha in northern Tanzania in January 1967. The declaration captured Nyerere's desire to establish a more egalitarian society by narrowing the gap between government and party officials and the mass of the people. It placed emphasis on self-reliance. Tanzania was to avoid being dependent upon foreign loans. In order to attain such a goal, Nyerere argued that the means of production and important services should be owned by the state. In short, it emphasised the themes of socialism and self-reliance. Consequently, the commercial banks, the mills and leading import and export houses were nationalised. For Nyerere, the Arusha Declaration was a necessary way to radically restructure Tanzania and a strategy that sought to introduce a new way of life for the population based on the principles of equality, co-operation and democracy.

Central to the strategy was the development of the agrarian sector, which was to play a key role in reducing dependence on foreign capital. Nyerere's particular version of socialism was based on the principles of *Ujamaa* (Nyerere 1973a). The values which he sought to encapsulate in the notion of *Ujamaa* were those of the strong family solidarity found within traditional African societies. This Nyerere brand of socialism rejected scientific socialism and was rooted firmly in the values of traditional African society (Civille 1972). By deploying the merits of *Ujamaa*, Nyerere sought to unite Tanzania placing particular emphasis on communal living in *Ujamaa* villages. The pursuit of such a strategy was based on the reality of Tanzania's predominately rural population, which the government sought to reach and encourage to unite in co-operative production villages in order to promote equality throughout the society. For Nyerere, these villages were essential entities which would promote equality and prevent the emergence of rich farmers. *Ujamaa* sought also to strengthen national identity, which had been undermined by colonial domination. The emphasis on co-operation, self-reliance and belief in the nation aimed to promote the role and capacity of all citizens to establish and contribute to the nation and its socialist development (*ibid.*: 171–2).[10]

Remarkably, utilising his immense popularity, Nyerere was able to implement the broad aims of the Arusha Declaration. The core actions taken included the Africanisation of the bureaucracy and the incorporation of the military and the trade unions into the one-party state, as well as the nationalisation of banks, insurance agencies, key companies, wholesale and foreign trade, manufacturing industries and plantations. In addition, the government introduced state marketing monopolies (parastatals) for the handling of crops and consumer goods. In 1970, under the Buildings Act, all buildings valued in excess of Shs. 100,000 were nationalised. The aim to promote equality was reflected in the manner in which public-sector wages were controlled. This led to greater equality between the urban and rural sections of the population. Furthermore, the TANU leadership code, which prevented party officials from accruing more than one salary, was vigorously enforced.

The policy of villagisation or *Ujamaa vijijini* represents one of the key strategies of Nyerere's socialist programme. Although the villagisation programme had begun prior to the Arusha Declaration, the declaration provided the impetus to further promote the concept. Initially, the government relied upon voluntary association setting up villages in remote areas and providing inducements for settlement. However, the President indicated his dissatisfaction with the progress of villagisation and, in 1973, the leadership moved to a programme of enforced villagisation (Scott 1998). The success of the enforced programme can be discerned in the statistic that, by 1980, 91 per cent of the rural population lived in *Ujamaa* villages.[11]

By the mid-1970s, despite the rhetoric of self-reliance which dominated official policy pronouncements in the aftermath of the Arusha Declaration, Tanzania continued to receive increasing rates of foreign aid, in particular from the Scandinavian countries. Nevertheless, its economy rapidly began to falter as a result of the ambitious and, in most cases, unrealistic development policies which had been adopted (Hyden and Karlstrom 1993: 1397). The economy hit crisis point by the end of the decade, when Tanzania was finding it increasingly difficult to meet its debt obligations. At the same time, inflation and corruption became uncontrollable. In the light of these difficulties, the IMF and the World Bank urged the Tanzanian government to abandon its socialist policies and adopt a structural adjustment plan which included liberalisation of the economy and a drastic reduction in the size of the burgeoning public sector in order to receive assistance. President Nyerere, undaunted, refused to accede to these demands (Baregu 1995: 1). The economic crisis was exacerbated by the rapid decline in exports and Tanzania's inability to import even the most basic commodities. The villagisation programme also proved to be a colossal failure – it became evident that peasant farmers were not producing as effectively on a co-operative basis as they had individually, leading to an overall decrease in agricultural production (Berg-Schlosser and Siegler 1990: 70–7). The failure of the socialist strategy in promoting a better life for the citizens of Tanzania was admitted by Nyerere who recognised that:

> The real price we paid was in the acquisition of a top-heavy bureaucracy. We replaced local governments and cooperatives by parastatal organiza-tions. We thought these organizations run by the state would contribute to progress because they would be under parliamentary control. We ended up with a huge machine which we cannot operate efficiently.
>
> (Nyerere, cited in Barratt Brown 1995)

It is important to note that not all Tanzania's problems were of its own making. The economy was affected adversely by the oil shocks caused by the OPEC cartel in the 1970s, significant shortfalls of rain, and the war with Uganda which led to Idi Amin's removal from power. In addition, Tanzania was at the forefront of the anti-apartheid struggle and was thus subject to the destabilising policies of the South African regime. Nevertheless, both the one-party state and African socialism plunged the African state into a deep crisis. There are a number of explanations emanating within African studies which seek to understand the nature of the crisis that pervades Africa and the role of the state.

The patrimonial state

The failure of the one-party state, African socialism and its variants has led to an evaluation of Africa in terms of the existence of a patrimonial state (Boyle 1988; Callaghy 1984, 1987; Sandbrook 1985; Steeves 1997). Such a state is based upon, and mirrors, earlier state formations in Europe and is characterised by Mamdani as exhibiting 'a tendency toward corruption among those within the system and toward exit among those marginal to it' (1996a: 11). The latter position, that of exit, was developed by Goran Hyden, who claimed that the lack of development can be explained by the inability of the state to capture the peasantry, because of an 'economy of affection', based on familial and kinship ties, which means that the peasantry does not have to participate in the formal economy (1980). In recent times, the former position has been articulated most clearly by Michael Bratton and Nicholas van de Walle:

> the distinctive institutional hallmark of African regimes is neopatrimonialism. In neopatrimonial regimes, the chief executive maintains authority through personal patronage, rather than through ideology or law ... relationships of loyalty and dependence pervade a formal political and administrative system and leaders occupy bureaucratic offices less to perform public service than to acquire personal wealth and status. The distinction between private and public interests is purposely blurred ... personal relationships ... constitute the foundation and superstructure of political institutions. The interaction between the 'big man' and his extended retinue defines African politics, from the highest reaches of the presidential palace to the humblest village assembly. As such, analysts of African politics have embraced the neopatrimonial model.
>
> (Bratton and van de Walle 1994: 458–9)

This mode of analysis, however, has been under attack on the grounds that it only highlights the role of key political actors and leaders whilst marginalising significant and important sections of the political sphere as well as the structures of power upon which such rule is based.[12] In contrast, a notion of the 'integral state' has been suggested by Crawford Young, who argues that such a state acts directly upon civil society through its hegemonic apparatus, so that 'the state is free to engage in rational pursuit of its design for the future and to amply reward the ruling class for its governance services' (1994: 39).

The black man's burden

In his magisterial, *The Black Man's Burden*, Basil Davidson argues that the creation of artificial states in Africa is a major cause of the lack of development. This is necessarily so because of the authoritarian nature of colonial rule which was bequeathed to African nations at the time of independence. Not only is the post-colonial nation-state firmly rooted in the authoritarian tradition but, more importantly, the acceptance of the post-colonial nation-state meant 'acceptance of the legacy of colonial partition, and of the moral and political practices of colonial rule in its institutional dimensions' (1992: 162). In that sense, Davidson sees the African crisis essentially as a 'crisis of institutions'. The institutions which he claims have thwarted development are the contemporary nation-states that emerged out of the decolonisation movements. These movements appeared to be heading initially towards genuine liberation. In the event, such liberation did not occur, and in practice turned out to be merely a 'new period of indirect subjection to the history of Europe' (*ibid.*: 10).

The central proposition advanced by Davidson is that colonialism prevented the natural development of pre-colonial institutions, replacing these by the nation-state without any reference to traditional political formations. He points out how different have been the trajectories of societies such as Japan, where traditional institutions were incorporated into the modern through the Meiji reforms. Davidson urges his readers to imagine what would have happened had Japan been colonised in the second half of the nineteenth century at precisely the time that it was instituting major reforms. He writes:

> Supposing that Western enclosure and dispossession could have succeeded and did succeed … had taken from the Japanese all scope for their initiative and enterprise? One may reasonably reply that in this case the modernizing revolution of Japan could not have been carried through: repression and stagnation would have replaced all those self-adjustments comprised in and after the Meiji reforms that brought Japan into the modern world and on its own feet.
>
> (Davidson 1992: 65–6)

In contrast, the Asante state, which was perhaps the most 'developed' in Africa, was easily dismantled without regard to the traditional modes of power on which it rested. The implication of Davidson's argument is that it is possible to imagine a form of modernity that would have allowed the Asante state to operate within its own specificity, had it not been thwarted by colonialism. It is this comparison between the Asante state and Japan which Colin Leys finds disturbing. He argues that the key to Japan was its high level of economic development, which meant that under the 'Meiji regime it rapidly became a strong, centralized, rationalized, militarist-bureaucratic state resting on a homogeneous national culture', which for Leys amounts to a 'real nation-state' (Leys 1994: 38). The essential difference between Africa and other parts of the world, he argues, was the extreme backwardness of African economies, which meant that they were no match for the highly developed economies of Europe that penetrated Africa in the nineteenth century. While it is difficult to argue with Leys's assertion, it is problematic simply to ignore Davidson's argument precisely because it is not possible to imagine in Eurocentric terms what sort of modernity would have emerged.[13]

The lessons of the pessimism which engulfed Africa in the 1980s also led to the assertion that the African crisis could be explained by conceptualising the state as either 'weak' or 'strong'. The contention was that a strong state tended towards dictatorship, while a weak state collapsed into clientelism. The way out of this conundrum, Davidson points out, has been to devolve power to local bodies and to re-establish democratic mass participation. Through this process it is possible to imagine the emergence of a strong state, 'the kind of state ... that would be able to promote and protect civil society' (1992: 295). This is, for him, by no means a new innovation but rather one that had been practised widely in pre-colonial times and an important 'route of escape' for a continent desperately in need of solutions.

While Davidson recognises some of the problems with this notion of the 'route of escape' into mass participation, he nevertheless, ultimately sees it as a 'route that can offer a crucial means of moral and political restoration' in which the 'making of the journey will count, not the arrival' (*ibid.*: 316). Such an optimistic conclusion perhaps was possible in the early 1990s, when a new second wave of democratisation swept through Africa in what appeared to be an outpouring of mass participation. It is unclear what Davidson would make of the current malaise that has plagued most African countries, making genuine democratic reform appear all the more elusive.[14] What he failed to take into account was the potential for entrenched African rulers to use existing structures and institutions while at the same time adapting in a minimalist way to the new political realities and demands placed on them. Leys rightly questions what incentive African rulers had to 'sustain civil, egalitarian political processes' at the very time that these countries were unable to reproduce themselves economically (Leys 1994: 40).[15] It is in this way that Leys' analysis differs fundamentally from Davidson's, and he concludes that, it 'is not the state but the weaknesses of the social formations on which the state rests' that 'accounts for Africa's tragedy' (*ibid.*: 46). Although Leys mounts a plausible case, it needs to be acknowledged that he remains entrapped within a certain epistemology which fails to acknowledge the specificity of the African case, viewing it instead as part of the all-encompassing story of capitalism, one in which African history can be viewed as part of the 'grand' story of Western modernity.

Longue durée

The notion of development and Western modernity is one that underpins the dependency and modernisation paradigms that have dominated the analyses of the 'South'. The crucial weaknesses of both schools of thought lie in their assertion that external factors determine political change. Jean-François Bayart argues that this reliance leads to the invention of the 'Third World' and 'to the theory of the radical extraneity of the modern state based on the model of Western bureaucracy. This alienation is then held responsible for most of the problems associated with political underdevelopment' (1991: 51). Bayart argues that the state in Africa should not be seen simply as a product of colonisation but that these so-called artificial states and the territorial boundaries which demarcate them 'have contributed to the distinct historicity of societies', which in turn has had the effect of 'diminishing the usefulness of the over-arching binary distinctions between East and West, and North and South' (*ibid.*: 53). Consequently, he advocates that the African state be analysed in the light of the '*longue durée*'.

Drawing on the work of Michel Foucault, Bayart seeks to abandon universalising categories which ignore the particular trajectories of individual states. Three different ways are suggested to reconstruct a *longue-durée* perspective of the state. First, it is possible to focus on civilisations and the forms of power and exploitation which underpin them. Second, regional or national scenarios can be defined in order to construct the state. Finally (Bayart's preferred method) the cultural logic underlying configurations of power may be identified (*ibid.*: 58–9). Bayart argues that a cultural construction of politics is essential to an understanding of the social foundations of the state. He finds the current preoccupation with the state and civil society debate disturbing not only because of its Western European roots but also because it seeks to deny the historicity of the African state. He argues that this 'theory is nothing but "a method of schematization belonging to one particular technology of government" (that of the West) except that (and this is the root of all difficulties) this "particular technology of government" was exported into non-Western countries, took root there, and penetrated their imaginary conception of politics' (*ibid.*: 61).

Bayart proposes that, by coming to terms with cultural historicity, one is able to understand political historicity. Here, he is particularly careful in illustrating the discursive genre of politics. He warns against emphasising one discursive genre in coming to terms with a particular political identification of societies, such as the Marxism-Leninism, the British system of government or Islamic thought. Instead, for him, 'contemporary cultures of the state are created by all social actors, including those from "below" even if their contribution does not contradict that of the powerful' (*ibid.*: 65). Again utilising Foucault, Bayart advocates a governmentality approach,[16] because through such an approach it is possible to come to terms with the 'politics of the belly'. It is this governmentality that 'has hemmed in all strategies and institutions which have worked to create modern Africa, especially administrations, the nationalist or revolutionary parties, and the Christian churches' (*ibid.*: 67).

Bayart fully develops this thesis in his now widely-acclaimed *The State in Africa: The Politics of the Belly*. His task is to understand the historicity of the African post-colonial state by transcending previously constraining theoretical works based on paradigms such as modernisation, dependency and Marxism. By taking a *longue-durée* approach, he is able to demonstrate that, although Africans have not been major players on the global scene, they none the less play an important, albeit minor, role. To this end, he argues that Africans have engaged in a politics of 'extraversion', furthering their own goals by forging alliances and extracting resources from external actors in order to deal with domestic political imperatives. Such a process entails the construction of historical blocs 'rhizomatically' linked to underlying societies and grouped around the state. The 'politics of the belly' means that ethnicity, class, etc., are all related in a 'reciprocal assimilation of elites', whereby elites collaborate to eat and then further their interests by drawing upon the outside world. In a trenchant critique, Colin Leys has observed that, 'Bayart makes a resolute separation of politics from economics and says virtually nothing about the relation between them. In his account of Africa, what matters is only how economic resources are appropriated to service the endless cycle of the reciprocal assimilation of élites' (1996: 43).

Disorder as a political instrument

In an attempt to understand why African states have continued to function in the face of what appear to be insurmountable challenges, Patrick Chabal and Jean-Pascal Daloz argue that there exists in Africa a new political system, in which politics have been informalised, stemming from the very disorder which pervades the continent. The propositions on which their argument hinges are twofold. First, the root of the African crisis is a crisis of modernity and, second, 'this crisis of modernity is rooted in the deep history of the societies in which it is taking place' (1999: xviii). They argue that there is a generalised system of patrimonial-ism which defines the conduct of politics that is characterised by an acute degree of disorder. The evidence for this disorder lies in the very inability of the state to function along rational lines: that is, its administrative arm fails to function in a neutral way. This form of disorder, however, is not to be understood as part of the 'backwardness of Africa' or the irrationality of the African political system. Rather, Chabal and Daloz seek to make 'explicit the observation that political action operates rationally, but largely in the realm of the informal, uncodified and unpoliced – that is, in a world that is not ordered in the sense in which we usually take *our* own polities in the West to be' (*ibid.*: xix, emphasis added).

The state is contextualised in the light of the thesis of the informalisation of politics. It is not surprising that the conclusion that is drawn is that the state is weak and vacuous when measured against a Weberian ideal type. Chabal and Daloz argue that the 'state in Africa was never properly institutionalised because it was never significantly emancipated from society' (*ibid.*: 4). Despite the rhetoric of the specificity of the African case and the need to analyse what is happening in Africa on its terms, this analysis is bedevilled by Eurocentrism, which becomes evident in the manner in which the Weberian model that can be distinctly observed in 'our' polities does not appear to have taken root in 'Black Africa'. There the defining characteristics are the failure of an independent bureaucracy to emerge and the continuance of patrimonialism, which does not allow for a separation of the public and private sphere. Further evidence of the lack of the development of the modern African state can be observed in the lack of the concept of citizenship which 'binds individuals to the state – above and beyond the more proximate ties of kinship, community or faction' (*ibid.*: 6).

The centrality of colonialism as a defining moment for the African state is rejected on the grounds that it is not clear that the colonial state eradicated pre-colonial political traditions. The inability of the colonial state to alter these political practices, largely because it was concerned with maintaining order at the lowest cost, means that the independent African state rapidly disintegrated and became weak and vacuous and easily captured by factional interests. This leads to the conclusion that there is no incentive for African political elites to dismantle political systems which have served their interests. As Chabal and Daloz note, 'the instrumentalization of the political (dis)order is thus a disincentive to the establishment of a more properly institutionalized state on the Weberian model' (*ibid.*: 14).

The criminalisation of the state in Africa

A recent, if somewhat perplexing, thesis has emerged in *The Criminalisation of The State in Africa* by Jean-François Bayart, Stephen Ellis and Béatrice Hibou. This work carries to the extreme the current Afro-pessimism which dominates analyses of the continent and is clearly captured in Bayart's assertion that Africa is returning to the 'heart of darkness' (Bayart *et al.* 1999: 114). The authors argue that this return needs to be examined through the lens of illicit activity and its relationship with ruling classes which determines the processes of state formation and economic accumulation. This allows them to speculate that 'the participation of the sub-continent in illicit finance and trade may favour its growth and alter the manner of its insertion in the world economy' (*ibid.*: xvii).

Bayart *et al.* posit five symptoms of change which have led inevitably to the criminalisation of the state: first, the relegation of sub-Saharan Africa in diplomacy, economics and finance; second, the failure of successive waves of democratisation and mass mobilisation; third, the speed and spread of wars even into areas that were free of violence; fourth, the realignment of the sub-continent around new foreign influences and axes of power; and, finally, the presence of new actors engaged in illegal criminal activity, particularly organised crime.[17] Because of these changes, they hypothesise, 'politics in Africa is becoming markedly interconnected with crime' and thus needs to be seen as the criminalisation of the state as opposed to processes of corruption, predation or kleptocracy (*ibid.*: 25). It is a process that has not as yet 'reached its apogee' but certainly has the potential to do so (*ibid.*: 30). This analysis is reminiscent of dependency analyses, in that it argues that Africa is being incorporated into the international system through international crime syndicates which have local African partners who have the capacity to marshal considerable armed force to further their interests. The evidence used to sustain the argument is that, increasingly, even so-called legitimately elected rulers are prepared to resort to violence in order to maintain their sources of revenue, which are allocated through patrimonial relations.

The African warlord state

The apparent collapse of a number of African states in the 1990s – such as Somalia, Liberia, Chad and the former Zaire – has given rise to the notion of warlord politics (Allen 1999; Cliffe and Luckham 1999; Goulding 1999; Reyntjens 1999). In such cases there is no attempt to create a state for the common good. Rather, the primary purpose of warlord rule is to increase power and accumulate wealth which is distributed along patronage lines. In this context the warlord state may appear to resemble the weak state, but William Reno points out that the distinction lies in the pursuit of private as opposed to collective interests. In the warlord state, 'rulers and their associates resemble a mafia rather than a government, if one thinks of the latter as necessarily serving some collective interest, however faint and by whatever means, to be distinguished from the mafia' (1999: 3).

For Reno, the distinction between what constitutes a ruler of a weak state and a warlord depends on a judgement based upon an observation that broad-based patronage politics have collapsed. The conditions which give rise to such a transition, paradoxically, arise from the liberalisation of markets and the reform agenda of the World Bank.[18] As Reno notes:

> A central paradox of this book is that in this context reform that emphasizes economic and political liberalization further undermines weak-state rulers' incentives to pursue conventional strategies for maximizing power through generating economic growth and, hence, state revenues.
>
> (Reno 1999: 4)

In the absence of conventional strategies, the weak-state ruler has few options but to resort to measures which allow for the retention of power. It is this which potentially leads to the warlord state.

Post-colonialism, modernity and the African state

The African crisis has certainly led to the emergence of an expansive literature on the state in Africa. The works discussed above are by no means an exhaustive list, but they do represent major trends and paradigms which have emerged within African studies. All the same, these explanations of the African state have been found wanting. But this is inevitable, given the compartmentalisation of theory that occurs because of the inability of First World theory to engage with Third World cultures and predicaments. For theory to transcend these limits, it needs to come together in what Mary Louise Pratt (1992) has called the 'contact zone' and to engage critically through a process of transculturation. It is in this context that post-colonial theory can be helpful in understanding that the African state is itself the product of transculturation. The institution of the nation-state is one which has European roots and origins, and one which was introduced into Africa. The state in Africa, however, has been inflected over time. Whilst retaining its linkages to its European past, most clearly manifested in the project of colonisation, the state in Africa is constantly evolving. In short, through the process of hybridisation and transculturation, the African state has been and continues to be inflected locally. It is important, however, to recognise that it is colonialism which fundamentally alters and ruptures pre-colonial forms of state formation. The idea that there is a reversion to pre-colonial forms is one that is not tenable. The African state, despite its emergence through the establishment of artificial boundaries, is one that fails to whither away, as evidenced by the fact that we continue to refer to these states as sovereign entities just as they were constituted with the inauguration of colonial rule. But this does not mean that the African state has remained a simulacrum of the colonial state. On the contrary, it is a hybrid entity that has developed differently in different contexts. Hence, it should not be too surprising to note that the state in Kenya is significantly different from the state in the Democratic Republic of Congo, just as the colonial states in both countries were significantly different. Nevertheless, a compelling feature of the colonial state was that it locked the post-colonial state into a certain conception of Western modernity with its emphases on development and progress. It is this process that is central to an understanding of a post-colonial perspective on the African state and it is a task that is discussed below.

Nationalism and the post-colonial developmentalist state

For post-colonial theory the issue of nationalism is particularly vexed. On the one hand, it was a necessary and essential part of the struggle for independence, and, on the other, it was one which both Fanon and Said claim needed to be transcended. Leela Ghandi has traced the linkages between nationalism and modernity and argues that, 'nationalism outside the West can only ever be premature and partial – a threat to the enlightened principles of the liberal state and, thereby, symptomatic of a failed or "incomplete" modernity' (1998: 108; Lazarus 1999). The need to reclaim and celebrate a culture denigrated by colonialism was at the heart of the nationalisms which led to the fight for independence. It is not surprising that such 'other' nationalisms are seen as perversions in the West. It is important to remember that it is from this nationalism that a new national identity is forged. The nation has to be reconstructed not only to survive but also to re-imagine and reconfigure its past. Said notes that, 'nationalism is an assertion of belonging to a place, a people, a heritage. It affirms the home created by a community of language, culture, and customs' (1984: 50; 1993).

Benedict Anderson demonstrates that nations are not merely the products of sociological factors, such as language, race or religion (Deutsch 1966; Kedourie 1978; Kohn 1965), but that, in both Europe and elsewhere, they are imagined into existence (Anderson 1983, 1991). The major institutional form that allowed such imagination to take shape is what he terms 'print-capitalism'. Anderson claims that Western nationalism provided for all subsequent 'other' nationalisms – such as Africa – a set of modular forms from which the nationalist leaders in the colonies were able to select the particular form they deemed appropriate. The colonial state achieved this through education and established 'bilingual intelligentsias'. These intelligentsias had access to 'models of nation, nation-ness, and nationalism distilled from turbulent, chaotic experiences of more than a century of American and European history' (1983: 140).

Nationalism, as in Anderson's framework, is a European construction that had been exported to the colonies. As Partha Chatterjee points out, nationalism was portrayed as one of 'Europe's most magnificent gifts to the rest of the world' (1993: 4).[19] In Africa, at independence, nationalism was seen as an important means to attain unity and became a central part of the dictum of the modernisation school which assumed that assimilation of diverse ethnic groups would occur with rapid modernisation. This process was called nation-building and had strong adherents in both the metropole and the colonies (Connor 1994). Basil Davidson's comparison of Africa with the former 'Communist' countries of Eastern Europe appears to be particularly poignant at a time when the term ethnic cleansing has become part of our lexicon. For Davidson, in Africa as in Eastern Europe, 'the black man's burden' has its roots in the nation-state and nationalism (1992: 10).[20] Davidson taps into the pervasively pessimistic mood which dominates analyses of post-colonial Africa that document the manner in which the promises that brought the nationalist leadership to power at independence have not been delivered, albeit due largely to the colonial legacy.

The heightening of difference between competing ethnicities in several African countries illustrates that national identity is relational. For example, in the case of Rwanda, Tutsi and Hutu identities are determined in relation to each other.[21] Michael Ignatieff points out that such identity is divided, and that nationalism 'does not simply "express" a pre-existent identity: it "constitutes" one. It divides/separates/re-classifies difference. It does so by abstracting from real life. It is a fiction, an invented identity. A form of narcissism' (1995a: 14; 1995b). He argues that it is the minor differences between groups that are most likely to become the major issues in their imagination. Hence, in the case of the Tutsi and the Hutu, given that they share a common language, religion and culture, it is the minor differences that erupt and manifest themselves into a nationalism that tears them apart. And this is where the narcissistic character of nationalism emerges. This narcissism 'turns difference into a mirror' which rejects anything foreign that does not confirm the narcissist's prejudices. Ignatieff argues:

> Nationalism is the transformation of identity into narcissism. It is a language game that takes the facts of difference and turns them into a narrative justifying political self-determination. In the process of providing legitimacy for a political project – the attainment of statehood – it glorifies identity. It turns neighbours into strangers, turns the permeable boundaries of identity into impassable frontiers.
>
> (Ignatieff 1995a: 19)

This narcissistic imagery is important when deployed in the African context. The imposition of colonialism had the effect of exacerbating differences between the ethnic groups and of turning neighbours into enemies prepared to kill each other. In most African states, then, a situation developed where separate identities were forged which gave way to different nationalisms. What is critical is that the only space that they can imagine for themselves is a common nation-state as delineated by the colonisers. The capturing of the state by ethnic groups has meant that access to scarce resources is guaranteed. In other words, what we witness is separate identities in search of a single state.

The common imagination of a single state by different identities has resulted inevitably in a great deal of turmoil. However, what is surprising is that the most enduring phenomenon of the colonial legacy, the partition of the continent itself, is not open to debate. The colonial boundaries established at the time of partition not only have endured but have been defended resolutely in the post-independence period. The Organisation of African Unity (OAU), whilst recognising that inherited borders were problematic, feared endless conflicts over them and decided that these European-drawn borders were to remain uncontested. The question of colonial boundaries until recently has remained sacrosanct within the African context (Nugent and Asiwaju 1996).

In his later work, Michel Foucault elaborated the theme of modern political power. What Foucault sought to do was undertake a re-evaluation of the state/civil society nexus in which the state was conceptualised as the site of power, and civil society as the site of attaining freedom. As David Scott aptly puts it, what concerns Foucault 'is the emergence in early modern Europe of a new form of political rationality which combines simultaneously two seemingly contradictory modalities of power: one, totalizing and centralizing, the other individualizing and normalizing' (1995: 201–2). It is this rationality which Foucault terms governmentality. It is about the 'problematic of government' – about how to rule and how to be ruled. In order to illustrate his point, Foucault examines Machiavelli's *The Prince*. He stresses the absolute power and authority of the prince, whose sovereignty is exercised on a territory and on all the subjects who reside within that territory. Government, for Foucault, is a 'question not of imposing law on men, but of disposing things: that is to say, of employing tactics rather than laws, and even of using laws themselves as tactics to arrange things in such a way that, through a certain number of means, such and such ends may be achieved' (cited in Scott 1995: 202). Governmentality, then, can be seen as a process through which a population can be categorised and regulated into manageable groupings, and hence come to be policed and subject to bureau-cratic regimes and disciplines (Foucault 1991).

Under colonialism, the objective was to create productive subjects who could be governed efficiently and effectively. This was achieved by altering the political and social world of the colonised. As Scott points out, the 'political problem of modern colonial power was therefore not merely to contain resistance and encourage accommodation but to seek to ensure that both could only be defined in relation to the categories and structures of modern political rationalities' (1995: 214). In contrast to such modes of power is the new art of government, which is characterised by self-regulation and the manner in which individuals are constrained, leading to new forms of knowledges, analyses and discourses through which individuals are 'disciplined' and 'civilised'. In such a configuration, the modern state, the panopticon state, normalises its citizens by deploying a host of complex disciplines, practices and discourses. Although Foucault was concerned with Europe, his work can be instructive in the African context. The processes of colonialism brought with them forms of the European state. However, to think of this merely as an extension or replication would be a misreading of the specificity of the African case. As Scott points out, in order to 'understand the project of colonial power at any given historical moment one has to understand the character of the political rationality that constituted it .... what is crucial is trying to discern the colonial power's point of application, its target, and the discursive and nondiscursive fields it sought to encompass' (*ibid.*: 204).

Through an elaboration of Foucault's ideas, we can see that the colonial state was not only one which had to fulfil the role of policing but one which had to meet the development objectives of both its metropolitan master and its subjects. It was in this sense that the very practice of colonialism was justified as the 'civilising mission', and it was one which Lugard, amongst others, argued was there for the good of the indigenous population. The colonial state was a paradoxical entity from its inception. Its policing role under all forms of colonialism was carried out, as Mamdani (1996a) has observed, through indirect rule practised on the principle of 'divide and rule', and yet at the same time it was underpinned by notions of development which required the forging of a unified nation with a common society.

The post-colonial state and civil society grew out of the nationalist project, in which nationalism served a hegemonic function of effecting decolonisation. The goal of such incipient nationalism was independence. But, once this independence was achieved, the nationalist project rapidly collapsed and was 'disciplined and normalized under the conceptual rubrics of "development" and "modernization"' (Chatterjee 1993: 3). The normalisation process was one that usually began well before independence and was part of the decolonisation process. One only has to examine the recent example of the African National Congress (ANC) in South Africa to realise how the ANC was disciplined prior to the first national election through a process of 'rational' planning in which this party articulated its goals and aspirations in its Reconstruction and Development Programme. The plan not only illustrated how the goals of the ANC were to become synonymous with the South African state but also clarified the process by which the South African state was permitted to become part of the global system under the regimentation of the West's hegemonic power. As Partha Chatterjee notes, 'the very institution of a process of planning became a means for the determination of priorities on behalf of the "nation"' (*ibid.*: 202). The planning process serves an important function of power in that it removes the allocation of productive resources from the political process, and hence the goals of the state become conflated with the nation.

This is necessarily so because part of the nationalist project was to demonstrate the manner in which the colonial state inhibited development, and therefore the post-colonial state 'represented the only legitimate form of exercise of power because it was a necessary condition for the development of the nation' (*ibid.*: 203). Once again, the South African case is instructive. The ANC had to demonstrate how the apartheid state economically marginalised the majority of the population. The major goal of the post-colonial state was to empower the majority economically, infusing a developmental ideology for the state in the process. Chatterjee argues that the state is connected to the people not only through the doctrine of representative government but also through its commitment to direct an economic development programme on behalf of the people, thereby connecting 'the sovereign powers of the state directly with the economic well-being of the people' (*ibid.*: 203).

The conflation between the nation and the state leads to tensions between the aspirations of the people and those of the state. Hence, in most post-colonial states, those detracting from state ideology were, and are, being repressed. This, it is claimed, is necessary because the state has to subsume particular interests in the general interest. One need only think of the examples of Indonesia and Malaysia to recognise the zeal with which development ideology is applied by the state while at the same time marginalising the political process.[22] The developmentalist ideology is not restricted to socialist or capitalist states. The essential difference in the former, as Arif Dirlik points out, is the desire of the socialist leadership to forge, 'a new culture which is neither of the West nor of the past' (1991: 400). This was certainly a characteristic of Nyerere's Tanzania.

The nationalist project, and the anti-colonial nationalism which it generated, sought to create a national culture which would enable colonial subjects to attain independence and decolonise their minds. Frantz Fanon argued that this could be achieved only through struggle and the forging of a national culture which represented 'the whole body of efforts made by a people in the sphere of thought to describe, justify and praise the action through which the people created itself and keeps itself in existence' (1967: 188). After decolonisation, the post-colonial state has to create a new national culture which can legitimate its rule.[23] As noted above, the post-colonial state achieves this through the exercise of planning and conflating the values of development with the values of the nation. The main tenets of the new national culture, then, are an essential reworking of the centrality of development and modernisation, the twin planks for the justification and civilising mission of colonialism. The state effectively dismantles the liberationist potential generated by the anti-colonial nationalism.

Conclusion

This analysis suggests that the post-colonial state is first and foremost a product of colonialism. Critically, post-colonial does not mean merely 'after independence'. Rather, the term carries with it the legacy of colonialism which was fundamental to its very development and evolution. Homi Bhabha notes in his discussion of the nation-state that, 'despite the certainty with which historians speak of the "origins" of nation as a sign of the "modernity" of society, the cultural temporality of the nation inscribes a much more transitional social reality' (1990: 1). It is the ambivalence of the nation's emergence which Bhabha seeks to capture, and it is this that defines the post-colonial state in Africa.

In the context of sub-Saharan Africa, where the post-colonial state is prevalent, one needs to examine closely the power relations which allow the goals of the developmentalist state to be furthered. As globalisation and cultural imperialism intensify, it is vital for the nation-states of Africa to consider the costs of a modernist project that celebrates economic development above all else. Certainly, tensions already are evident with the assertion of African values, albeit these values are being subsumed rapidly by the development conundrum. The African countries also need to examine the global system and to discern the patterns through which hegemony is maintained. Post-colonial theory offers a way to break down the tyranny of the structures of power which continue to entrap post-colonial subjects. As Edward Said has pointed out, the strengths of post-colonial theory lie in its attempts to grapple with issues of local and regional significance whilst retaining an emancipatory perspective (1995: 350). It is this task that needs to be confronted by Africanists. For too long, Africa has been subjected to a history of analogy, in which it is compared to other parts of the world, notably Europe. By taking into account the specificity of the African case, it is possible to move beyond such analyses as the patrimonial state, the black man's burden, the *longue durée*, disorder as political instrument, the criminalisation of the state and the warlord state. A post-colonial perspective on Africa points to the formation of a hybrid African state, one which has appeared through a process of transculturation and cannot easily be understood simply as part of the structures of Western modernity.[24] At the same time, post-colonial studies needs to take account of African studies if it is to avoid eliding culture with the state.

4 Striving for democratisation

The complexities of civil society and human rights

It is often declared that democracy demands such a high level of political sophistication from citizens as to make it doubtful that it can be mastered by Third World peoples. Thus democracy is too simple for complex societies and too complex for simple ones.

Sheldon Wolin

If one day *apartheid* is abolished, its demise will not be credited only to the account of moral standards ... because, on the scale which is that of a worldwide computer, the law of the marketplace will have imposed another standard of calculation.

Jacques Derrida

Over the course of two centuries, Americans have found that advancing democratic values and human rights serves our deepest values as well as our practical interests .... That each of us comes from different countries absolves none of us from our obligations to comply with the Universal Declaration of Human Rights .... We cannot let cultural relativism become the last refuge of repression.

Warren Christopher

At the beginning of the 1990s sub-Saharan African states were engulfed in 'democratisation' processes which most analysts claimed rested on growing and thriving civil societies. While the full outcome of these democratic transitions have yet to be determined, the early promise of new configurations of power based upon the full participation of all citizens remains elusive.[1] In a number of countries, the authoritarian incumbents have either clung on to power or, at best, the transition has amounted to little more than intra-regime and intra-elite circulation. Michael Bratton and Nicholas van de Walle point out that, by 1994, there had been democratic transitions in sixteen African countries, with flawed transitions in twelve countries and blocked or impossible transitions in fourteen countries (1997: 120).[2] Despite the obvious obstacles, Larry Diamond argues that the very fact that African dictators were forced to legalise opposition parties and hold elections 'represents a seachange in the postindependence politics of Africa' (1999: xi). While there has been an unquestionably significant shift in the formal conduct of politics, it is difficult not to share Richard Joseph's observation that what have emerged are 'virtual democracies' (1999: 3; 1997). Although a considerable debate exists over whether the causes of the moves towards democratisation were internal or external, it is inconceivable that it would have occurred if both types of force had not dovetailed and forced incumbent regimes to free up the political system (Chabal 1998; Howard 1996; Joseph 1999; Lawson 1999). While both internal and external forces placed political liberalisation on the agenda, more than fifteen years of structural adjustment have failed to provide the institutional infrastructure essential to deliver the economic freedom so critical for the betterment of the people. The failure to effect meaningful change has meant that Africans are disillusioned and rapidly losing faith in the latest wave of democratisation. The optimism that marked the beginning of this decade has dissipated as economic conditions continue to deteriorate. It is in this context that Patrick Chabal has warned against the upsurge of Africanist literature that has focused merely on the democratisation and multi-party elections. He points out that:

> a focus on multi-party political liberalization is liable to distract us from enquiring into the deep causes of the present political crisis in Africa. This is because in order to identify the reason for the apparent disorder of black Africa we must begin by making sense of the multifarious and complex ways in which political accountability operated in the neo-patrimonial political systems that developed everywhere after independence.
>
> (Chabal 1998: 303)

This suggests that the patterns of power and the edifice of the system of rule established under colonialism continue to dominate the political landscape. In this chapter, the focus is on understanding the modes of power which character-ise the contemporary nation-state. It is necessary therefore to examine contemporary debates about governance and democracy. In addition, a critical analysis is included of current debates on civil society as well as of the key role of civil society – the protection of human rights.

The rise of authoritarian rule

The literature provides a myriad of explanations for the emergence and consolidation of authoritarian rule in sub-Saharan Africa. The explanations offered for such authoritarianism are encapsulated, for example, in Larry Diamond's (1988: 5) list of factors which includes: ethnic divisions, a shallow sense of nationhood, weak political institutions, lack of indigenous managerial and technical talent, extreme economic dependence and rising popular expectations. Another commentator argues that political instability can be attributed to one or more of five factors: cultural heterogeneity, low regime legitimacy, lack of coercive power, economic backwardness and structural simplicity.[3] These lists are by no means exhaustive,[4] and indeed several writers attribute the rise of authoritarianism to the overwhelming nature of personal rule in Africa (Bayart 1993; Decalo 1985; Hyden 1983; Jackson and Rosberg 1988, 1992; Oyugi *et al.* 1988; Sandbrook 1985; Young 1981; Zolberg 1966). Although the salience of personal rule has come to dominate recent analyses of African politics, there seems to be little attention paid to the phenomenon of 'founding-father' presidencies (Ahluwalia 1996, 1997).

Africa has produced many such 'founding fathers': Nkrumah in Ghana, Touré in Guinea, Senghor in Senegal, Nyerere in Tanzania, Kaunda in Zambia, Banda in Malawi, Kenyatta in Kenya and, more recently, Mandela in South Africa. The end of colonial rule in Africa represented the beginning of a new era in which power was assumed by the dominant personality, however symbolic, within the nationalist movement, who almost by default became the 'founding father' of the nation. The challenge to colonial authority, the definition of national being, as well as the transition to political independence and beyond, all focused attention on the leader. Such an individual attained mythical status, symbolising both the struggle for freedom and the continuation of the independent state. The association between leader and nation approximated unity. All these 'founding fathers' seemed to be the embodiment of the nation-state.

The endurance and the continuing legacy of the founding-father president can be attributed to what Ali Mazrui terms, 'heroes and uhuru-worship'. He argues:

> Next to forgetting past enemies, the most important element in building up national consciousness is perhaps the faculty of remembering past heroes. This involves recognizing the heroes as common heroes. And this act of recognition is itself an exercise in national self-identification ... To give the idea of a nation warmth, it is often necessary either to personify it meta-phorically, or, more effectively, to give it specific human form in national heroes.
>
> (Mazrui 1967: 21)

The worshipping of the hero is not merely an exercise in the beatification of the founding father but also a cathartic expression of freedom. In addition, hero-worship insulated the founding fathers when they were unable to deliver the 'fruits of freedom'. The legacy of the founding fathers was inscribed deeply within the imagination of the polity, which rapidly came to accept the assertion that, if the founding fathers had suffered in the interests of the nation, then so could they. Founding-father presidencies have virtually come to an end. In their place, new political imperatives dictate not only new forms of governance but also a reconceptualisation of the analytical framework that has dominated our understanding of African political realities.

African perspectives on 'good governance'

Although the need for 'good governance' on the African continent is a problem ultimately requiring an African solution, a vast amount of Western writing has dominated debates about governance in Africa.[5] In this context, it is important to examine recent African thinking and contributions to the general debate about good governance (Hyden *et al.* 2000). Bingu Wa Mutharika, the Secretary-General of the Common Market for Eastern and Southern Africa, brings to bear the experience of someone committed to regionalism and integration. His recent book *One Africa One Destiny: Towards Democracy, Good Governance and Development*, is in essence an appraisal of the failures of African development thinking over the past thirty years. It makes the case for transcending Africa's past in order to forge ahead into the new millennium. Wa Mutharika argues that, for too long, Africa has remained entrapped in various externally driven ideologies and asks whether 'human rights and multiparty democracy' will 'be the last of conditionalities for increased resource flows into Africa?' (1995: 3)

Wa Mutharika argues that if Africa is to get out of its current malaise, it has to embrace new directions which are grounded firmly in regionalism, democracy and good governance, whilst recognising at the same time that these have to emanate from within civil society. Civil society, despite the influences and ravages of colonialism and neo-colonialism, is founded upon traditional values which continue to mould its direction and identity. It is this sense of tradition that is essential for change in the future. He notes that 'economic philosophies that are not rooted in traditionalism, are not readily applicable as a solution to the continued underdevelopment in our continent' (*ibid.*: 9). It is against this background that a new development agenda for Africa is advocated – taking a holistic approach, covering all sectors of the economy, with a prime objective to reach all people at all levels. For Wa Mutharika, the most important aspects of civil society in Africa are not only its traditionalism but also its emphasis on regional economic co-operation. In this context, he argues that, 'African civil societies and the social framework should be redesigned to form the new basis for economic liberalisation, political reforms and democratisation' (*ibid.*: 18).

The focus on contemporary debates about democracy and the relationship between state and civil society is also the subject of Lloyd Sachikonye's *Democracy, Civil Society and the State*. Sachikonye examines the role of social movements which have been neglected in most analyses of civil society and democratisation processes in Southern Africa. He challenges the liberal conceptions of both democracy and civil society, arguing that any analysis which seeks to separate civil society from the state is fraught with difficulty. Sachikonye argues that the relationship between state and civil society is 'a continuous and dialectic one' (1995: iv). This dialectic relationship is central to the argument on social movements, which, it is asserted, have been seen as autonomous from the state. Hence, he argues that social movements have a complex relationship with the state and the political process.

Chole and Ibrahim question the kind of democratisation that has been taking place, whether it is 'merely in form or, more exactly, how much substance and how much form does it involve' (1995: 2). More importantly, they seek to understand the link between economic reform and democratisation. They question the reasons behind the oscillations between arguments that a strong state was essential for economic growth and the current orthodoxy which ties growth to liberalisation. The authors urge that uncritical adulation should not be foisted upon countries merely for holding multi-party elections. This has been vindicated clearly by the disillusionment with the processes of democratisation which have occurred in much of the continent. As they point out, 'the essence of democracy resides in the relationship between the state and the people, especially on how much control the latter have over the former' (*ibid.*: 3). Peter Anyang' Nyong'o makes the case that democracy is necessary in Africa on philosophical and moral grounds 'before it becomes a political and economic' debate (1995: 40). For Mamdani, it is the epistemological questions about democracy that are central when contextualised in different cultural locations – 'democracy is not an artefact that can be introduced and sustained regardless of context, either as an intellectual enterprise or as part of a foreign aid package' (1995: 56). While there is little doubt that change has occurred on the continent, it is equally important to note that, in most cases, there has been little more than an intra-elite transfer of power. For the bulk of Africans, these debates have not only *not* led to better conditions, on the contrary, conditions have become decidedly worse.

Both Western and African perspectives have emphasised the centrality of civil society in order to attain the necessary conditions essential for the attainment of 'good governance'. In a recent report, the World Bank made its views on civil society clear, arguing that, 'the reinforcement of civil society is a way of increasing the resilience of social institutions that may be able to fend off anarchy even if the state is very weak' (World Bank 1997: 160). This insistence of the importance of civil society and its necessity warrants a closer examination of the civil society debate.

The centrality of civil society

The attraction of civil society is obvious in the light of the revolutions which swept through Eastern Europe, leading to the collapse of communist states. It was here that the notion that civil society had triumphed over the state first emerged. The attraction of civil society to East European intellectuals has been captured by Michael Ignatieff, who claims that, 'it renounced an enforceable vision of the good life toward which unhappy souls could be force-marched' (1995b: 129). The idea of civil society emerged in Europe as philosophers and historians sought to understand the emergence of modernity. However, the idea that democracy and economic liberalisation were equated with civil society, as is commonly held in contemporary Africanist discourse, was not the manner in which eighteenth century theorists understood the concept. Ignatieff points out that civil society was not conceivable without a market. More importantly, it was the pressure of public opinion that, 'determined how free, efficient, and honest a market would emerge' (*ibid.*: 130). A new notion of public opinion, Taylor points out, is one that developed in the eighteenth century, creating a different model of public space. This arises out of the development of print-capitalism and from this 'there emerges a sense of nation, or its literate segment, an opinion which deserves to be called "public"' (1990: 109).

In the Western tradition, the demarcation between state and civil society can be seen from the eighteenth century onwards. This delineation entailed recognition that civil society constituted an autonomous space which was distinct from the state. Charles Taylor has outlined three different ways in which civil society can be located within the European tradition:

1   In a minimal sense, civil society exists where there are free associations, not under the tutelage of state power.
2   In a stronger sense, civil society only exists where society as a whole can structure itself and co-ordinate its actions through such associations which are free of state tutelage.
3   As an alternative or supplement to the second sense, we can speak of civil society wherever the ensemble of associations can significantly determine or inflect the course of state policy.

(1990: 98)

These three notions of civil society have developed out of a number of ideas which have contributed to the demarcation between state and civil society. Taylor points out that this separation between state and civil society has arisen due to the following ideas:

A   the medieval idea that society and political organization cannot be conflated;
B   the idea of the independence of the church;
C   the legal notion of subjective rights which arises out of feudalism;
D   the growth of self-governing cities in medieval Europe; and
E   the secular dualism of the medieval polity in which the monarch ruled with the support of a body of estates.

(Taylor 1990: 101–3)

It is against this background that he traces the manner in which these ideas were amalgamated in quite different ways by both Locke and Montesquieu in order to produce two differing conceptions of state–society relations which have become central to the Western tradition. It is not intended here to point out at length the differences between the two, but rather to note in particular the commonality of the notion of subjective rights which have become implicated in the history of capital (Chatterjee 1990: 122).

For both Locke and Montesquieu, Chatterjee argues, subjective rights are grounded in a notion of community. In the case of Locke, subjective rights are grounded in the state of nature where 'men' are already constituted as subjects by the 'community of natural law, even before the emergence of society' (*ibid.*: 122). It is this condition that allows them to establish a society and then a government which is designed to protect their subjective rights. For Montesquieu, subjective rights are related in institutional terms to the forces existent in D and E above. It is this relationship between rights and community that is central to the history of state–civil society relations in Europe. Taylor describes how state–society relations have subsequently been shaped by the manner in which the relations between rights and community have been conceptualised. The Locke and Montesquieu positions, he argues, were brought together by Hegel, although they do not sit comfortably with each other. For Hegel, civil society constitutes a separate private realm, distinct from the state, where private individuals pursue their interests. More importantly, civil society is the domain of the 'market economy and civil law' (Taylor 1990: 126). However, what is germane to the discussion here is that Hegel and liberal theory have suppressed the notion of community which was evident in both Locke and Montesquieu. It is this suppression which creates the possibility within European social theory of having both the distinction between state and civil society as well as the very erasure of that distinction. As Chatterjee argues:

> These divergences are framed within two extreme positions: on the one hand, abolishing community altogether and thinking of rights as grounded solely in the self-determining will, and on the other, attributing to community a single determinate form, delegitimizing all other forms of community.
>
> (Chatterjee 1990: 123)

It is these divergences which, on the one hand, lead to arguments that the state has no place in constraining the activities of private individuals, who are free to enter into contractual arrangements, while, on the other hand, there are arguments 'that would have *one* political community, given the single, determinate, demographically enumerable form of the nation-state … usurping the domain of civil society' (Chatterjee 1990: 128). It is this recognition which necessitates that state–civil society relations cannot be viewed as being in simple opposition. For Chatterjee, the possibilities arise because the individual and the nation-state become embedded within the grand narrative of capital, which seeks to suppress the narrative of community, and it is this which leads to the disciplinary technologies of power that seek to normalise the individual.

It is this argument that problematises the European historical specificity of Taylor's A to E conditions. The condition which universalises the European experience is the narrative of capital. In the case of Africa, it is this narrative which allows the ravages of colonialism and conquest to be cast as a universalising discourse that emphasises progress, modernisation and freedom. This is only possible, Chatterjee argues, due to the destruction of the notion of community. It is a condition which Marx was well aware of in his formulation of primitive accumulation, which was based on the destruction of pre-capitalist community. In such a conceptualisation, community is relegated to capital's prehistory in order to ensure that progress and modernisation are unhindered. The universalising of capital necessitates that community 'becomes the universal prehistory of progress, identified with medievalism in Europe and the stagnant, backward, undeveloped present in the rest of the world' (*ibid.*: 129).

However, it has not been possible to fully suppress community. While Marx was able to envisage society becoming divided along the lines of opposed classes of capital and labour, he was unable to comprehend adequately the ability of these classes to come together in the political community of the nation. It is here that Benedict Anderson's (1991) formulation of 'imagined communities' takes on a poignant relevance. The inability of capital to fully suppress or destroy community has meant that there exists a tension that gives community the potential to become either good or bad nationalism. It is in this context that Chatterjee has asserted that community, which should have been eradicated from the narrative of capital, 'continues to lead a subterranean, potentially subversive life within it because it refuses to go away' (1990: 130).

Nowhere are these tensions more evident than in the anti-colonial nationalist movements. The state and civil society were imported into African countries as a result of the processes of colonisation. These institutions were reproduced in the colonies just as they existed in Europe. In the case of civil society, it was seen as the site where colonial rule could be legitimated. Although there are significant differences in the manner in which such institutions developed within settler and non-settler colonies, in non-settler colonies 'native others' were conferred the status of subjects, as opposed to citizens. It is from within this domain that resistance to colonial rule emanated when subjects refused to accept that they were members of such a civil society. It is this distinction which allowed them to forge a national identity by utilising the narrative of community. In the post-colonial period, however, the narrative of community once again comes into tension with capital while the journey of modernisation and progress is resumed with considerable zeal. It is important to turn now to that process and examine the tensions that arise as a result of the predominance of the 'developmentalist' state.

It is argued here that the post-colonial state as well as civil society are a product of colonialism. While certain notions of civil society were introduced within the colonies, they were 'limited by the fact that the colonial state could confer only subjecthood on the colonized; it could not grant them citizenship' (Chatterjee 1993: 237). The anti-colonial nationalism which led to the end of colonial rule was predicated upon a different narrative: a narrative of community which could not be suppressed by the narrative of capital. However, this alternative narrative was displaced by the post-colonial state, which adopted the goals of rationality, progress, modernisation and development. Chatterjee captures this as follows:

> The modern state, embedded as it is within the universal narrative of capital, cannot recognize within its jurisdiction any form of community except the single, determinate, demographically enumerable form of the nation. It must therefore subjugate, if necessary by the use of state violence, all such aspirations of community identity.
>
> (Chatterjee 1990: 238)

As globalisation and cultural imperialism intensify, it is vital for sub-Saharan Africa to consider the costs of a modernist project that celebrates economic development above all else. It is in this way that contemporary African debates, emphases and hopes which are tied to the notion of civil society need to be examined. The post-colonial state, enmeshed with the universalising nature of capital, is unable to recognise different forms of community other than a single nation. In Africa, the sense of community is heightened and linked mostly to questions of ethnicity. In these cases the state has a tendency to subjugate any sense of community identity by violence. Steven Friedman has noted astutely that there is an assumption that 'democratic modernity requires the obliteration of traditional identities and authority', a view that is a 'pervasive tenet of much of an African intelligentsia firmly committed to democracy' (1999: 830). Nevertheless, what is surprising is that there have not been greater moves towards secession and the break-up of the nation-state system which was bequeathed by the colonial powers along ethnic lines.

The distinction between state and civil society, which is tied to the history of Europe, needs to be viewed in the context of the narrative of capital. Such a distinction does reproduce strategies which reflect, and seek to replicate, the historical experiences of Europe and in the process imply the superiority of the European historical experience over the historical experiences of others. As Gyan Prakash points out, this is where post-colonialism is instructive in allowing us to rethink, relocate or reclaim lost narratives. He argues:

> Based on the belief that we do not have the option of saying no to the determinate conditions of history – capitalist modernity, discourses of liberty, citizenship, individual rights, nation-state – postcolonial criticism attempts to identify in the displaced historical functioning in these discourses the basis for other articulations ... [It] directs attention to those relocations of dominant discourses that emerge from elsewhere – not from the space of the nation state ... but from contingent, contentious, and heterogeneous subaltern positions.
>
> (Prakash 1996: 201)

Civil society in Africa

Jacques Derrida's astute observation in the early 1980s that apartheid did not have an everlasting relationship with capitalism met with considerable hostility (McClintock and Nixon 1986). And yet, he appears to have been vindicated. The recent transitions not only in South Africa but across much of sub-Saharan Africa have taken place neither as a result of the overthrow of the capitalist system nor through a socialist revolution. Indeed, they might well have been aided by capitalism itself, as in the case of South Africa.[6] Eric Hobsbawm noted that 'in the late 1980s and early 1990s an era in world history ended and a new one began' (1994: 4). For Africanists, particularly on the left, this has meant a need to reconceptualise the very foundations of their theoretical assumptions which ultimately rested upon the linkages between the international capitalist system, the state and the local bourgeoisie. But it was not only the left that was unable to contemplate and comprehend the rapid changes that occurred. The right also had difficulty in explaining the African crisis and the transitions which swept through the continent. After all, theoretically they had been linked inextricably to the state, under the rubric of modernisation which they had advocated vehemently in the immediate post-independence period. Such reconceptualisation, has meant that both the left and the right are now focusing much attention on the role of civil society in the light of the perceived failure of a state-centred approach.

The concept of civil society is not only complex but, given the plethora of definitions, its adoption into African political discourse has rendered it controversial as well as problematic. It is a concept that is rapidly evolving and, in the African context, is being inflected in particular ways. Some writers see it as being inappropriate for Africa, given its obvious European roots (Bayart 1986; Mamdani 1996a). Nevertheless, the predominance of the state system has meant that the notion of civil society has become an integral part of, and an important analytical tool for, Africanists. The linkages to the state mean that the concept is intertwined with, and inseparable from, that of the state. It is in this way that Chabal defines civil society:

> civil society, in so far as it can be defined, consists not just of what is obviously not part of the state but also of all who may have become powerless or disenfranchised: not just villagers, fishermen, nomads, members of different age groups, village councillors or slum dwellers, but also professionals, politicians, priests and *mullahs*, intellectuals, military officers and all others who are, or feel they are without access to the state. Civil society is a vast ensemble of constantly changing groups and individuals whose only common ground is their being outside the state and who have … acquired some consciousness of their externality and opposition to the state.
>
> (Chabal 1986: 15)

So, for Chabal, civil society is all that which is excluded from the state. But, for Bayart, it is civil society which seeks to counteract the totalising tendencies of the state (Bayart 1986: 112). The independent African state is, Bayart argues, one that has been 'deliberately set up against civil society rather than evolved in continual conflict with it' (*ibid.*: 112). Regardless of the numerous definitions of civil society within Africa, the importance of the concept has arisen as a result of the need to remove authoritarian and repressive African rulers who have dominated the political space since independence. Recently, the very notion of civil society has become a panacea for democratisation. Eboe Hutchful has claimed that, 'indeed the term has come to be virtually synonymous with democracy' (1996: 54).

A number of critics have pointed out the fragility of civil society in Africa where the one-party state has dominated the political sphere; the one-party state has been in many ways not significantly different from the colonial state. John Mw Makumbe points out that civil society has been responsible for the demise of colonialism, and that it was highly successful during the decolonisation process. Its success, however, has meant that independent regimes threatened by a strong and viable civil society have inaugurated coercive means to ensure that the one-party state would remain unchallenged (1998: 310). For him, despite the numerous hurdles that civil society faces:

> civil society exists in Africa today. African civil society is, however, fairly weak and beset with constraints of a financial, organizational, operational and environmental nature. Naturally, these multi-faceted constraints make it rather difficult for civil society in Africa effectively to represent, promote and protect the interests of the people.
>
> (Makumbe 1998: 316)

In the African context, the role of civil society has been emphasised and advocated by the World Bank, the IMF and the international donor community. This represents another instance of the discourse of Africanism[7] and is illustrative of the triumphalism of the West. This triumphalism has resulted in the export, or even invention, of civil societies from the West to Africa.

However, Nelson Kasfir argues that the recent emphasis on civil society and its linkages to democracy are exaggerated. Such exaggeration can be attributed to a misreading of the role of the state which, far from having receded, remains a potent force in Africa. The conventional view of civil society in Africa[8] is one that attributes it a great deal of autonomy: 'By definition, then, much, probably most, public associational life is excluded from civil society and thus from any proper analysis of the impact of civil society on the struggle for democracy or its consolidation' (1998a: 5). These exclusions characterise civil society as playing an adversarial role in relation to the state. Further, they cause Kasfir to question the ability of civil society to play a key role in consolidating democracy. A central problem with the conventional literature is that it 'requires a notion of civil society which evaluates what is happening, not what ought to happen' (1998b: 126).

The idea that civil society is an effective check on the state and that it can serve a policing role is one that is central to the conventional view of civil society. It is this view which Kasfir seeks to debunk, claiming that such a proposition is based on the notion that the state is an equal actor along with other elements of civil society.[9] A notion of the 'integral state' is one that Crawford Young has developed, arguing that such a state acts directly upon civil society through its hegemonic apparatuses whereby 'the state is free to engage in rational pursuit of its design for the future and to amply reward the ruling class for its governance services' (1994: 39). In the African case, the colonial state was predicated upon the almost complete suppression of African civil society, and this has remained a hallmark of the state after independence. From the conventional viewpoint, in the aftermath of the democratic transitions which swept Eastern Europe as well as Africa, the state has weakened considerably. As a consequence, the state has retreated. While this is true in terms of the economic sphere, largely as a result of growing demands, escalating population growth as well as mismanagement and structural adjustment programmes, there is little evidence that the state has weakened or retreated from the political sphere. On the contrary, the overwhelming evidence suggests that the democratic transitions have been extremely fragile. Nowhere is this more evident then in the case of Kenya, where the early promise manifested within civil society has failed to alter fundamentally the power structures established by President Moi. Moi has been so successful in exploiting elements of civil society that it has not challenged his rule in two successive elections (Ahluwalia 1996a, 1997a). Hence, for Kasfir, a fundamental weakness of the conventional view is that it fails to ask 'how possible can organisational autonomy be, given the existing states in contemporary Africa – no matter how much they would like these states to change' (1998a: 10).

In order to move beyond the confines of the conventional approach to civil society, Kasfir advocates adopting a notion of civility, which he takes from Laurence Whitehead (1997). The emphasis on civility necessitates that two kinds of civil society be considered in order to assess their propensity towards democracy. He states:

> In the case of an authoritarian state, the denser the civil society, the more likely it could be forced to begin a democratic transition – to liberalise. In the case of a state undergoing democratisation, a more selective civil society, one that excludes uncivil, inegalitarian and anti-democratic organisations, may be more effective in achieving democracy – to consolidate ... noticing differences in civil society may help explain why some countries achieve more successful democracies than do others.
>
> (Kasfir 1998: 12)

The conventional model which Kasfir attacks is one that has been adopted from the American case. However, he points out that the model is being advocated as a panacea for Africa at precisely the time when civic association and participation in the United States is at its lowest. Kasfir urges caution, arguing that, 'either civil society has less to do with democracy in the West ... or the nature of Western democracy is changing in ways that make it less desirable as a model for Africa' (1998b: 143).

Irving Markovitz challenges the assertion that the state can be viewed as being separate from civil society, arguing that they are not in a 'precarious balance' but that they intertwine. Drawing on the work of Ellen Meiksins Wood (1991), he points out that, in order to gain a comprehensive understanding of contemporary African politics, it is essential to view capitalism and the state as repressive instruments of social control, and that an examination of class is essential to understand civil society. The literature on civil society in Africa is dominated by writings that draw on the work of John Keane (1988). His views of civil society fail to deal adequately with the significance of capitalist development. As an example, Markovitz shows how the works of Naomi Chazan and Jean-François Bayart reproduce such omissions:

> Bayart joins Keane in playing down the significance of the economic, especially the significance of class. He questions the existence of capitalism in Africa. He is in the forefront of those Africanists who have adopted the postmodernist tropes that Wood finds so problematic ...
>
> (Markovitz 1998: 39)

The need to examine the class dimension of civil society and the manner in which it deals with the state is central to understanding the ways in which democracy develops. Markovitz warns of the dangers of forgetting crucial variables, such as exploitation and domination, which for him remain an integral feature of politics in Africa.

Civil society has come to be seen as the key site which can lead to democratisation. The faith in civil society is premised upon Joel Migdal's (1988) positive correlation between a weak state and a strong society: that is, if the former is weak the latter will necessarily be stronger. It is on the basis of this binary relationship that much contemporary Africanist discourse has focused on civil society. This is where post-colonial theory is instructive, for it seeks to move beyond simple binary distinctions, which in practice are not sustainable. The argument mounted here is that such a binary is not helpful because the state and civil society have to be analytically conceptualised as constituting a symbiotic relationship. Civil society is tied integrally to modernity and to the narrative of capital which sought to suppress the notion of community. In Africa, where colonialism created artificial nation-states, both the colonial and post-independence states have been steeped in the language of modernisation and nation-building. The result has been to 'commit one of democratic theory's cardinal sins – to suppress difference' (Friedman 1999: 830). It is not surprising that the current efforts to democratise have been problematic, particularly in the light of the unresolved issues between narratives of capital and the suppression of community which are being carried out within the discursive space of the post-colonial African state. It is important in this context to reiterate the argument mounted in the previous chapter that in Africa a hybrid state and civil society have emerged, which were inherited from the European colonial powers but which are continually being inflected locally.

This discussion of civil society is an important backdrop to examining the issue of human rights in Africa. The abuse of human rights has been widely documented and has formed the cornerstone of analyses which seek to deploy a civil-society perspective, arguing that civil society is the only effective mechanism whereby human rights can be protected.

Human rights in Africa

Despite ever-increasing tensions in several different areas of the globe, in the post-Cold-War period there has come to be a general (almost unquestioned) acceptance of the universality of human rights. While the assertion of human rights represents the triumph of liberalism, the violation of these rights (under such terms) continues unabated. In this section, human rights in Africa are investigated by deploying a post-colonial perspective. Such a perspective is necessary in order to delineate the complexities of the post-colonial condition, which is pervasive in the African case.

Although sub-Saharan Africa has been independent for more than thirty years, the continent is at present being subjected to perhaps the greatest scrutiny it has ever endured. Africa is under constant attention and surveillance, as a plethora of organisations monitor virtually every aspect of African lives. This intrusion is legitimised by the inauguration of a host of successive World Bank and IMF structural adjustment programmes, and there is an ever-increasing number of organisations which are dedicated to monitoring the human-rights record of the continent. The presence and intensification of the European gaze is made all the more possible because of the dominance of a single, imperial power that sets the agenda under which African countries operate in the post-Cold-War period. This agenda is exemplified in an influential 1989 World Bank document, which argued that 'underlying the litany of Africa's development problems is a crisis of governance' (World Bank 1989: 60). This has meant the advent of the imposition of conditionality to effect liberal democratic government. As a corollary, such a stance has pushed for the dignity and sanctity of human beings and argued for the universality of human rights.

There is little doubt that the 'human-rights record' in sub-Saharan Africa after independence has been dismal (Thomas 1997). There is now a massive record which details the manner in which significant sections of the population have suffered the excesses of various regimes on the continent, in regions as diverse as Kenya, Uganda, South Africa and Rwanda. Despite such obvious injustices, the literature on human rights in Africa is polarised between those who claim the universality of such rights and those who seek to argue the specificity of the African case. It is necessary therefore to examine closely the divergent positions advanced.

Universal rights v. cultural specificity

The universality of human rights is asserted on the grounds that, as a human being, each person is entitled to certain human rights which are part of the fundamental values that all cultures share. This view of human rights is articulated clearly by Jack Donnelly, who argues:

> The very idea of human rights does entail a certain individualism. Human rights are those rights that one has simply as a human being, irrespective of one's membership or place in society ... each person, regardless of status or past actions, has certain fundamental human rights that ordinarily take priority over other moral and political claims and obligations. The idea of *human* rights, in other words, implies that there is a certain irreducible moral value in each individual being.
>
> (Donnelly 1990: 35)

It is the individualism that is associated with human-rights discourse which elicits considerable controversy. While it is not intended here to trace the epistemological roots of human-rights discourse, it is important to note that the modern notion of human rights can be traced to the eighteenth-century Western philosophical tradition. Here, the individual's rights against the state, and the protection of private property as an essential part of the individual's autonomy, were stressed.[10] The culmination of this discourse can be seen in the Universal Declaration of Human Rights in 1948 and two subsequent covenants – one on civil and political rights, the other on economic, social and cultural rights – which were approved in 1966. The need for two covenants arose from the West's opposition to the latter covenant, which is seen as containing demands and claims rather than intrinsic human rights. Economic, social and cultural rights, it is contended, require positive state action, and hence differ from fundamental human rights (Koshy 1999).[11] The emphasis on the individual in this tradition renders any notion of the community or communal rights virtually impossible, and it also evokes passion, as it represents yet another dominating discourse from the West which seeks to normalise African subjects.

The stress on individualism and a failure to place economic, social and cultural rights on an equal footing have meant that there are those who challenge the acceptance of this tradition as one which is universal.[12] This is largely due to the legislation's Western-liberal underpinnings, which are not seen as being consistent with the African communitarian views and values. This view maintains that Africans have their own rich heritage and tradition of rights inherent within the community, which is drawn, although not exclusively, from traditional African society. As Rhoda Howard notes, such a claim is based on the communitarian ideal in which, 'the group is more important than the individual, decisions are made by consensus rather than by competition, and economic surpluses are generated and disposed of on a redistributive rather than profit oriented basis' (1986a: 13).[13] In addition, universal rights are seen to be incompatible with the challenges of development, which necessitate an interventionist state.[14] Sakah Mahmud has pointed out that collective rights 'would be meaningless if individuals do not benefit from them equally' (1993: 487). For Mahmud, the only way to ensure communal rights is through 'true' democracy, which is a collective right.[15]

The politics of human rights in Africa

Although the debate on human rights has revolved around the issue of whether or not such rights are universal, the practice of human rights under either theoretical conceptualisation has been wanting in virtually all parts of the world. The idea of a unique set of rights established on a group or communal basis has been founded on notions of the 'traditional' African society with roots in the pre-colonial era. A considerable debate exists about the validity of such assertions. It is not intended to engage in this debate, but it is important to recognise that colonial contact fundamentally altered the culture of African societies. The impact of colonisation is such that there is no turning back, making it impossible to revert to pre-colonial modes. This is necessarily so, because culture is not a static entity which can be invoked after the colonisers leave. Rather, culture is a dynamic entity which makes and remakes itself continuously. Consequently, the colonial experience fundamentally alters the very dimensions of the debate.

Regardless of the pre-colonial experience, there is no doubt that with the advent of colonialism African peoples' human rights were affected adversely. Under the guise of the civilising mission, colonial powers systematically impinged upon every vestige of African life, denying the African humanity itself. Fanon captures the dehumanising of the African:

> Native society is not simply described as society lacking in values .... the native represents not only the absence of values, but also the negation of values .... At times this manichaeism goes to the logical conclusion and dehumanizes the native. In fact, the terms the settler uses when he mentions the native are zoological terms.
>
> (Fanon 1967: 32)

It is against this background that the Universal Declaration of Human Rights needs to be evaluated – it was certainly in existence at the very time that colonialism was at its zenith in Africa. In the struggle for independence, the declaration served as a useful reference point and an important political tool in exposing the hypocrisy of the colonial powers for whom the rights embodied in the declaration were the exclusive preserve of the European. African leaders asserted their equality and sought the same rights which had been granted to the European. In 1945 the fifth Pan African Congress endorsed the principles of the Universal Declaration and urged Africans to organise themselves in order to support the struggle for independence (Nkrumah 1971: 53). It was Julius

Nyerere who emphasised the importance of international human rights discourse:

> Here we are, building up the sympathy of the outside world on the theme of Human Rights. We are telling the world that we are fighting for our rights as human beings .... Does anybody really believe that we ourselves will trample on human rights? I do not believe the leaders of a people are going to behave as hypocrites to gain their ends, and then turn around and do exactly the things which they have been fighting against.
>
> (Nyerere 1966: 70)

Human rights were thus an integral part of the African struggle for independence. In the period immediately following the end of direct colonial rule, African political leaders reaffirmed their commitment to international human rights either by directly referring to the Universal Declaration or by expressing similar sentiments in their country's constitutions or in party documents. For example, in Tanzania the TANU (at that time, Tanganyika African National Union) Constitution included the objective of safeguarding 'the inherent dignity of the individual in accordance with the Universal Declaration of Human Rights' (Minouge and Molloy 1974: 68). Similarly, in Zambia the ruling party's stated objectives were 'to ensure that freedom of speech, worship and freedom of the press shall not be infringed and that the people of Zambia shall be free to think, speak, write, assemble, work and trade' (*ibid.*: 104).

While the achievement of independence heralded a new phase for Africa, the drive for modernisation meant that the rights for which Africans struggled were subordinated to the development imperative. In the event, African leaders adopted measures that were authoritarian and similar to those of the colonial masters whom they had just replaced. Critically, the development–rights trade-off became an important tool for political regimes to repress their citizens. It was not only to some pure and authentic pre-colonial African heritage that they turned for justifying their actions. One of the most influential defences can be found in the work of John Rawls (perhaps the most important liberal theorist of the century), where he claims that, as an exception to his general rule, a poor country can justify the sacrifice of civil liberties for an increase in economic well-being, thereby suggesting a trade-off (Rawls 1971: section 82).[16] African regimes, buoyed up by the Cold War and the super-power rivalry, were permitted to engage in repressive actions, reprimanded only when Western interests were threatened.[17]

In this way, supported by the West, African governments were able to argue that the realisation of full human rights was an ideal for the future, and not something that could be attained in the short-term. It is not surprising therefore that Julius Nyerere, who earlier had championed the cause of human rights, argued that:

I have myself signed Detention Orders. I have done these things as an inevitable part of my responsibilities as President .... Our Union has neither the long tradition of nationhood, nor the strong physical means of national security which other states take for granted. While the vast mass of people give full and active support to their country and its government, a handful of individuals can still put our nation into jeopardy and reduce the efforts of millions.

(Nyerere, cited in Duggan and Civille 1976: 184)

It is this political manoeuvring that has undermined the notion of a unique set of African human rights. However, it must be noted that the political machinations in Africa are no different from the abuses of rights endured by sections of the population in the West. For example, the purging of communists during the McCarthy era and the infringement of the rights of the Socialist Workers Party by the FBI during various US administrations are reminiscent of strategies deployed by political regimes everywhere. What is surprising, however, is that the West's abuses remain largely unadmonished.

In the 1980s, as Africa's economic crisis intensified, an evaluation of Africa's problems led to a rethinking of the development–rights trade-off. It now was asserted that the only way for Africa to progress was to embrace the positive correlation between human rights and economic development. It is in this context that the democratisation wave which swept much of Africa in the early 1990s must be viewed. African citizens openly protested, expressing their frustration at both the economic crisis as well as the repression which they had endured. The single-party system, which had become characteristic, came under attack not only within African nations but critically also amongst the donor community. It was the support of the West that forced onto the agenda not only democratic reform but also human rights. Yash Tandon captures the change of heart:

the paradox of 'democracy' is that every slave master eventually turns his whip on the slave supervisors for allowing things to deteriorate so badly that the slaves are in revolt .... This is what the World Bank and the donor agencies are now doing with African governments.

(Tandon 1991: 1495)

The solutions to Africa's crisis are now articulated and co-ordinated by the World Bank and the IMF under the strict regimen of structural adjustment programmes (SAPs) (Green 1998). The changed policy is endorsed fully by the most influential donor, the US Agency for International Development, which holds that, 'there is growing evidence that open societies that value individual rights, respect the rule of the law, and have open and accountable governments, provide better opportunities for sustained economic development than do closed systems which stifle individual initiative' (Decalo 1992: 23). Pita Ogaba Agbese points out that SAPs and the push towards democratisation are not compatible. SAPs require a repressive regime to be implemented and reflect imperial interests rather than citizens' interests (Agbese 1994; Riddell 1999). For a human-rights culture to exist in Africa, Shivji (1989) points out, it must be anti-imperialist because imperialism itself is a deterrent to freedom and democracy.[18] The double standards and the rhetoric of the West are all too evident in a country such as Uganda, which has received only a muted response to its particular form of democratic governance, which in many ways resembles the one-party state of the past.[19]

Post-colonial theory and human rights

In current debates, the 'post' in post-colonial no longer accepts the mere periodisation of the 1970s debates which signalled a new era after decolonisation. Rather, the post-colonial seeks to problematise the cultural interactions between both the colonised and the colonisers from the moment of colonisation onwards (Ashcroft *et al.* 1989; Said 1993a). Such a reworking of the post-colonial means that the post-colonial condition is not universal and cannot be generalised as a theory. As Bill Ashcroft notes:

> 'post-colonial' does not mean 'after colonialism' … It begins when the colonisers arrive and doesn't finish when they go home. In that sense, post-colonial analysis examines the full range of responses to colonialism … All of these may exist in a single society, so the term 'post-colonial society' does not mean an historical left over of colonialism, but a society continuously responding in all its myriad ways to the experience of colonial contact …
>
> (Ashcroft 1997: 21)

A particularly important trope in post-colonial theory is the notion of binarism. If one looks at Western rationalism as a product of modernity, and development as its social signifier, we begin to see how the notion of 'traditional' society is embedded deeply within imperial culture and the colonial imagination. Binarisms allow us to establish meaning by defining concepts in contradistinction to each other. Hence, when we look at reason or rationality, it can be juxtaposed to emotion or madness. What such binarisms suggest is that there are no positive terms in isolation, 'in language, there are only differences *without positive terms*' (de Saussure 1974: 120). Just as feminist theory has demonstrated that binarisms operate within Western patriarchal thought, where reason is associated with masculinity and emotion and hysteria with femininity, there is a similar binarism that operates within developed and developing or First and Third World countries. As Cixous points out:

> I saw that the great, noble, 'advanced' countries established themselves by expelling what was 'strange'; excluding it but not dismissing it; enslaving it. A commonplace gesture of [Hegelian] History: there have to be *two* races – the masters and the slaves. We know the implied irony in the master/slave dialectic: the body of what is strange must not disappear, but its force must be

conquered and returned to the master. Both the appropriate and the inappropriate must exist: the clean, hence the dirty, the rich, hence the poor, etc.

(Cixous 1995: 210)

These binarisms are clearly in opposition, but, more importantly, they are unequal and hierarchical – replicating the master/slave relationship. This is precisely the kind of relationship which Frantz Fanon captures in his *The Wretched of the Earth*, where there are two opposed zones. First, there is the settler's town, occupied by white people which is a 'well-fed town, an easy-going town, its belly is always full of good things'. The other zone is the town of colonised people, 'a hungry town, starved of bread, of meat, of shoes, of coal, of light ... a town of niggers and dirty arabs' (Fanon 1967: 30).

The examples of both Cixous and Fanon and the binary oppositions which they deploy confirm the binary logic of imperialism, which represents the way in which Western thought in general sees the world. This is where post-colonial theory differs. It seeks to break down the tyranny of imperial structures and binaries which dominate the subject. In post-colonial formulations, such dichotomies are no longer adequate. As Ashcroft *et al.* point out, this is the

> domain of overlap between these imperial binary oppositions, the area in which ambivalence, hybridity, and complexity continually disrupt the certainties of imperial logic. Thus the ambiguous regions, the interstitial spaces which inevitably emerge in the binary logic of imperial ideology, are the fertile ground of post-colonial analysis.
>
> (Ashcroft *et al.* 1998: 23)

By seeking to disrupt imperial binarisms, post-colonial theory investigates the interstitial space arising out of the post-colonial condition, which raises the possibility of an ambivalent and hybrid subjectivity. It is this which leads to the possibility of social transformation. This sense of agency makes the 'post' in post-colonial different from other 'post' formulations. An important dimension of such disruptions is that, while imperial binaries suggest a unilinear movement of domination from coloniser to colonised, post-colonialism opens up the possibility of movements in both directions. The African Charter of Rights contains perhaps the beginnings of such a movement.[20]

The African Charter of Rights

A problem exists between the universal and the African notion of rights, with the former characterising the latter as culturally relativist. While these positions are not easily reconcilable, it is important to examine how African nations have dealt with their particularities and specificities through a close examination of the African Charter of Rights.

The African Charter of Human and Peoples' Rights, 'the Banjul Charter', was adopted by the Organisation of African Unity (OAU) in 1980. [21] The adoption of the Charter many years after the formation of the OAU can be traced to the origins of the organisation, which was established initially to fight colonial rule. In the aftermath of colonialism the OAU has been particularly adamant and consistent in its views about interfering in another state's internal affairs. However, in the light of considerable criticism that it faced as a result of severe injustices committed against citizens of several African states, including Uganda, Equatorial Guinea and the Central African Empire, the organisation embarked upon an African Charter of Rights. A typical characterisation of the OAU can be discerned by the following observation:

> If we do not learn to criticize injustice within our continent, we will soon be tolerating fascism in Africa as long as it is practiced by African governments, against African peoples. Consider what our reaction would have been if the 30,000 Ibos (killed by Amin) had been massacred by whites in South Africa …. Yet those people are dead; the colour of those who killed them is irrelevant …. Justice is indivisible. Africa and the OAU must act accordingly.
>
> (Emerson 1975: 224)

The African Charter was influenced in part by the Universal Declaration of Human Rights, but in no way was it a simple adoption of the UN document. Rather, it was guided by the principle that it should 'reflect the African conception of human rights, [and] should take as a pattern the African philosophy and law to meet the needs of Africa' (Amnesty International 1991: 10). The preamble to the Charter captures the spirit of this principle pointing out 'the virtues of [African] historical tradition and the values of African civilization which should inspire and characterize their reflection on the concept of human and people's rights' (International Commission of Jurists 1986). The preamble stresses the importance of the community, stating that, 'the enjoyment of rights and freedoms also implies the performance of duties on the part of everyone'.

Perhaps the most significant distinguishing feature of the Charter is its commitment to peoples' rights. The notion of peoples' rights is that these are 'collective rights to national sovereignty free from external influence (sometimes said to be grounded in a nation-state's right to self-determination) and rights to national "control over the country's natural resources", and the state is seen as a surrogate of "the people" – a protector of their culture, liberty, and development' (Paul 1990: 216; Howard 1986b). This is amplified in the Charter's emphasis on the duties of the individual toward the community and the state (Articles 27–9). This emphasis is at the heart of the tension between the universal and culturally specific rights which was examined above. Nevertheless, the African Charter does not reject the notion of rights as developed in the Universal Declaration. Rather, it incorporates such rights: 'fundamental human rights stem from the attributes of human beings, which justifies their international protection …' (Paul 1990: 216). The African Charter clearly benefited from and drew upon the Universal Declaration, recognising that it was 'prudent not to deviate from international norms' (Amnesty International 1991).

While most African countries are signatories to the African Charter, critics point out that 'claw-back' clauses 'essentially confine the charter's protections to rights as they are defined in national law' (Welch 1992: 43). For the West, one of the most controversial aspects of the Charter has been its ambivalence towards the right to liberty and the security of the individual. It is here that it is seen to be vulnerable and open to abuse by the state, primarily because of the clauses which subject the Charter to the laws of individual states. It is in this context that the African Charter has been characterised as being 'incapable of supplying even a scintilla of external restraint upon a government's power to create laws contrary to the spirit of the rights granted' (*ibid.*: 46).

Critics of the Charter emphasise also the lack of power vested in the African Commission on Human and Peoples' Rights, the body responsible for policing the abuse of rights as set out in the Charter. The Commission is appointed by and reports to the OAU Assembly, which is comprised of the Heads of State and Government. This has led to the criticism that the OAU is prepared in principle to promote human rights but not to protect them. Furthermore, critics point out that the African region lacks a court to complement the Commission, unlike other regions where such commissions exist (*ibid.*: 47). The most damning criticism, however, concerns the inability of the Commission to act independently, as it is subject to scrutiny by the OAU Assembly. As one critic notes, 'the Commission's only real sanction – publicity – is severely limited by the powers the African Charter vests in the Assembly (of Heads of State), which is a political body that is not likely to be an enthusiastic guardian of human rights' (Buergenthal 1988: 189).

The problems of implementation that critics of the African Charter raise are not unique nor restricted to Africa. In virtually every part of the world, including the West, human-rights abuses occur despite the formulation of an elaborate web of legal frameworks and structures. What is different about the African Charter is that it is a unique document which seeks to include African values whilst recognising the importance of the internationally accepted declarations and covenants on human rights.

Both the theory and practice of human rights in Africa evokes a great deal of controversy. The politics of human rights on the continent have been punctuated by rhetoric, while its citizens have had their most basic rights denied by both colonial and post-colonial regimes. The polarisation of human-rights discourse into universalism *or* cultural specificity has not been beneficial to the people of Africa. The clouding of African and Western human-rights rhetoric, as a result of political imperatives affecting both African leaders and Western interests, has been a powerful mechanism for shifting responsibility from the state to the people. While political conditionality has opened up the political space in some African countries, the terms imposed on African states by the donor community and the ever-increasing interventionist policies of the West are not ideal for ensuring that human rights will be protected. Africans are wary about foreign intervention, particularly as debates about recolonising Africa gain promi-nence.[22] Hence, it is not altogether clear that a mere policing and surveillance of Africa along with an enhancement of the European gaze will necessarily produce the desired outcome of societies more attuned to the protection of their citizens, albeit according to a universal or culturally-specific African notion of rights.

This is where post-colonial theory is instructive. It recognises the complexities of post-colonial societies, particularly at a time when there is increasing globalisation. Post-colonialism recognises that, as a result of the post-colonial condition, there are no pure cultures. It seeks, therefore, to break down binaries which have been produced by the logic of imperialism – such as universal and culturally-specific, or Western and African, human rights. Post-colonial theory seeks to examine the interstitial spaces which arise out of the disruption of such simple binaries. By tearing down those elements of colonial discourse which objectify and negate the African subject, post-colonial theory is able to create discursive space for previously oppressed peoples.[23] It is in this context that the African Charter of Rights, when stripped of its most obvious political constraints, has some long-term significance for the people of the continent. It is a charter which seeks to acknowledge the complexities of the African condition whilst recognising the value of the Universal Charter, and, most importantly, it is an African document which Africa may well be prepared to own.

Conclusion

The emphases on good governance and democracy which have dominated contemporary African politics are rooted firmly in conceptions of civil society. Africanists, frustrated with the lack of 'progress' on the continent, have sought salvation in new tools of analysis. To this end, civil society has appeared as the key variable which has been ignored in African studies. It has become the single most important variable through which it is expected that Africa can be transformed. The promise of civil society is predicated on the belief that the state has failed, and that, in the wake of its retreat, civil society has the potential to radically transform African societies. Certainly, it is seen as the primary vehicle through which democratisation can be achieved.

There is little doubt that civil society has received scant attention, and that it has a considerable role to play in any society, not just in the case of Africa. Yet simply to focus all our attention on civil society, as has been the case recently, when academics as well as NGOs and donor agencies have privileged it as the moving force capable of transforming Africa, is problematic. It is essential to consider the relationship between the state and civil society. More importantly, it is crucial to recognise that not all actors in civil society have the capacity to operate on a level playing field. In the case of Africa, the state might well have retreated from the economic sphere as a result of scarce resources as well as donor pressure, but it has by no means retreated from the political sphere. This is where post-colonial theory is helpful. It urges that a polity be examined in its totality – from the moment of colonisation, when its politics are ruptured and defined in new ways. It is in this way that we need to examine the impact of colonialism and the effect it had on the key issues of governance, democracy and civil society. It is colonialism which defines the modes of power that continue to determine the shape of contemporary African society. It is with such a perspective that an examination of human rights in Africa has been carried out. Such an analysis points out that, once those modes of power have been traced, it is possible to understand the local inflections which individual African states deploy after independence in order to carry out governance. As the discussion of human rights has illustrated, it is not possible to view Africa as outside the dynamics of global politics. Rather, all cultures are now intertwined inextricably, and this fundamentally affects the manner in which they adopt and inflect institutions and practices. The case of the African Charter illustrates the manner in which African specificity is tied to the universalism of human rights.

5 Citizenship, subjectivity and the crisis of modernity

> In all these countries the ruling party – or rather the ruling bureaucracy, for the concept of political party in every legitimate sense had ceased to apply – was itself the state; and this state had ceased to have any citizens .... Citizens might remain present as existential phenomena; they were absent as participating actors.
>
> Basil Davidson

> I have been working to change the way I speak and write, to incorporate in the manner of telling a sense of place, of not just who I am in the present but where I am coming from, the multiple voices within me. I have confronted silence, inarticulateness. When I say then, that these words emerge from suffering, I refer to that personal struggle to name the location from which I come to voice – that space of my theorizing.
>
> bell hooks

Since independence, the countries of Sub-Saharan Africa have been subjected to various forms of intervention aimed at modernisation. The modernisation imperative has meant that the continent has endured various theoretical positions as diverse as modernisation theory, dependency and Marxist analyses. All of these have failed to provide the elusive salvation which Africa so desperately seeks. Mahmood Mamdani's *Citizen and Subject: Contemporary Africa and the Legacy of Late Colonialism* is a monumental effort to rethink the current impasse facing Africanists. It is an important book which seeks to engage with, and point towards new theoretical referents at a time when traditional paradigms have failed Africa. It seeks to do so by examining closely the dividing line between citizen and subject. As such, this work warrants closer examination. The advent of colonisation entailed differentiating between peoples in the colony. The movement of administrators and settlers to the colonies necessitated that these individuals were seen to be separate from the indigenous population. In this way the former were accorded citizenship and certain rights, while the latter were ascribed the status of subjecthood, with none of the attendant rights enjoyed by citizens. This chapter critically engages with Mamdani's book, reflecting on its core thesis. More importantly, it seeks to extend the analysis presented by Mamdani by deploying a post-colonial perspective. This perspective illustrates that the distinction between subject and citizen which Mamdani establishes is itself a simple binary which is untenable. It does this by bringing questions of subjectivity to the foreground, highlighting the complexities of post-colonial identity. It is argued that it is critical to view post-colonial identities as complex formulations – constituted as citizen/subjects.

Citizen and subject: the argument

Mamdani's intervention begins by discussing Africa's impasse. He contends that contemporary thinking has been polarised between modernists and communitarians. For the former, the 'problem is that civil society is an embryonic and marginal construct', while for the latter it is 'that real flesh-and-blood communities that comprise Africa are marginalized from public life as so many "tribes" ' (1996a: 3). His stated purpose is not to privilege any one position but to attempt a synthesis by highlighting the centrality of the colonial experience. There is a shift in perspective whereby the emphasis is more on the 'mode of incorporation than that of marginalization' (*ibid.*: 295).

In this book, Mamdani is concerned with institutional segregation not only on the obvious basis of race but also on the basis of the modes of power which underpinned colonial rule. It is also about resistance, the manner in which Africans responded to colonial rule. The book is, at its core, concerned with three questions. First, is the structure of power in contemporary Africa inherited from the colonial power? Second, what was the role of local ethnic powers both in enforcing power and in being the locus of resistance? Finally, why have African states failed to transcend ethnic differences in the post-independence period? In asking these three questions, Mamdani seeks to fulfil four objectives. First, he wants to emphasise the centrality of Africa as a historical unit of analysis. Second, he attempts to illustrate that apartheid does not need to be seen as an aberration or exceptional case, but rather that it is the consummate colonial state. Third, Mamdani sets out to illustrate the contradictory nature of ethnicity. Finally, he tries to show that, while the colonial state was deracialised, it was not democratised (*ibid.*: 7–8).

Mamdani traces the major trends within African studies by pointing out that Africa remains entrapped in 'history by analogy', which either exoticises Africa or simply represents it as part of European history. In both extremes, Africa's specificity is denied. The idea that Africa exemplifies earlier historical experiences, or that it is part of a unilinear historical continuum, is evident amongst North American Africanists, who hold two extreme positions which can be described as state-centric or society-centric. He points out that, 'for the state-centrists, the state has failed to penetrate society sufficiently and is therefore hostage to it; for the society-centrists, society has failed to hold the state accountable and is therefore prey to it' (*ibid.*: 11).

Mamdani is particularly good at showing the manner in which African studies is dominated by, and rife with, binaries. For example, studies of exit focus on the peasantry, where the debate is polarised, with one side seeing the peasantry as being linked inextricably with the market, while the other views the market as irrelevant in a situation where the 'economy of affection' predominates (Hyden 1980, 1983). For Mamdani, both positions are simply different ways to dismiss African specificity. The emphasis on civil society, he claims, mirrors the debate on socialism, and in a similar manner is underpinned by analogy rather than by any rigorous theoretical foundation. In particular, this is because of the arguments that equate civil society in Africa with civil society in Europe whilst also claiming that the forces underlying democratisation are the result of the contention between state and civil society. For Mamdani, it is important to come to terms with the manner in which those excluded from civil society are ruled. By showing how subject populations are incorporated, he argues 'that no reform of contemporary civil society institutions can by itself unravel this decentralized despotism. To do this will require nothing less than dismantling that form of power' (1996: 15–16).

Whilst recognising the specificity of the colonial state in each particular colony, Mamdani argues that everywhere it was concerned fundamentally with one overarching issue: 'the native question'. In short, the basic problem existing in all colonies was how a minority European colonial power was to rule over a majority indigenous population. The solution was twofold: direct and indirect rule. Direct rule meant that the majority of the population was represented as uncivilised and was 'excluded from the rights of citizenship, direct rule signified an unmediated – centralized – despotism'. Direct rule was founded on the basis of a single legal order which was based on the colonial power's conception of 'modern' law. Indirect rule, on the other hand, 'signified a mediated – decentralized – despotism' (*ibid.*: 17). Indirect rule was grounded in a legal dualism where 'alongside the received law was implemented a customary law that regulated nonmarket relations in land and in personal (family) and community affairs' (Mamdani 1996b: 145). In theory, direct rule was applied in white settler colonies, and indirect rule in all other colonies. In practice, however, such a line of demarcation was not always possible, and eventually:

> Direct rule was the form of urban civil power. It was about the exclusion of natives from civil freedoms guaranteed to citizens in civil society. Indirect rule, however, signified a rural tribal authority. It was about incorporating natives into a state-enforced customary order. Reformulated, direct and indirect rule are better understood as variants of despotism: the former centralized, the latter decentralized. As they learned from experience – of both the ongoing resistance of the colonized and of earlier and parallel colonial encounters – colonial powers generalized decentralized despotism as their principle answer to the native question.
>
> (Mamdani 1996a: 18)

The dovetailing of both direct and indirect rule and the demarcation between urban and rural sites meant that the colonial state was a bifurcated state in which two systems of rule co-existed under a single hegemonic authority. This system of rule was not restricted to any single colonising nation. Although it was developed by the British, it was adopted eventually by all others. For example, in the case of the French colonisers, the system of indirect rule was known as 'association'.

Furthermore, the colonial state was governed by racism. On the one hand, it functioned on the rule of law and rights when it came to settlers, who were defined as citizens, and, on the other hand, it was a state that ruled over subjects who were not entitled to any rights associated with the settler population. It was only at the moment of decolonisation that the boundaries of civil society were extended to create an indigenous civil society. However, Mamdani points out that this was of limited significance because independence merely de-racialised the state without doing the same in civil society. To illustrate his argument, Mamdani points to the successful politics of Africanisation which removed racial barriers facing the African population. However, on the important issue of redistribution, the very population which united to disband racial categories reverted to ethnic or familial ties. He notes that the tendency of the literature on corruption 'has been to detach the two moments and thereby to isolate and decontextualize the moment of redistribution (corruption) from that of expropriation (redress) through ahistorical analogies that describe it as the politics of patrimonialism' ([Mamdani 1996a]: 20). The effect of this was that, while substantial changes were made in urban areas, not much changed in the rural sector; as a result, the 'unreformed Native Authority came to contaminate civil society, so that the more civil society was deracialized, the more it took on a tribalized form' (*ibid.*: 21).

Mamdani stresses that it was the 'native question' which determined the form of rule which shaped the colonial experience. Here, it was indirect rule which exacerbated ethnic allegiance and 'came to be simultaneously the form of colonial control over natives and the form of revolt against it. It defined the parameters of both the Native Authority in charge of the local state apparatus and of resistance to it' (*ibid.*: 24). This allows Mamdani to argue that, not only was the local apparatus of the colonial state based on ethnicity and the customary, but more importantly, so was every instance of resistance. It is this emphasis on the Native Authority that has remained intact and has served as a deterrent to democratising processes. In order to attain democratisation, Mamdani argues, it is essential to reform the local state. Hence, he claims that the colonial state was deracialised but not democratised. This scenario is currently being played out in South Africa which, until 1994, was the colonial state *par excellence*. Although the system of direct rule or apartheid may well have been dismantled, indirect rule continues to shape its future. In this way, South Africa is not to be seen as an exceptional case but merely as part of the enduring legacy of colonialism.

In short, Mamdani's central thesis is that the institutional framework forged during late colonialism was based upon the use of indirect rule over the 'native' population by the local state apparatus in which chiefs ruled on the basis of customary law. The power of the chiefs was directly attributable to the colonial state to which they were beholden – their appointment was subject to state scrutiny. This meant that the chiefs were no longer accountable to members of their community – which fundamentally altered the basis of power which existed prior to colonisation. For example, in the case of the Tswana, adult males served as a check on the authority of the chief in a public assembly which was designed to discuss any public issue. However, under colonialism, 'this public assembly was turned into a forum where decisions were announced but not debated' (*ibid.*: 46). The effect of this system of rule was to dichotomise African societies into citizens and subjects. Citizens were those individuals not covered by customary law, and included principally white settlers as well as black urban elites. Subjects, on the other hand, included the bulk of the population, who were lumped together according to ethnicity and then ruled under Native Authority and customary law – in Mamdani's terms, under 'decentralized despotism'. Citizens and subjects 'derive their rights, customary or civil, through membership in a *patri*: tribe for the subject, a nation for the citizen' (*ibid.*: 292).

The colonial state in Africa needs to be placed within the trajectory of Europe's overall colonial project. When viewed from such a perspective, Africa – the last of Europe's colonial experiments – was the site where the notion of the 'civilising mission' was abandoned, in the face of resistance, in order to maintain power through the use of indirect rule based on customary law. The key features of the system were:

> First, the customary was considered synonymous with the tribal; each tribe was defined as a cultural group with its own customary law. Second, the world of the customary came to be all-encompassing; more so than in any other colonial experience, it came to include a customary access to land. Third, custom was defined and enforced by customary Native Authorities in the local state – backed up by the armed might of the central state
>
> (Mamdani [1996a]: 286)

By centring indirect rule as the key unit of analysis, it is possible for Mamdani to reach the conclusion that the African state was by no means a mere tropical replication of the European nation-state. Rather, it was a state that rested on a different structure, where the peasants were ruled by 'Native Authorities', which in turn were responsible to white officials, who were at the epicentre of colonial rule.

At independence, Africa faced an agenda which entailed three imperatives: 'deracializing civil society, detribalizing Native Authority, and developing the economy in the context of unequal international relations' ([Mamdani 1996a]: 287). Of the three, deracialisation was carried out with the greatest degree of success. The failure to 'detribalise' Native Authority meant that it was not possible to attain democratisation. As a corollary, the lack of democratisation meant that development could only be a 'top-down agenda enforced on the peasantry' (*ibid.*: 287). The effect of such an enforced agenda is that the post-colonial state in Africa has become a 'regime of compulsions', not unlike its predecessor, which extracted tribute from the peasantry, thus rendering them subjects (*ibid.*: 178). The inability to reform the local state remains the most important task, and without it the democratisation processes of the 1990s remain vulnerable. The way out of this impasse is to link the rural with the urban, a phenomenon that has occurred successfully only through the militant nationalism which brought about an end to colonial rule. For Mamdani, the way forward for Africa is to transform both the urban and rural at the same time. He argues, 'only then will the distinction rural–urban – and interethnic – be more fluid than rigid, more an outcome of social processes than a state-enforced artifact' (*ibid.*: 301).

The state inherited at independence by the nationalist movement focused on urban reform and failed to 'detribalise' the Native Authorities system of the colonial power. In such a context, electoral politics necessarily became more than the representation of civil society. It was concerned also with providing access to a rural system of rule as well as with resources. For Mamdani, this factor ensures that urban politicians establish patron–client relationships with rural constituencies, and it is this that results in patrimonialism. He argues:

> In the absence of the democratization of Native Authorities and the custom they enforced, the more civil society was deracialized, the more it came to be tribalized. Urban tribalism appeared as a postindependence problem in states that reproduced customary forms of power precisely because deracialization was a postindependence achievement of those states.
>
> (Mamdani [1996a]: 290)

It was not in all cases that there remained a divide between the urban and the rural, between the deracialisation of civil society and the 'detribalisation' of the Native Authorities. In a number of cases, where a radical agenda was adopted under the aegis of socialism, these authorities were dismantled, but only to be replaced by a strong single party. Here, the single party emerged as the major institution which mediated power between the urban and the rural. In this situation the reform of decentralised despotism created centralised despotism. It is this that presents itself as a dilemma: 'on the one hand, decentralized despotism exacerbates ethnic divisions, and so the solution appears as a centralization. On the other hand, centralized despotism exacerbates the urban–rural division and the solution appears decentralization. But, as variants, both continue to revolve around a shared axis – despotism' (*ibid.*: 291).

Problems with the Mamdani thesis

Mahmood Mamdani's book is an important contribution, particularly given that he is an African scholar reflecting on the impasse within African studies. This book represents a major shift of perspective for the author. Mamdani is recognised as the foremost Uganda scholar, and his book, *Politics and Class Formation in Uganda*, was amongst a number of important books written in the 1970s from a dependency perspective. While he has been locked firmly into what can be described broadly as a political-economy approach, in *Citizen and Subject* he attempts to takes into account the impact of the modes of power on which colonial rule rested. This is not surprising, given the general turn in social theory, where traditional modes of inquiry have come under sustained attack by the 'post' phenomena. Although Mamdani attempts to break out of the constraints imposed by traditional modes of inquiry, he nevertheless remains entrapped within those very discourses.

Mamdani, both carefully and successfully, has delineated the predominance of binaries which dominate analyses of Africa. Despite being aware of the problems of such dichotomisation, he nevertheless succumbs to it. The distinction between citizen and subject on which his project rests, in itself reinforces a binary representation. Mamdani shows how colonialism set up and maintained structures of power through the system of indirect rule and decentralised despotism. More importantly, he demonstrates that, during decolonisation, it was this system of rule that was challenged successfully by nationalist and revolutionary movements. It is well before the moment of decolonisation that the inhabitants of a particular country recognise that they are part of a larger conglomerate and imagine themselves as part of a unified nation (Anderson 1983). This liberation and emancipatory exercise, the decolonisation of the mind, leads to the dismantling of the colonial structures of power. This decolonisation of the mind welds and forges the nation.

In the cases cited by Mamdani – the Mau Mau in Kenya, the Rwenzururu uprising in Uganda, and the Simba revolt in the Congo – all three attacked the 'despotic Native Authority'. Although Mamdani points out that in these cases the urban and rural combined to overcome colonial modes of power, there is no explanation of the manner or reasons which led to a recolonisation of the mind – for that is the implication of rendering these agents of social change as mere subjects. It is imperative to question how, after decolonisation, the very population that had freed itself from colonisation would allow itself to be entrapped in the manner in which Mamdani suggests. Mamdani's argument is particularly weak in the South African context where, as he points out, industrialisation led to the massive urbanisation of the black population, and the policy of indirect rule and decentralised despotism was played out as an urban phenomenon through the policy of forced removals and Bantustans. His argument hinges on the Zulu migrant workers who straddle the urban and the rural and the role which they played in the 1994 elections. He claims that the African National Congress (ANC) was unable to reach these migrant workers, and that this allowed the Inkatha Freedom Party (IFP) to 'embrace those Zulu as the custodian of their customary rights in KwaZulu' ([Mamdani 1996a]: 294). The more the IFP penetrated Zulu migrant workers, the more 'the tribal logic of customary authorities came to contaminate urban civil society' (*ibid.*: 294). In order to avoid further conflict, the ANC agreed to form a government of national unity. However, such a compromise came at the expense of 'unreformed customary power in the reserves' (*ibid.*: 294).

What is disturbing about this account is the failure to scrutinise the election results, which indicated the level of support for the ANC not only in IFP strongholds but also in the rest of the country. This support, as in all other decolonisation movements, is testimony to the nationalist movement's ability to transcend simple ethnic politics (Ahluwalia and Nursey-Bray 1994). Similarly, one need only examine the Tanzanian case, where the nationalist struggle under Julius Nyerere was so successful that no other party other than TANU (Tanganyika African National Union) gained seats in Parliament (Tordoff 1967; Pratt 1976). In short, the questions that need to be asked are: What forces led to decolonisation, which necessarily brought the urban and rural together? Why were founding-father Presidents such as Kenyatta and Nyerere successful in maintaining and forging a national identity? Why have African countries managed to remain intact, preserving borders demarcated by the colonial powers? All these questions suggest that, if Mamdani is correct in asserting that a system of decentralised despotism was imposed upon rural peoples who had successfully fought colonial rule, then we should have witnessed a severe crisis of legitimacy that would have made rule in the post-independence period unsustainable. It is important to point out that Africa has been rife with coups and counter-coups, which have dominated its political history. Despite the political turmoil, though, African countries have not reverted to some pre-colonial basis of territorial sovereignty based on ethnic grounds. On the contrary, despite the massive problems faced by Africans, they have not simply carved the continent into hundreds of nation-states based on ethnicity. Rather, the nation-state has continued to endure, indicating that some sense of national identity, however fragmented, has been forged.

The attack on Goran Hyden, for dichotomising the economy between modern capitalists and African peasants who are locked into an economy of affection, is mirrored in Mamdani's thesis by his reinforcement of the binary between deracialisation and democratisation, the urban sector and the rural sector. By establishing such a dichotomy, Mamdani leaves himself open to the charge that he merely is reverting to the categories of the modernisation school – the traditional, as opposed to the modern – of which he has been an ardent critic. It is important also to examine instances outside Africa where indirect rule was utilised. It was in India that both the system of indirect rule and that of 'divide and rule' were first used. In India, and in Pakistan, the customary was prevalent.[1] After decolonisation, the British colonial system based on local authorities was adapted and retained. Nevertheless, the system of decentralised despotism as characterised by Mamdani, with civil society being deracialised but not democratised, did not ensue. On the contrary, despite the economic difficulties India has endured, it has remained relatively democratic with fair and free elections at the federal level. It is pertinent to question what forces have permitted this to occur.

The complexities of contemporary society are not factored into Mamdani's analysis. The rural and urban divide is not as striking as it appears. New forms of communication, new technologies and globalisation have made the world a smaller place.[2] Mamdani has argued for new forms of analysis, citing the impasse within African studies, and, while his work goes a long way to providing such an answer, it ultimately fails to do so. This is because Mamdani has reverted to another set of binaries, citizen and subject, which cannot be sustained under careful analysis. It is important, therefore, to examine recent debates on citizenship in order to explore the complexities entailed in such a characterisation.

The complexities of citizenship and subjectivity

One might well begin by questioning who is a citizen and who is a subject? In Western political thought, subjects are individuals who have consented to a sovereign's rule and who, by according that consent, have certain rights and obligations. It is on the basis of the relationship between the sovereign and the subject that a polity functions. The consent of the subject 'is thought to provide the sovereign with the *right* to govern, the attendant obligations of those subjects are supposed to provide the sovereign with the capacity to do so' (Hindess 1996: 13). In response to the problematic of who comes after the subject, Etienne Balibar has responded forcefully: the citizen. The citizen, he notes, 'is that "nonsubject" who comes after the subject, and whose constitution and recognition put an end (in principle) to the subjection of the subject' (Balibar 1991: 38–9).

The claim that citizens succeed subjects is one that Balibar develops by questioning 'who is the subject of the prince? And who is the citizen who comes after the subject' (*ibid.*: 40). While a sovereign's power was traditionally based on divine right, with the implication that subjects essentially were obeying God, the modern notion is grounded in the idea that all people are born 'free and equal in rights'. This rupture arises as a result of the *Declaration of the Rights of Man and of the Citizen* of 1789, which evokes the sovereignty of the revolutionary citizen. This entails the process whereby the citizen becomes a subject, '*the citizen is the subject*, the citizen is always a *supposed subject* (legal subject, psychological subject, transcendental subject)' (*ibid.*: 45). In this way, the citizen is '*neither* the individual *nor* the collective ... *neither* an exclusionary being *nor* a private being' (*ibid.*: 51). For Balibar, citizenship is a kind of freedom which is rooted in 'natural rights'. Such a perspective shifts the debate that arises in questions of nationality and immigration, which are based on 'who are citizens', to one which fundamentally asks 'who is *the* citizen'.

In her empirical study of citizenship, Pamela Johnston Conover points out that citizen identities are the defining elements which shape the character of communities. Such identities can be socially cohesive. However, when they are found to be lacking, legitimacy itself becomes problematic. She points out that there are three key components to citizenship. The first is membership in a political community signified by some legal notion. Although in the modern world citizenship is embedded strongly in the nation-state, individuals are also members of other political communities, and 'thus citizens experience multiple levels of citizenship nested within each other' (1995: 134). It is important to recognise that, despite the association of nation-states with citizenship, it is at the local level and in the local contexts that people experience being and express themselves as citizens. The second component is a *sense of citizenship*. This sense is based on the 'affective significance that people give their membership in a particular political community' (*ibid.*: 134). Finally, there is the practice of citizenship, which entails both political participation as well as civic activity. A number of differing conceptions of citizenship have developed, depending upon perspective:

> From a liberal perspective, to be a citizen is to be an individual 'bearer of rights'. That universal status is what we have in common. In contrast, from a communitarian perspective, to be a citizen is to be a member of a particular community. That shared life is what we have in common. And different still, from a cultural pluralist perspective, to be a citizen would mean to be a member of a particular social group, one of many in the political community ... The difference in these conceptions is considerable as are their consequences, for the ontological nature of citizen identities shapes the nature of the civic bond.
>
> (Conover 1995: 139–40)

The pluralist position on citizenship is one that postulates that citizens are 'those in a body politic who share in the allocation of power' (Laswell and Kaplan 1952: 217). Such a conception entails the most common perception of citizenship – that it allows one to engage in the political sphere. This is epitomised by being permitted to stand for public office or by voting for those who seek public office. Citizenship evokes also feelings of patriotism, with strong allegiance to the flag and institutions which are analogous with the nation. In contemporary societies citizenship, as opposed to residency, means that one is allowed access to state resources as well as being allowed to participate in the political process.

In his lectures on 'governmentality', Michel Foucault maintained that, despite the different manner in which the term is utilised, there is, nevertheless, continuity between the government of the self, the government of a household and the government of a community or state. The importance of Foucault's views lies in his different conception of government. The work of government is performed by both state and non-state agencies which are more 'involved in moulding the public and private behaviour – and even the personalities – of individuals than any conception of those individuals as citizens would allow' (Hindess 1996: 131).

For Foucault, the relationship between ruler and ruled is more complex and nuanced than one which simply operates on the basis of consent. It is as citizen-subjects that individuals are able to be governed. This conception rests on the acknowledgement that there is a great deal of power that lies beyond the state. As Hindess points out:

> Far from being restricted to the actions of *the* government ... the government of societies takes place in a variety of state and non-state contexts.

The family, for example, can be seen not only as a potential object of government policy, but also as a means of governing the behaviour of its own members.

(Hindess 1996: 134–5)

In short, Foucault's argument rests on a notion of power that is pervasive and operates at different levels in order to carry out its function.

Chantal Mouffe points out that citizenship is a form of political identity which is based on modern pluralist democracy founded on the principles of liberty and equality for all. She argues:

A citizen is not … as in liberalism, someone who is the passive recipient of rights and who enjoys the protection of the law. It is rather a common political identity of persons who might be engaged in many different communities and who have differing conceptions of the good, but who accept submission to certain authoritative rules of conduct.

(Mouffe 1993: 82)

This conception of citizenship is based upon the recognition that individuals have more than a single identity, that within society individuals occupy a multiplicity of positions, depending upon circumstances at a particular time.

James Donald, claims that 'the citizen' needs to be seen as a position and not as an identity. Viewed from such a perspective, it is a position which can be 'occupied in the sense of being spoken from, not in the sense of being given a substantial identity' (1996: 174). The citizen as an empty space in such a conceptualisation entails that the 'status of citizenship is contingent on an operative symbolic order that needs to be distinguished from any claims to a cultural identity for the citizen' (*ibid.*: 175). Hence, to become a citizen is 'therefore to become a subject within this symbolic order' (*ibid.*: 175).

Toby Miller has divided citizenship into four moods. First, there is the right to association which was decreed by classical political theory. Second, liberal political theory extended this right by adding the doctrine of the civil right to relative freedom. Third, there exists the social right to a minimum standard of living guaranteed by the welfare state. The final mood is the postmodern guarantee of access to technologies of communication which are central to one's identity and polity. Miller argues that there is a perceptible shift between the modern and the postmodern. In the former, subjects recognised their debt to the great institutions of the state whilst the postmodern:

derives its power from a sense that such institutions need to relearn what sovereignty is about in polymorphous sovereign states and transnational business and social milieux that are diminishingly homogenous in demographic terms and increasingly heteroglossic in their cultural competence.

(Miller 1993: 25)

Citizenship has become an important trope in which civil society is seen to be a powerful agent of social change. The notion of shared rights which citizenship evokes is one that has been advocated by all modern emancipatory movements. For example, it was one of the central arguments mounted by the nationalist movements which sought decolonisation. As Miller points out, equal access to citizenship has not translated into equal justice 'because of the propensity toward economic anarchy and political oligarchy and because the discourse of justice increasingly presumes a space of autonomy between person, economy, and polity rather than a policy of assurance by the last on behalf of the first, or some other variant' (*ibid.*: 223).

Citizenship in itself has a tendency to universalism and fails to recognise difference. As Ruth Lister has noted:

> to link citizenship and difference is an oxymoron. On the one hand, citizen-ship is an intrinsically universalistic concept. On the other, its denial of difference has served to exclude those who do not fit its universalist template … Janus-faced citizenship operates simultaneously as a force for inclusion and exclusion both within and at the borders of nation-states.
>
> (Lister 1998: 71)

It is this need to recognise difference which has meant the problematising of citizenship by feminist scholarship (Benhabib 1996; Mouffe 1995; Lister 1997; Young 1990). It is because the discourse of citizenship has a tendency to homogenise that it allows for a limited questioning which seeks only to evaluate the 'spread of services within a given type of social organization, not the shape of that society or the means of defining and dividing it' (Miller 1993: 230).

This discussion has demonstrated the complexities of citizenship and the difficulty in dichotomising individuals simply into either citizens or subjects. What is clear is that the distinction between citizen and subject is complex and entails questions of responsibility and participation. In short, individuals in all communities are citizen-subjects. It is with this in mind that we now can turn to examine a post-colonial perspective.

Citizenship and subjectivity: post-colonial reflections

The questioning of European forms of knowledge, with their universalist prescriptions, is a task that has been undertaken by post-structuralism. However, the notion of the subject is one that is central to post-colonial theory, for it affects the manner in which colonised peoples come to terms with the conditions which entrap them. It is this perception of their conditions of domination which is vital to their being able to develop strategies of resistance. Hence, Martina Michel has pointed out that post-colonial theory has effectively reformulated the postmod-ern notion of the subject 'by shifting our attention from the (fractured) Self to processes of subject formation' (1995: 89). The liberal humanist conception of the unified autonomous subject who has the capacity to determine his or her destiny is one that has been challenged. The subject now 'is considered meaningless in itself, a mere cocoon, which, once opened, dissolves into a multiplicity of discursive facets. The subject does not speak, but is spoken by, language. The effect of such analysis is often to assign to the subject a position of passivity' (*ibid.*: 90).

Benita Parry argues that the effect of the recognition of the fractured self, however, is the fixing of the marginalised other into a position of silence (Parry 1987). It is the quest to recover this silenced other which gives post-colonial theory its impetus over other 'post' phenomena. Ascribing agency to the subject allows post-colonialism to insist that the subject has the capacity to act (Lister 1997; 1998). Michel points out that this in itself does not allow the subject to determine their own position because:

> Subject positions continue to be seen as constructs; but as agent the subject constantly acts out, reformulates, challenges, and potentially re-locates these constructs/discourses that assign to her or him a place from which to speak.
>
> (Michel 1995: 91)

The ability to resist is one which was examined earlier in the discussion of decolonisation and is central to the work of Frantz Fanon and Edward Said (Ashcroft and Ahluwalia 1999). It is the notion of resistance that 'lies at the heart of postcolonial debate' (Michel 1995: 92). However, the centrality of resistance does not entail a return to a past essentialised identity. For, there is no possibility of such a return. Rather, it is the continual reconstitution of identity under different circumstances which becomes important. It is a process which Said captures in his assertion that the dismantling of binary oppositions challenges 'the fundamentally static notion of *identity* that has been the core of cultural thought during the era of imperialism' (1993a: xxviii).

This is where post-colonial theory is instructive. It infuses a normative dimension into the debate, rupturing the dominant decolonisation discourses. It suggests that there are other narratives, other histories which have been subsumed and which need to be recovered. Edward Said offers one way in which this process of recovery can proceed. He makes a distinction between the potentate and the traveller in his writing on the role of the intellectual. Said urges intellectuals to adopt the identity of the traveller, because thereby they 'suspend the claim of customary routine in order to live in new rhythms and rituals' unlike the potentate 'who must guard only one place and defend its frontiers, the traveler crosses over, traverses territory, and abandons fixed positions, all the time' (Said 1991: 18).

The identity and location of intellectuals means that they need to be contextualised within their own cultural specificity. At the same time, the intense globalisation that has occurred has important implications for the individual intellectual who seems to embody more 'than strictly local application' (Said 1994: 20). The intellectual makes political choices to follow the difficult path.

The modern intellectual's role, then, is to disrupt prevailing norms because 'dominant norms are today so intimately connected … to the nation, which is always triumphalist, always in a position of authority, always exacting loyalty and subservience' (*ibid.*: 27). Said urges the intellectual to push the boundaries, to reconcile one's own identity with the reality of other identities, other peoples rather than dominating other cultures. He argues that, despite a proliferation of the liberal rhetoric of equality and justice, injustices continue in many parts of the globe. The task for the intellectual is to apply these notions and bring them to 'bear on actual situations' (*ibid.*: 71).

The post-colonial state is locked inextricably into a modernist discourse which has its epistemological roots located within nineteenth-century liberal philosophy, in which the nation-state is conceived as a sovereign subject of development. Furthermore, it is based upon Orientalist assumptions which stress that Western models of growth are appropriate for the Third World to follow (Said 1978). In this context, the post-colonial subjects are subsumed by the dominant narratives emanating from the state and made manageable by the institutions and discourses of the state and civil society. Within the constraints of the state's ideology of economic development and modernisation the normalisation and disciplining of the subject takes place. In this way these manageable subjects are formed and governed through institutions and discourses in which individuals are private subjects and public citizens at the same time. It is these shifts that discern the manner in which loyal citizens learn to govern themselves in the interests of the cultural-capitalist polity.

Michel Foucault points out that governance of the self effectively carries out the policing role of the state (1982: 790). However, this mode of self-governance means that, 'subjects are also expected to recognise themselves as part of a public' (Miller 1993: xxi). In this way they are not only subjects but also citizens. In the context of the developmentalist state, it is through these modes of self-governance that subjects relinquish their individual interests for the general interest as citizens. As citizens these subjects are to re-imagine themselves, along the lines of Benedict Anderson's well-known analysis of nationalism, into an imagined community espousing goals determined by the state (Anderson 1983). These citizen/subjects are to become the agents and tools of development. This is necessarily so in this heightened and intensified period of globalisation in which nation-states have little capacity to control the movement of capital and commodities. Surely, this is nowhere better exemplified than in the cultural imperialism that is currently under way. In this globalised world, the post-colonial state is charged with control over an essential element, labour, which it has to regulate, discipline and normalise, whilst at the same time ensuring that, as citizens, the labour subjects become local consumers.[3] As the goals of progress, modernisation and development become paramount, new histories and narratives are constructed, whilst older narratives are displaced as they prove little use to the new order. The imperatives of the modern developmentalist state and civil society – the mere replication of the Western model, albeit with local inflections – raises the question of the extent of suppression of the narrative of community.

As pointed out in the last chapter, to view state–civil society relations in mere opposition is problematic. We noted the manner in which the narrative of community is suppressed by the grand narrative of capital leading to the sorts of disciplinary techniques of power which ensure the normalisation of the individual. This narrative of community leads to decolonisation, but it is one that is displaced by the imperatives of modernisation and development. However, such imperatives do not mean that the distinction between citizen and subject, in Mamdani's terms, is reinforced both by a lack of 'detribalisation' and by democratisation. Rather, it is the crisis of modernity which renders individuals both citizens and subjects. While the system of indirect rule and Native Authorities in the colonial period was based upon a great degree of force and violence, in the period after independence it is not based on coercion alone. The system is used as an important means of distributing resources and serves a crucial legitimising function.

Colonialism, as Edward Said points out, is 'a fate with lasting, indeed grotesquely unfair results' (1989: 207) – particularly because of its propensity to irredeemably alter the cultural priorities of the colonised. Ashis Nandy provides an important reminder that, in the process, colonisation has a tendency to generalise 'the concept of the modern West from a geographical and temporal entity to a psychological category. The West is now everywhere, within the West and outside, in structures and in minds' (1983: xi). It is clear that, once colonisation occurs, it and the cultural shifts which it inevitably produces, leads to new configurations and new energies, as a result of which it is not possible to revert to pre-colonial forms. There is, in essence, no pre-colonial to return to, for no society is static; all societies are changing constantly, making and remaking themselves. Thus, once decolonisation has occurred and people in a particular country have tasted the fruits of freedom, whether they are from urban or rural locations, it is not possible to imagine that they willingly return to the very processes which had entrapped them during colonialism. In short, they are not willing once again to become mere subjects.

For example, even in repressive, one-party state systems people in both urban and rural areas had a considerable impact on who was elected to Parliament. In order to maintain a modicum of legitimacy, the one-party state had to permit inter-candidate rivalry. For example, at every election in Kenya, not only were a large number of incumbent MPs not returned but a great number of cabinet ministers were rejected (Ahluwalia 1996a). The same pattern was repeated in Tanzania under the one-party state. These trends suggest that merely to treat the population as subjects is to deny the manner in which they exercise their rights as citizens, even in a single-party system where the electorate is given an opportunity to choose between candidates, even if they belong to the same party. In short, it is not possible simply to dichotomise the population into citizens and subjects. Rather, it is important to examine the processes through which individuals, constituted as both citizens and subjects, govern themselves in order to engage in the practice of everyday life.

Conclusion

Mahmood Mamdani's recent work has been an important effort to rethink and reconceptualise the very practice of African politics. He correctly points out that the modes of power which operate in contemporary Africa are derived from the colonial state. While Mamdani aptly problematises binaries which dominate African studies, ultimately he falls into the same trap by establishing a binary on which his entire project rests – citizen and subject. Mamdani recognises the centrality of subjects in the decolonisation process but is not willing to grant them the freedom which they gain at independence, when the entire polity is granted citizenship. For him, these subjects remain entrapped under the post-colonial state through a system of decentralised despotism. The processes which lead to such a reversion, however, are not adequately explained. Mamdani renders these subjects passive and denies them the capacity to speak or to act. In short, he operates from a position where people are ascribed fixed identities by the state.

By deploying a post-colonial perspective, I have shown here how such a simple binary is rendered ineffective. Post-colonial theory brings questions of subjectivity to the foreground. It illustrates the complexities of post-colonial identity, particularly at a time of intense globalisation. It demonstrates that post-colonial subjects have multiple identities that are shaped continually by the practice of everyday life and that they have the capacity to resist, to speak and to act as citizen/subjects.

6   Globalisation and post-colonialism

Towards the reconstitution of identity

Today, the everyday culture of Africa is polyglot, and the sense of what languages these are needs to be explored. A striking feature of at least urban Africa is the number of languages that people have to possess to function at all. Almost everyone in any African city has to have access to at least two languages: the first is the language of home, and the second is whatever lingua franca is necessary to function in the marketplace.

Ioan Davies

It is now commonplace to speak of a global culture, the global village, as well as of the speed and spread of globalisation processes which are gripping the world. Yet, within such discourses, the absence and nullity of Africa is all the more prominent at this juncture of the millennium. Africa, which was at the centre of the economic forces which inaugurated modernity itself, as part of the transatlantic slave trade, sadly is now marginalised, with scant attention paid to it by those who proclaim a new globalised world. This chapter explores this nullity and absence as well as the impact of globalisation in Africa. It begins by examining the way in which globalisation is theorised in different ways across many disciplines. Then the importance of culture and globalisation is explored. Finally, it considers the relationship between globalisation and post-colonialism. The trope of inflections and the difference between active and passive globalisation are posited as a way to understand the manner in which Africa is engaging with globalisation.

Globalisation is not a new phenomenon. Nevertheless, new information, communication, transport and manufacturing technologies, as well as trade regimes (effected through such multilateral organisations as the GATT and tariff reductions) have allowed production, commerce and finance to be organised and operated on a global scale. The rise and spread of multinational corporations operating across nation-state boundaries raises questions about the capacity of the state to function in the national interest. In addition, the mass migration of peoples from different parts of the world has intensified. While there are considerable arguments for and against the extent and impact of globalisation, there is no denying that the phenomenon is going on (Appadurai 1990, 1996; Giddens 1990; Hoogvelt 1997; Jameson and Miyoshi 1998; Miyoshi 1996;

Robertson 1992; Wallerstein 1990; Waters 1995). Still, there is little agreement across disciplines on how to theorise globalisation. Malcolm Waters has claimed recently, that just as 'postmodernism was the concept of the 1980s, globalization may be the concept of the 1990s, a key idea by which we understand the transition of human society into the third millennium' (1995: 1).

Kwame Anthony Appiah (1992) argues that it is the exchange of commodities which has led to an international 'syncretic' culture. The rise of the multinational corporation as an institution which facilitates such an exchange of commodities at unprecedented levels, has not only problematised the sanctity of the nation-state by subverting national policies and priorities as well as pointing to new ways of flexible accumulation, it has also illustrated the amorphous capacity of capitalism. It is important to recognise that globalisation has linked diverse economies which seek to supply the insatiable demands of the West's consumption needs and to replicate those very consumption patterns, often by inflecting them locally. As Gyan Prakash argues, 'it is necessary to remember that Marx himself had argued that the universalization of capital requires difference; it spreads only by reconstituting otherness' (1996: 199).

David Held and Anthony McGrew note that globalisation's spatial connotation has two dimensions: 'stretching', where what happens in one part of the world has important ramifications and significances for other parts of the world, and 'deepening', which 'involves a growing penetration of the "global human condition" with the particularities of place and individuality' (1993: 262–3). Spatiality entails viewing the intersections between peoples and cultures as part of a global space, the result of late modernity. Globalisation discourses have done much to highlight the importance of space in their wake, thereby disrupting the centrality of historicism and temporality. As Paolini argues, 'the emphasis on space has gone hand in hand with a rethinking of politics along global lines and an embracing of identity as a relational interaction between global and local processes' (1997: 56). The term globalisation has been defined by Robertson, as 'the crystallization of the entire world as a single place' (1987a: 38) which leads towards a 'global human condition' (1987b: 23). It is this that makes globalisation at once both universal and local.

Globalisation can be seen as a product of the massive expansionism of European economic, political and cultural influence throughout the world. It is certainly a process which intensified under colonisation. The fundamental guiding principles of globalisation, Malcolm Waters argues, are that 'material exchanges localize; political exchanges internationalize; and symbolic exchanges globalize' (1995: 9). Globalisation processes are therefore intimately related to modernity and capitalism, which facilitate such exchanges.

Enrique Dussel, in examining the world system and its inherent Eurocentrism, points out that modernity is 'not a phenomenon of Europe as an *independent* system but, of Europe as center' (1998: 4). For him, such a proposition alters the very notion of modernity, which has been tied to Europe. He considers the process of modernity:

as the already indicated rational management of the world-system. This position intends to recoup what is redeemable in modernity, and to halt the practices of domination and exclusion in the world-system. It is a project of liberation of a periphery negated from the very beginning of modernity.

(Dussel 1998: 19)

Dussel sees the world system threatened by three key limitations of modernity. The first is the ecological destruction of the planet which has been unhindered in the pursuit of ever-increasing rates of profit. The second is the destruction of humanity itself. The third limitation is modernity's inability to subsume the 'populations, economies, nations, and cultures that it has been attacking since its origin and has excluded from its horizon and cornered into poverty' (*ibid.*: 21). It is through these limitations that the process of resistance and liberation must begin.

Globalisation is a multidimensional process whose impact on the modern liberal state, as well as civil society, encroaches upon the idea that a community 'governs itself and determines its own future'. Hence, the very notions of sovereignty and democracy are 'being prised away from their traditional rootedness in the national community and the territorially bounded nation-state' (Held and McGrew 1993: 264). The practice and meaning of democratisation needs to be examined in the light of the emergence of local, regional and global processes and structures which are currently under way. In this context, several elements need to be recognised. First, the manner in which different spheres – such as economic, legal, political and military – are intertwined and the manner in which these connections problematise the ability of the state to regulate needs to be made clear. Second, the manner in which the liberal-democratic state faces challenges from below is significant. Finally, it is important to heed the manner in which increasing interaction 'creates chains of interlocking political decisions and outcomes among states and their citizens, reconstituting in the process the relationship between sovereignty, democracy and the territorial political community' (*ibid.*: 284–5).

A common theme amongst globalisation theorists from a wide variety of disciplinary backgrounds is that the processes of globalisation threaten the very sovereignty of the state. However, for David Armstrong, such an assertion is problematic, and he argues that the state needs to be set in an international context 'as a self-seeking entity, with its membership of international society helping to confirm and preserve its identity as a state, while also shaping and changing it' (1998: 462). He summarises the manner in which globalisation discourses have problematised state sovereignty. First, contemporary issues have challenged the state. It is argued that issues such as the environment, drugs, crime and migration are no longer subject to a single state's regulation. Second, non-state actors, such as transnational corporations, media empires and crime syndicates, increasingly challenge the state. Third, the emergence of global financial markets makes it difficult for states even to regulate their own currencies. Fourth, new communication technologies make it virtually impossible to control the flow of information across states. Fifth, the very idea of national culture promoted by the nation-state is challenged by modernity and global capitalism. Sixth, the very legitimacy of the state over a given territory is being called into question by globalising processes. Finally, it is argued that the crisis of modernity and the uncertainty it generates threatens the nation-state, which has been linked inextricably to modernity (*ibid.*: 462–5).

In contrast to such assertions by globalisation theorists, the counter-arguments posited are that such processes are neither new nor as intensified as they were at the beginning of this century, at the height of imperialism (Rodrik 1997: 22). Before World War I it was claimed that the interdependence of the world made it virtually impossible for war to break out. Armstrong therefore argues that it is important to examine the interaction between globalisation and international society. It is through such an interaction that

> a fuller picture of the immensely complex changes currently under way in world politics … begin to emerge. One process tends to break down territorial boundaries and replace them with new, uniform configurations of power, money, and culture. The other reconfirms territorial boundaries and the structures and processes contained by them, but also permits some change. The two exist in a relationship of dialectic tension and, given the evident strength of each, are likely to do so for the foreseeable future.
>
> (Armstrong 1998: 478)

Paul Hirst and Grahame Thompson argue also along similar lines, pointing out that globalisation as conceived by its more extreme proponents is largely a myth, for five reasons. First, the present internationalisation of the economy is not new and is not even as integrated as it was between 1870 and 1914. Second, there are few genuine transnational corporations. Rather, most companies are nationally based. Third, there is little capital mobility between the First and the Third Worlds, the bulk of foreign investment is concentrated in the advanced industrialised economies. Fourth, the world economy is not global: trade and financial flows are concentrated in Europe, North America and Japan, with little indication that this pattern is likely to change. Finally, these three areas have the capacity to exercise governance pressures over financial and economic markets (1996: 3). These factors allow Hirst and Thompson to conclude that, 'we are well short of dissolving distinct national economies in the major advanced industrial countries or of preventing the development of new forms of economic governance at the national and international levels' (*ibid.*: 4).

The contested nature of globalisation means that the articulation between the local and the global must be raised. In this conceptualisation, capitalism constitutes and reconstitutes itself in a variety of forms in order to be able to penetrate different areas of the world. If globalisation manifests itself in such a manner, what room is there for the role of the state and civil society? What does this mean for the post-colonial state which pursued a nationalist project after decolonisation?

Culture and globalisation

After decolonisation, the globe was generally thought of as being divided into three 'worlds'. Immanuel Wallerstein's (1979) work was most influential in dismantling the idea of 'three worlds' by proclaiming a single capitalist world system which, he argued, had been developing since the sixteenth century. However, Wallerstein himself erred in totalising and generalising different cultural and historical experiences. John Tagg captures this when he challenges world systems theory:

> I would suggest that the very desire for such an account is tied to notions of social totality and historiographical representation that are untenable. If we are to talk of global systems, then we shall have to ask whether concepts of globalization can be separated from theoretical totalizations.
>
> (Tagg 1991:156)

In criticising world systems theory, Jan Nederveen Pieterse points out that its close association with notions of globalisation has meant that it has 'made "society", as the unit of analysis, appear as a narrow focus, while on the other hand it has faithfully replicated the familiar constraints of Marxist determinism' (1995: 46). For Pieterse, the focus on either modernity or capitalism means that globalisation is plagued by Westernisation and Eurocentrism and is in danger of being associated with the modernisation theories of the 1950s. Consequently, the prevailing interpretations of globalisation, which stress that the world is becoming homogenised as well as promoting the idea that globalisation is inextricably linked to modernity, are problematic. Instead, Pieterse argues that globalisation processes need to be viewed as 'hybridisation which gives rise to a global mélange' (*ibid.*: 45).

In the aftermath of the collapse of communism and the success of south-east Asian economies, the very notion of the Third World has been challenged. It is in this context that the term 'post-colonial world' has been adopted in preference to 'Third World'. For Hoogvelt, this designation has merit because

> it groups together all formerly colonial societies despite differences in their relation to the global capitalist system, while at the same time offering a point of entry for the study of those differences. This point of entry is the 'aftermath' of the colonial relation and the manner in which this becomes reconstituted *and* contested in the process of the present transformation of the global political economy.
>
> (Hoogvelt 1997: xv)

Hoogvelt illustrates the manner in which Africa has been integrated into the global economy and yet at the same time remains excluded. This is shown by examining the debt crisis which has plagued the African continent. For him, the debt crisis has had a dual function. First, it has allowed the periphery to be managed by the core economies of the world capitalist system and, second, it has permitted an intense and effective means of extracting economic surplus from the periphery (1997: 163). This has occurred largely due to financial integration as well as deregulation, which denies African countries the capacity to regulate their currencies.

In the African context, the IMF and the World Bank have led the assault, through structural adjustment programmes. The record of such programmes in improving the lot of African peoples has been dismally poor. Nevertheless, they have been highly successful in integrating and intensifying globalisation processes. Hoogvelt argues that:

> Structural adjustment has helped to tie the physical economic resources of the African region more tightly into servicing the global system, while at the same time oiling the financial machinery by which wealth can be transported out of Africa and into the global system.
>
> (Hoogvelt 1997: 171)

Frederick Buell points out that the classification of the world into three components produced a particular image of culture within the Third World. He argues:

> Third World cultures are simultaneously depicted by some as defective versions of metropolitan originals and imaged by other observers as premodern plenums. As 'local' cultures supposedly in touch with their traditional roots, they represent the continuation of the past, not the rupture that produces modernity. As a collection of plenums, they represent the many particular, not the universal one. A full-blown description would style them separate bounded wholes, and each culture would appear as consensual, tacit, and enduring in its essence.
>
> (Buell 1994: 28)

It is in this context that Terence Ranger (1983) provides an important example, claiming that the very notion of the African 'tribe' is an invention which is imbued with all the trappings of European ideas of the nation-state and the idea that other societies needed to be viewed in contradistinction. In imposing such a model, the Europeans obliterated the minute and delicate balance on which rested the relationship between the different peoples of Africa.

In contrast to such totalising narratives as world systems theory, contemporary globalisation theory needs to be viewed as analogous to Anthony Appiah's (1992) notion of postmodernism as a space-clearing gesture. The growing awareness of global cultural complexities is a profoundly transformative project, much in line with the work of cultural theorists such as Edward Said. Buell correctly points out that the 'theorization and representation of culture has changed in the postwar period in response to a succession of geopolitical and geocultural shifts' (1994: 337). The effect of globalisation on culture, for Anthony King, who examines leading proponents of the globalisation phenomenon, is that, 'despite their different positions, and very different conceptual languages, all share at least two perspectives: the rejection of the nationally-constituted society as the appropriate object of discourse, or unit of analysis, and to varying degrees, a commitment to conceptualising "the world as a whole" ' (1991: ix).

Cultural globalisation, Roland Robertson argues, has intensified because of two factors: the 'compression of the world' and 'global consciousness'. The former is the product of the interrelationship and interconnectedness of the world, where what happens in one part of the world has consequences for other parts. The latter makes globalisation processes more immediate precisely because people begin to perceive the world differently once it is embedded into the consciousness.

Stuart Hall has described the process of globalisation in cultural terms as a

> new form of global mass culture, very different from that associated with English identity, and the cultural identities associated with the nation-state in an earlier phase. Global mass culture is dominated by the modern means of cultural production, dominated by the image which crosses and re-crosses linguistic frontiers more rapidly and more easily, and which speaks across languages in a more immediate way. It is dominated by all the ways in which visual and graphic arts have entered directly into the reconstitution of popular life, of entertainment and of leisure. It is dominated by television and film, and by the image, imagery and styles of mass advertising. Its epitomy is in all those forms of mass communication of which one might think of satellite television as the prime example. Not because it is the only example but because you could not understand satellite television without understanding its grounding in a particular advanced national economy and culture and yet its whole purpose is precisely that it cannot be limited any longer by national boundaries.
>
> (Hall 1991: 27)

Hall points out two important components of global mass culture. The first is that it is centred in the West, embodies all the technological and industrial techniques with which it is replete and is dominated by the languages of the West. Second, it is particularly homogenising. However, this form of homogenisation does not entail recreating Western forms, rather it recognises and absorbs 'differences within the larger, overarching framework of what is essentially an American conception of the world' (Hall 1991: 28). Hall points out the importance of thinking of globalisation as an articulation between the global and the local, stressing that these formulations are often contradictory.

A particularly compelling feature of contemporary late modernity is the manner in which two contradictory processes – globalisation and localisation – appear to be operating simultaneously. Increasingly, production, consumption and distribution are globalised. This, coupled with a period of mass tourism and travel as well as technological advances, has given rise to an intense period of cross-cultural movement. The intensity and speed and spread of globalisation mean that increasingly it is thought of as a process that is wiping out local cultural identities. As Susantha Goonatilake points out, 'a vast reservoir of culturally learned responses of humankind, built up over thousands of years, is being threatened, a parallel – one should note – to the loss of genetic diversity in the biological world' (1995: 229).

The multiplicity of identities which we all embody, with allegiances to kin, group and nation, has meant that we are always negotiating and putting forward different identities at different times. While such identities were at one time largely based in a single nation-state, the process is now more complicated, due to the changes in global cultural processes, rapid economic changes, communications, travel and migration. As Goonatilake illustrates:

> Thus one may be born in country A, get primary socialization through a religion B, secondary socialization through predominantly European science C, military training D on Chinese military strategy, work in country E, have as employer an internationally traded company F, upgrade or change the profession through a new training G, receive a transnational global package H through radio and television, and travel in country J. Today's self is encroached upon dynamically by many shifting cultures.
>
> (Goonatilake 1995: 231)

For her, it is in this multiplicity of identities that the processes of globalisation and localisation are being carried out. More importantly, just as Fanon pointed out the importance of decolonisation of the mind, it is similarly in the mind that the processes of globalisation and localisation are played out: 'It is in these mental reservoirs that the various urges for, as well as the human results of, globalization and localization occur' (*ibid.*: 231).

In addressing the issue of universalism and particularism, Roland Robertson points out that we are, in this latter part of the century, 'witnesses to – and participants in – a massive, twofold process involving *the interpenetration of the universalization of particularism and the particularization of universalism*' (1991: 73). In any analysis of globalisation, he argues, there are four elemental points of reference, 'national *societies, individuals, the world system of societies* (international relations) and *humankind*' (*ibid.*: 79). These four elements define the nature of contemporary globalisation, which operates within the confines of these elements.

Roland Robertson has introduced the concept of 'glocalization' as a way of explaining the assumption that globalisation subsumes the local. For him, such a characterisation is problematic because 'it neglects the extent to which what is called local is in large degree constructed on a trans- or super-local basis' (1995: 26). He traces the origins of the term to a telescoping of the terms 'global' and 'local' in Japan, where business was oriented globally while at the same time being adapted to local conditions (*ibid.*: 28). He argues that, viewed from such a perspective, the term 'globalisation' involves the 'simultaneity and the interpenetration of what are conventionally called the global and the local, or – in more abstract vein – the universal and the particular' (*ibid.*: 30). In short, 'glocalization' is an attempt to rectify the implication inherent in the term 'globalisation' that it is in tension with the local.

Rob Wilson and Wimal Dissanayake look at the local and global relationship as one where the local needs to be linked to the global 'at all points, to global processes without falling into the by-now-tired modernist binary of the universal (global) sublating the particular (local), explained through a colonizing master-narrative of undifferentiated homogenizing forces meeting endlessly specific and hyper-detailed adaptations doomed to defeat' (1996: 6). As the world becomes more complex, and globalisation processes more prevalent, replacing national institutions and frameworks, a large number of theorists question the centrality of the nation-state.

Richard Madsen argues that, in the aftermath of the collapse of the former Soviet Union, a global monoculture has emerged centred around the common themes of freedom, rationality and justice. The emergence of this global monoculture can be attributed to three main linguistic categories, which Madsen labels 'languages' or global conversations. The first is the language of the market, which is based on the principle of comparative advantage. The second is the language of the behavioural sciences, which has become dominant and mediates human organisation and efficiency world-wide. The third is the language of the community, which sets out and defines identity in terms of responsibility and commitment (1993: 495–6). During the Cold War, the inconsistencies between these 'languages' was justified in terms of combating the enemy, but in the aftermath of the collapse of the Soviet Union has seen the emergence of a global monoculture.

The discourse of globalisation is unquestionably founded upon modernity and its capacity to reach beyond its merely European bounds. Nevertheless, globalisation, with its linkages to Western modernity, is not only a highly Eurocentric conception but also a universalist one. It therefore tends to obfuscate the specificities of non-Western, particularly African, societies. A particular problem of recent globalisation theory has been its tendency to homogenise the world, proclaiming a postmodern world which has transcended traditional borders, with cyberspace occupying a key role in that process. In the light of such accounts, it is only fair to question what space Africa occupies (Paolini 1997, 1999). While theoretically Africa may not feature prominently (and whether or not Africa wishes to be part of this globalised space), it is increasingly finding itself within its vortex. Nevertheless, it is important to recognise that the disillusionment with modernity that has led to postmodern critiques and a lamenting of modernity is not necessarily applicable to Africa – for in Africa, and other parts of the non-Western world, there appears to be a celebration of modernity. In this context critics such as Dirlik argue for a different conception of modernity which is relevant to the third world (Chatterjee 1993; Dirlik 1994). However, it is Africa's marginality which calls for an urgent reassessment of the homogenising tendencies of globalisation (Mazrui 1999). This marginality demands a more nuanced approach to the global/local nexus if globalisation is to avoid being seen as merely another manifestation of Eurocentric theory which seeks to dominate Africans. In short, it is important to recognise that within the local/global configuration there are numerous dimensions, inconsistencies and conflicts which often produce unpredictable outcomes.

Post-colonialism and globalisation

Arjun Appadurai (1996) argues that we have embarked upon a new era of globalisation marked by two key features, electronic mediation and mass migration, both of which operate not as technological advances themselves but rather as the work of the imagination. While not everyone migrates or is exposed to global communication networks, it is extremely rare to find someone who has not been affected by events elsewhere. He notes:

> both persons and images often meet unpredictably, outside the certainties of home and the cordon sanitaire of local and national media effects. This mobile and unforeseeable relationship between mass-mediated events and migratory audiences defines the core of the link between globalization and the modern.
>
> (Appadurai 1996: 4)

The effect of this process is that it has created new diasporic public spheres which cannot be contained by nation-state boundaries (Anderson 1994).

The globalisation processes that are under way are threatening the very notion of the nation-state. What Appadurai questions is the hyphen between nation and state, which he argues is being challenged increasingly by the mass migrations and movements which have been going on for some time. He argues that the complexities of the global system are the result of certain disjunctures between economy, culture and politics and suggests a framework for understanding this by proposing five dimensions of global cultural flows. These are ethnoscapes, mediascapes, technoscapes, financescapes and ideoscapes (1996: 33).

These scapes constitute the building blocks of what he refers to as the imagined worlds of the 'historically situated imaginations of persons and groups spread around the globe' (*ibid.*: 33). Appadurai explains that ethnoscapes includes the tourists, immigrants, exiles, guest workers and other individuals and groups who affect the relations between nations in an unprecedented manner. Technoscapes are the sum of global transfers of technology, both mechanical and informational, which do not recognise previously defined boundaries. Financescapes are the rapid flows and movements of global capital across nation-state boundaries that are increasingly difficult to monitor. Mediascapes include the capacity to rapidly distribute and disseminate information in the world through newspapers, television, film and other multimedia resources. Finally, ideoscapes are political ideologies which states themselves, or those wanting to capture state power, propagate. These scapes do not operate under a system of order and rationality, which has been characteristic of previous epochs, but rather through *chaos* (*ibid.*: 47).

In a recent article, Partha Chatterjee (1998) questions Appadurai's thesis that the nation-state's demise is inevitable and imminent. He argues that the so-called crisis of the nation-state can be attributed to two sets of arguments. The first concerns the inability of the state to govern effectively: that is, its inability to meet the 'welfare' needs of its population. The second outlines the 'decay or lack of appropriate civil-social institutions that could provide a secure foundation for a proper relationship between autonomous individual lives in society and the collective political domain of the state' (*ibid.*: 65). It is this that explains the dictatorial and authoritarian role of the nation-state. Chatterjee argues that Appadurai collapses these two arguments and in turn sets up a dichotomy between globality and modernity which nation-states are unable to mediate. Rather, Chatterjee points out that what is required is two kinds of mediation: 'one between globality and modernity, and the other between globality and democracy. The two, at least apparently, cannot be performed by the same set of institutions. This, as I see it, is the current crisis of the nation-state' (*ibid.*: 65–6). The way in which global modernity is being advanced is 'profoundly colonial', whereas the articulation of democracy 'will pronounce modernity itself as inappropriate and deeply flawed' (*ibid.*: 68). It is the awareness of these twin pressures that will permit any movement beyond the nation-state.

As noted in an earlier chapter, decolonisation entailed more than the mere removal of the colonisers. It was an essential step towards liberation, but in most cases, decolonisation merely reverted to what Said has termed 'nativism' (1993: 275–7). It is the possibility, indeed the necessity, to transcend such nativism that Said sees as essential for the project of post-colonialism, and that idea of transcendence has global implications. As Edward Said points out,

> No one today is purely *one* thing. Labels like, Indian, or woman, or Muslim, or American are no more than starting-points, which if followed into actual experience for only a moment are quickly left behind. Imperialism consolidated the mixture of cultures and identities on a global scale.
>
> (Said 1993a: 407)

The experience of colonialism bound disparate societies and peoples together, making the world a closer place; 'although in the process the separation between Europeans and natives was an insidious and fundamentally unjust one, most of us should now regard the historical experience of empire as a common one' (*ibid.*: xxiv). It is this implication of the commonality between the colonisers and the colonised, the sense of hybridity and transculturation that it invokes, that post-colonialism shares with globalisation discourses. It is, in short, the continuing legacy of imperialism, now led by the United States, which makes globalisation so relevant to post-colonialism. The process of transculturation between the local and the global is what defines relations, albeit unequally, between disparate cultures, and that process is being productively reproduced under globalisation. However, under globalisation in this era of late modernity, this process does not move from the imperial centre to the colonial outposts. Rather, as Ashcroft notes, it is rhizomic and transcultural. It is this that

> links it to the dynamic of imperialism, in which the movements in culture proceed not only two ways but in many ways between the dominated and dominating societies. The rhizomic reality of colonial space continually subverts the hierarchical and filiative metaphors of colonial discourse.
>
> (Ashcroft 1998: 6)

Leela Ghandi, however, urges caution, pointing out that, 'we need to ensure that the euphoric utopianism of this discourse does not degenerate into a premature political amnesia' (1998: 140). It is a point that resonates with Masao Miyoshi who argues that, contrary to proclamations of post-coloniality, what we are witnessing is a form of intensified colonialism which is 'even more active now in the form of transnational corporatism' (1996: 80).

While taking heed of Ghandi and Miyoshi, it is possible to see the engagement between post-colonialism and globalisation through the interaction of the local and the global. It is an engagement which Bill Ashcroft has described as transformation (Ashcroft 1998). This is similar to what James Clifford terms 'travelling cultures', in which 'cultural action, the making and remaking of identities, takes place in the contact zones, along the policed and transgressive intercultural frontiers of nations, peoples and locales' (1997: 7). This is not merely a matter of appropriation, as previous Eurocentric models – such as development and in its most degenerate manifestation modernisation theory – suggested. Rather, contrary to development, which forced 'the local into globally normative patterns, "transformation" acts to adjust those patterns to the requirements of local values and needs' (Ashcroft 1998: 8).[1] How does one make sense of globalisation in the African context, given that it hardly features in globalisation discourses? It is here that the very notion of transformation or what I have been calling 'inflections' is important.

Globalisation and inflections

In his now much cited 'Is the "Post-" in "Postcolonial" the "Post-" in "Postmodern"?', Kwame Anthony Appiah looks closely at an art exhibition being held in New York. Among the artefacts on display, he focuses on a piece labelled, *Yoruba Man with a Bicycle*. He reproduces the description of the sculpture:

> Page 124
> Man with a bicycle
> Yoruba, Nigeria 20th century
> Wood and paint H. 35 in.
> The Newark Museum

The influence of the Western world is revealed in the clothes and bicycles of this neo-traditional Yoruba sculpture which probably represents a merchant enroute to market.

(Appiah 1997: 423)

It is not the task here to reiterate Appiah's arguments about post-colonialism and postmodernism. What is pertinent, however, is the conclusion he reaches:

Yoruba Man with a Bicycle was produced by someone who did not care that the bicycle is the white man's invention – it is not there to be the other to the Yoruba self; it is there because someone cared for its solidity; it is there because it will take us farther than our feet will take us; it is there because machines are now as African as novelists ... and as fabricated as the king-dom of Nakem.

(Appiah 1997: 441)

His conclusion is suggestive of the manner in which different cultures have been interacting and the inevitable hybridisation that results: 'If there is a lesson in the broad shape of this circulation of cultures, it is surely that we are all already contaminated by one another, that there is no longer a fully autochthonous, pure-African culture ... (just as there is ... no American culture without African roots)' (*ibid.*: 439). More importantly, it points to the transformative nature of globalisation. It illustrates the manner in which the bicycle has been appropri-ated, making it an African object and machine. Furthermore, it has become part of the aesthetic imagination which is reproduced in contemporary African art. It is, in short, a process whereby the pervasive globalising tendencies are being inflected locally in Africa.

The representations of Africa as the dark continent continue unabated, with the continent viewed as the repository of disease, war and pestilence. Neverthe-less, the global media have, as the institutions at the forefront of globalisation processes, 'sufficiently wired Africa to the West, from the public sphere to the bedrooms, to the extent that Africans are isolated from nation to nation but united in looking toward Europe and America for the latest news, politics and culture' (Diawara 1998: 103). This may well appear to be an entrenchment of the colonial process which linked infrastructure to the metropolitan centre at the expense of viewing individual countries as part of an integrated region. Nowhere is this better exemplified than in the manner in which it has always been easier to make phone calls to the former colonial powers than to neigh-bouring countries. Nevertheless, the current processes of globalisation are decidedly different, problematising simple assertions, such as colonisation is analogous to globalisation.

Diawara argues that this form of globalisation is one that Africans see as part of the mechanisms that are deployed to recolonise them, with the IMF and World Bank acting as the principal agents. The market-places of West Africa which have a long history, including the trade in slaves, are linked to globalisation and are venues of international consumption. While Diawara argues that they are sites of resistance to the World Bank's conception of globalisation, as espoused under the terms of structural adjustment programmes, it is possible to view the market-place as the site of transculturation and inflection. Rather than resisting globalisation, these market-places are constantly appropriating and transforming globalisation in the process ensuring that consumers have choice and availability of goods at affordable prices. This is only possible through illegal practices such as corruption and smuggling. Market corruption, Diawara argues, is different from state corruption which is largely the result of the interaction between the elites and donors. 'Market corruption ... benefits the masses by increasing the variety of goods in the marketplace, lowering prices, and making consumption possible' (*ibid.*: 123). It is consumption and the desire for commodities that makes globalisation a dynamic reality for sub-Saharan Africa. However, as Albert Paolini has pointed out, 'modernity is consumed, not merely as some fetishized commodity but as an appropriated, hybridized feature of everyday life. It thus becomes as much part of the local and particular as the traditional and "indigenous" ' (1999: 169).

This notion of inflections needs to be expounded, drawing upon another example, that of the petrol or gas station, which has become an important (indeed central) part of many local communities. Throughout East Africa, in the last few years, there has been a proliferation of petrol stations. The effects of structural adjustment and the mismanagement of the economy are outwardly evident and visible, with almost all areas appearing dilapidated. In most towns and cities, the buildings have not been repaired and are in desperate need of even the most basic maintenance, such as a coat of paint. Most roads are now in such disrepair that unemployed youth sit by the roadside crushing stones and rocks to fill the ever-burgeoning potholes in the hope that passing motorists will pay them something for their services. The state has simply stopped engaging in the maintenance of infrastructure. In the midst of this decaying infrastructure, one finds these flashy petrol stations, symbolising the invasion of global capital. The petrol stations are designed characteristically so that one could not differentiate them from other such locations in the world. In most of these stations, one usually finds a small supermarket attached, with a restaurant. They clearly stand out amongst the surrounding structures of any town.

At night, when most of the town is lit by candles and paraffin lights because the electricity inevitably vanishes, the petrol station, powered by its own generator, stands out with its glowing neon lights. The petrol station is obviously there to meet the needs of tourists and the local elite. We might well ask what this symbol of Western power and capital has to do with the local communities in which they are located?

In western Uganda, in the town of Mbarara, you encounter the local Shell station just as you reach the main roundabout on the road from Kampala. This petrol station stands out as a monument, and in that sense it is very different from its counterparts in other Western locations. It is the best lit place in town and the hub of activity; next to the station the local taxi service, the 'matatus' (mini-vans), as well as the 'bicycle taxis' operate, and bicycle-owners use the air-guns to inflate tyres, making a once onerous task relatively simple. The petrol station is by no means only engaged in merely selling petrol to motorists. It is continuously serving the needs of the community, as locals bring their Coca-Cola and other bottles to be filled with the paraffin they use for cooking and lighting. It is the site where virtually all people who are in the town converge. Here hawkers peddle their food and wares, making it an unofficial market-place. In this way the petrol station, a signifier of globalisation and Western extravagance, has been appropriated and given meaning at the local level. Like the *Yoruba Man with a Bicycle*, it matters little what the petrol station might signify elsewhere: in Mbarara it has been appropriated and locally inflected to meet the needs of the local community.

It is possible to point to other examples of this transculturation, hybridisation and local inflection.[2] All over East Africa one sees rubber sandals made from discarded tyres. This demonstrates the appropriation, transformation and consumption of global commodities which had no previous meaning for local cultures. But it also illustrates the importance of the informal sector and the prevailing conditions within Africa which necessitate the production and consumption of what are considered in the West to be waste materials. Through such processes Africa defines and consumes modernity, giving it meaning through the practice of everyday life. This process of transculturation has been described by Ulf Hannerz:

> creole cultures like creole languages are those that draw in some way on two or more historical sources, often originally widely different. They have had some time to develop and integrate, and to become elaborate and pervasive. People are formed from birth by these systems of meaning and largely live their lives in contexts shaped by them. There is that sense of a continuous spectrum of interacting forms, in which the various contributing sources of cultures are differentially visible and active. And, in relation to this, there is built-in political economy of culture, as social power and material resources are matched with the spectrum of culture.
>
> (Hannerz 1987: 552)

The very notion of post-colonialism which we have been elaborating is precisely this creolisation of cultures. Nowhere is this made more abundantly clear than in the way the practices and rituals of the Catholic Church are consumed locally in Africa: it is not unusual, for example, to find a stalwart of the Church practising polygamy. This Africanisation of the Christian Church is, for Mudimbe, an instance of the reinvention of Africa by Africans which has come about as a result of 'cross-cultural breeding' (1988: 63–4). It is through the trope of inflections that we can begin to understand how the Church has come to have meaning in the everyday life of its members, and why it is that as a global institution its strongest adherents are now found in Africa.

The notion of inflections is suggestive of hybridity. In post-colonial discourse it is Homi Bhabha who has most advanced the notion of hybridity. In *The Location of Culture* he argues that there is an in-between space which characterises identity, and that 'this interstitial passage between fixed identifications opens up the possibility of a cultural hybridity that entertains difference without an assumed or imposed hierarchy' (1994: 4). It may appear that the process of hybridisation entailed in the processes of globalisation is the exclusive preserve of the elite in Africa. However, our examples illustrate that such hybridisation is pervasive and occurs at all levels of society. The notion of multiple identities is not new in Africa. This is where post-colonialism is instructive. Since the advent of colonialism and its attendant mixing of cultures and processes of transculturation, African identities are hybrid. A form of globalisation has been taking place since at least the slave trade.

Ioan Davies' observation that the culture of Africa is polyglot, with most people speaking several languages in order to be able to function effectively, is testimony to the hybridity which exists within Africa. Such hybridity is the product of colonisation, which forced contact not only between the colonisers and the colonised but also between different African ethnic groups. In this way colonisation made it necessary for African peoples from different ethnic backgrounds to create and recreate their identities. Mary Louise Pratt's idea of the contact zone is helpful here; in this zone the culture of both groups is affected, and there is a 'creolisation' of identities (1992: 4–6). In most cases, disparate African peoples have successfully negotiated their everyday lives through such an undertaking. One of the most interesting cases has been the manner in which Kiswahili has become the lingua franca of East Africa, with the greatest success in Tanzania.

Such hybridity and the impact of globalisation can be discerned in the active participation of the elites of Africa – through the use of communication technologies now available throughout the world. In addition, the manner in which virtually every part of sub-Saharan Africa has been touched by globalisation needs to be examined more carefully. There is little doubt that people throughout Africa now have some conception of the world outside their own specific locality. However, what is less understood is that the processes of globalisation and their impact are not homogenous, and not uniformly nor equally felt. It is here that the engagement of the local and the global becomes paramount, and the idea of inflections and transformations is useful in distinguishing between active and passive globalisation. While the former appears to be the preserve of the elites, who are financially able to participate in and partake of the kinds of globalisation processes associated with the new technologies, there is a great deal of passive globalisation under way. Passive globalisation is common in urban locations because of the proximity between the mass of the population and the elites, as well as the relative affluence of the African city compared to the rural areas. In major regional cities, such as Nairobi, large expatriate populations as well as tourists inevitably allow people to imagine that they are part of a much larger world. From Johannesburg to

Nairobi, and Kinshasa to Lagos, the contemporary African city is ever-increasingly part of global networks linked by new communication technologies. And yet, at the same time, these cities bear and reflect their colonial past. AbdouMaliq Simone notes that it is this outward orientation of the African city, a product of the enduring legacy of colonialism, that makes 'many Africans still see the city as an "invasion", as an unwelcome and unexpected intrusion on their preferred life rhythms and sensibilities; it is something that must be accommodated, or at least tolerated, occasioning an entire vocabulary of microresistance expressed in how people maintain both its physical and cultural spaces' (1998: 71). However, this process is by no means restricted to the urban areas. Passive globalisation is very much part of the large number of small towns and rural locations throughout Africa. It is manifested in the market-place, where commodities are sold and/or exchanged.

The T-shirt, for example, which is found in almost all market-places, is, 'possibly one item of clothing which asserts, more strongly than any other, the dominance of sign value over use value. Its utility as clothing is well attested globally, but its reason for existence almost seems to lie entirely in its value as a sign' (Ashcroft 1998: 17). The T-shirt is a good example of the manner in which passive globalisation operates. It is manifest in the wearing of second-hand clothes amongst the poorer sections of the population in both urban and rural locations. It is common to see people in both these locations wearing T-shirts with 'Coca-Cola' or 'Harvard' embossed or printed on them. What is interesting, however, is that, for the most part, people wearing T-shirts with such global symbols see little sign value in them. This results from the brutality of structural adjustment programmes and liberalisation policies which have destroyed local industries: these industries are no longer able to compete on the global market, and their closure inevitably forces people to rely on second-hand goods. These goods, collected from the donation bins in the Western world, are recycled and made available to large numbers of people in Africa. Nevertheless, despite the utility and necessity of the T-shirt, as a much-needed article of clothing, it has an inadvertent sign value. It is in this way that local consumers encounter passive globalisation through such cultural signifiers.

It is a process similar to that which James Clifford writes about in *Routes*. Clifford reports the encounter between Amitav Ghosh and the inhabitants of an Egyptian village. Ghosh, expecting to find a 'settled and restful people', paints a completely different picture, which Clifford describes as, 'the traditional, rural village as airline transit lounge. It's hard to imagine a better figure for postmodernity, the new world order of mobility, of rootless histories' (1997: 1). But he notes Ghosh's observation:

> And none of this was new: their grandparents and ancestors and relatives had travelled and migrated too, in much the same way as mine had, in the Indian subcontinent – because of wars, or for money and jobs, or perhaps simply because they got tired of living always in one place. You could read the history of this restlessness in the villager's surnames: they had names

which derived from the cities in the Levant, from Turkey, from faraway towns in Nubia; it was as though people had drifted here from every corner of the Middle East. The wanderlust of its founders had been ploughed into the soil of the village: it seemed to me sometimes that every man in it was a traveller.

(Ghosh, in Clifford 1997: 2)

Ghosh's experience, by no means unique, is suggestive of active and passive globalisation. The movement of African peoples and their patterns of settlement as part of the process of capitalism is well documented (Illife 1983). African peoples have been restless and moving for a very long time in processes similar to those described by Clifford as 'travelling cultures'. Similarly, contemporary processes of globalisation are being appropriated and inflected constantly, allowing African identities to be created and recreated.

Conclusion

The term globalisation, particularly in its cultural manifestation, is linked to Americanisation and evokes fears that it will wipe out all that is local and in its wake produce a homogenised culture. Maryse Condé, however, urges that globalisation should not be feared, because it means, 'reaching out beyond national and linguistic borders both in actual exchanges and transatlantic influences and in the expressive imagination of diasporic black communities' (1998: 1). She views the dynamism expressed in Paris in the early part of the century as well as the emergence of the negritude movement there as constitutive of the trends towards globalisation. Paris had become 'an ideal space for exchange and communication' (*ibid.*: 1). Central to these processes of identity-formation were the linkages between 'black' peoples everywhere. Condé questions, 'what was negritude, what was Pan-Africanism if not forms of globalization, the implied project of complete identity and an active solidarity among the black peoples?' (*ibid.*: 2). It is in this way that globalisation needs to be viewed as an opportunity to return to a 'shattered dream of unity'. Condé is optimistic and takes heed of Malcolm X's adage that, 'If Africa changes, the fate of the black man throughout the world will change'. Thus, she argues,

> Globalization cannot only be controlled but used to our benefit. It may become the creation of a universe where the notions of race, nationality, and language, which for so long have divided us, are re-examined and find new expressions; where the notions of hybridity, metissage, multiculturalism are fully redefined. I see the mapping of a new world, a brave new world ...
>
> (Condé 1998: 5)

As globalisation processes intensify, this opens up opportunities for sub-Saharan Africa. It needs to examine the global system and discern the patterns through which hegemony is maintained. Post-colonial theory offers a way to break down the tyranny of the structures of power which continue to entrap post-colonial subjects. As Edward Said has pointed out, the strengths of post-colonial theory lie in its attempts to grapple with issues of local, regional and global significance whilst retaining an emancipatory perspective (Said 1995: 350). The task for Africa remains to move beyond decolonisation and to adopt a liberating perspective, particularly in the light of the failure of what Said has termed nativist projects, such as negritude and African socialism. This is where the notion of inflections and transformation may well provide a better understanding of the manner in which African identity constantly is constituted and reconstituted, thus forcing Africanists to rethink the manner in which Africa has been conceptualised through the dominant category of the nation-state.

Afterword

We are the number one race in the world; the more countries we spread to, the more we will contribute to the salvation of the human race.

Cecil Rhodes

I must see what it is to be black – and this means being sufficiently intelligent to know how the world is moving and how black people fare in the world. This is what it means to be black. Or an African – the same: what does Africa mean to the world? When you see an African, what does it mean to a white man?

Chinua Achebe

In his book *Africa in Chaos* George Ayittey tells how Keith Richburg, the African-American journalist, appalled by the Rwandan and other African crises, was tormented emotionally and moved to write *Out of America: A Black Man Confronts Africa*. Ayittey recounts the events at a book launch in Virginia, where Richburg, 'concluded that he was glad to be an "American" and the designation "African-American" was meaningless – devoid of content. Perhaps the slave traders did him a favour by shipping his ancestors out of Africa in slave ships for America' (1998: xiii). As one would expect, the audience, which Ayittey reports was about forty per cent black, did not share Richburg's sentiments. Ayittey also notes his own disgust at the images of the Rwandan genocide: 'I could say that one television scene probably did more to smash my African dignity and pride than 200 years of colonialism, but *non-African* blacks would probably misinterpret that statement' (*ibid.*: xiv, my emphasis).

Precisely those images of the Rwandan genocide appalled me also. As an Indian-African whose parents migrated to North America, and as somebody who now lives in Australia, it was difficult to fathom how such inhumanity and cruelty could be inflicted by one group of people upon another. In order to understand this process, in 1995 I spent nearly six months in Rwanda and Zaire. It quickly became clear to me that it was not African but human dignity which was at stake – all the more so because of the commitment of the world community after the Jewish holocaust that never again would there be another genocide. The roots of the Rwandan tragedy, I discovered, are located firmly in the continent's colonial past as well as in its post-colonial present (Ahluwalia

1997b). It is just this interaction between the coloniser and the colonised that post-colonialism seeks to understand – and also underlies this book, which deploys a post-colonial perspective in order to elucidate the complexities of the post-colonial condition. It is a process which recognises that Africa has to deal with its past in order to understand its present and confront its future. This is where post-colonialism is instructive, because it does not degenerate into establishing binaries which ascribe a politics characterised by a 'rhetoric of blame'.

It is hardly a new revelation that Africa is in crisis. The 'African crisis' has been recorded, reported and widely discussed for more than a decade (Chabal and Daloz 1999; Davidson 1992; Leys 1994, 1996; Mamdani 1996a; Rush and Szeftel 1994). Patrick Chabal provides a good summary, capturing the extent of the crisis by categorising it into four distinct but interrelated factors: 'an acute economic crisis, political instability, the so called "re-traditionalisation" of African societies, and the marginalisation of Africa on the international scene' (1996: 29). The African crisis feeds into the prevailing representations of both Africa and Africans, as the 'dark continent': primordial, tribal, violent, unable to feed itself and with a begging bowl permanently in its hand. If the power of representation in earlier centuries led to the colonisation of Africa by Europeans who embodied the civilising mission, at the beginning of the new millennium there are echoing calls for the recolonisation of the continent (Helman and Ratner 1992; Mazrui 1994, 1997; Pfaff 1995).

The ascendancy of Afro-pessimism, of which this type of thinking is representative, has a tendency to homogenise the 'African tragedy', concluding that Africa has neither the political will nor the capacity to deal with its problems. The African condition, it is claimed, is largely of Africa's own making, and therefore there is little or no hope for improvement. Afro-pessimism resonates in metropolitan centres where, in the aftermath of the Cold War, both former colonial powers and the United States are seeking ways to disengage themselves from Africa. This is a convenient way for the West to wash its hands of a problem that is largely of its making. Since at least the fifteenth century, Africa has been raped and plundered, first through the slave trade and then by formal colonisation. The assertion that Africa has gained full independence and that the transfer of power from coloniser to colonised is complete is one that is challenged by the post-colonial approach of this book.

V.Y. Mudimbe (1988) has noted poignantly that Africa is an invention. The very signifer 'Africa' is one that was constructed by the West, and one that is currently being reconstructed through Western institutions that decide and exert their power by 'knowing' what is best for Africa – namely development and modernity. It is through their amassing of statistics and surveillance that an underdeveloped, primordial, traditional and war-ravaged Africa is (re)produced. However, Kate Manzo captures the irony of this when she notes that, 'the majority [of developmentalists] never classified the countries of Western Europe, the United States or Great Britain as "developing" or "modernizing" societies;

they belonged to the realm of the logos, or pure and invariable presence in need of no explanation' (1991: 10).

This does not mean that Africans, and in particular their leaderships, can be absolved of responsibility for the African crises. Rather, it entails recognising the manner in which the cultures of both the coloniser and the colonised are deeply intertwined and implicated and that they are a product of colonialism and its continuing legacy. As Robert Young has observed, both have a responsibility:

> The means of administration may have often moved from coercive regiments to regimes supported by international aid and the banking system, the 'white man's burden' may have been transformed by the wind of change into the TV appeal for famine in Africa. But the burden of neocolonialism remains for all those who suffer its effects; and responsibility cannot be ignored by those who find themselves part of those societies which enforce it.
>
> (Young 1991: 3)

The notion of shared responsibility is an important one, for it marks its distance from a 'rhetoric of blame'. It calls for a different mode of analysis. The failure of Eurocentric theory in its various guises – modernization theory, dependency theory and various post-dependency and Marxist-inspired analyses – have all failed. These theories were imposed from the outside and were underpinned by the power of the West. As Slater notes, 'ethnocentric universalism receives its deepest and most pervasive expression in the domain of mainstream development theory' (1993: 99). The mode of analysis suggested here is based on the notion of post-colonial inflections. This is not a mere repudiation of everything that has occurred in the African past, but an engagement with the manner in which Africa has dealt with institutions and practices which it has inherited from the past, both pre-colonial and colonial.

These institutions have not remained static – they have become hybridised and have evolved with particular meanings attached to them in culturally specific locations. In this context, it needs to be remembered that post-colonialism is not another grand theory but one that recognises the centrality of colonialism and the manner in which each society that it encountered has been differently affected by it. A major preoccupation of contemporary post-colonial theory has been with literary texts and literary theory – which is not surprising, given that some of the most important works in the area have emerged from writers who are situated in literature departments. It is this analysis, this tension (often evoked via the charge that recent post-colonial theory fails to engage with the 'real' world) that is addressed. It illustrates the centrality of the negritude movement as an important project in the process of identity formation, the processes of decolonisation and liberation, the dilemmas of modernity and the nation-state, the importance of civil society and citizenship and the manner in which globalisation impacts upon the local, thereby reconstituting post-colonial identity. It is a mode of analysis which shows the complexity of African politics and the manner in which post-colonial African subjects negotiate their lives. It is a process in which, as Achille Mbembe has noted, 'the postcolonial "subject" mobilizes not just a single identity, but several fluid identities which, by their very nature, must be constantly "revised" in order to achieve maximum instrumentality and efficacy as and when required' (1992: 5). In short, post-colonialism forces one to think of the plurality and diversity of African identities and implores us to heed the ethical call of responsibility.

Notes

Introduction

1 It is important to note, however, Ahmad's own trajectory. He is an academic who works in one of India's most prestigious institutions, has worked in Western universities and published his book *In Theory* with a British publisher.
2 An extended discussion of good governance can be found below, in Chapter 4.
3 For an extended discussion of worldliness, see Ashcroft and Ahluwalia 1999. Ato Quayson appears to advocate a similar strategy without acknowledging his debt to Said. For an interesting discussion of the relationship between politics and literature, see his chapter 'Literature as a Politically Symbolic Act' in Quayson 2000.

1 'Negritude and nativism': in search of identity

1 For an excellent account of the child trope, see Ashcroft 1997; Valentine 1996.
2 The question of language is crucial and has been debated vigorously in African literature, see Ngugi wa Thiong'o 1981.
3 The slave trade was the single most important factor in the depopulation and denigration of the African continent. For an excellent account of the slave trade, see Blackburn 1997.
4 Although Senghor acknowledges the influence of the African-American movement, Koffi Anyinefa has recently demonstrated how African-Americans remained ambivalent to Senghor's work (Anyinefa 1996). For an excellent account of the Black renaissance, see Gates 1997. See also Jules-Rosette 1998.
5 For his major writings, see Senghor 1962, 1964a, 1964b, 1969, 1976.
6 For a detailed account of Spivak's 'strategic essentialism', see Childs and Williams 1997 and Moore-Gilbert 1997.
7 For an interesting account of Césaire's negritude as black surrealism, see Richardson and Fijalkowski 1996.
8 It is important to note however, that Benita Parry has recently raised the issue of ambivalence in Fanon's work in relation to the negritude movement. See Parry 1987, 1994.
9 Marion O'Callaghan has noted that, 'not only did neo-*négritude* pose no threat to the category of race, it reinforced this category. For it is exactly the racialization of history and of cultures that is the most serious, because seemingly evident, underpinning of racism. Moreover, neo-*négritude* refused and eliminated the real questions of today and the passage to today's technological conquest by the very nature of its return to a mythical yesterday' (1995: 34).

2 Decolonisation and national liberation

1 Lord Lugard defined indirect rule in the *Dual Mandate* as 'Rule by native chiefs, unfettered in their control of their people, yet subordinated to the control of the Protecting Power in certain well-defined directions' (cited in Robinson 1980: 68). The nature of indirect rule and its impact is discussed widely by Mahmood Mamdani (1996a). In Chapter 5 I discuss this system in detail whilst engaging with the thrust of the Mamdani thesis. Although it is generally argued that it was only the British who utilised indirect rule, Mamdani convincingly illustrates that all colonial powers succumbed to it.

2 On the phenomenon of founding fathers, see Ahluwalia 1996b.

3 Although the first conferences for Pan-Africanism were dominated largely by African-Americans, the fifth Pan-African Conference, held in Manchester in 1945, saw prominent African leaders such as Kenyatta and Nkrumah taking part. By the time the conference was held in Ghana in 1958, the movement had become focused essentially on Africa. There is, however, a renewed interest in the movement. See Lemelle and Kelley 1994; Kanneh 1998.

4 It is also one that Ngugi wa Thiong'o recognised as being vital. See his *Decolonising the Mind* (1986).

5 Fanon's biographical details can be found in Caute 1970. See also Bulhan 1985; Gendzier 1973; Gordon *et al.* 1996 and Hansen 1977. For a good discussion of the gender issue in Fanon's work, see Moore-Gilbert 1996.

6 The question of locating Fanon and positioning him is an important one. Arguing that it is particularly difficult to do this in the case of Fanon, Nicholas Harrison writes:

> to situate Fanon himself, one of the key figures of postcolonial theory, is a complex matter. It is complex partly, of course, because his situation changed; and one of the favourite ironies of his biographers is that young Fanon not only fought in the Free French armies in Morocco, Algeria and on the Swiss border, but was decorated by Colonel Salan, one of the future leaders of the French forces in the Algerian War and one of the founders of the OAS.
>
> (Harrison 1998: 57)

7 It is important to note Anne McClintock's point about the gender blindness in Fanon's work (1997). In the introduction to their Fanon reader, Gordon *et al.* make the point that 'Fanon devoted a number of pages to discussions of feminist theory and resistance that were in fact ahead of their time' (1996: 6). For a further elaboration of the gender question in Fanon, see Dubey 1998.

8 This binary opposition in language is explained by Derrida as not a condition of peaceful co-existence but rather one that entails a violent hierarchy, with one of the two terms in the binary being paramount (see Derrida 1981: 40).

9 For an interesting attack on these new readings of Fanon, see Gibson 1999; Sekyi-Otu 1996.

10 Gordon *et al.* have noted that there are five phases of Fanon studies. The first consisted of reactions to his work as well as the manner in which it could be applied; the second was biographical; the third stage was locating Fanon as a political theorist. The fourth stage is the postmodern and post-colonial revival of his work, and the final stage is the impact of Fanon on academic disciplines themselves (1996: 5–8).

11 This is where Said parts company with colonial discourse theorists and has much in common with Fanon. As Benita Parry notes:

> The significant differences in the critical practices of Spivak and Bhabha are submerged in a shared programme marked by the exorbitation of discourse and a related incuriosity about the enabling socio-economic and political institutions

and other forms of social praxis. Furthermore, because their theses admit no point outside of discourse from which opposition can be engendered, their project is concerned to place incendiary devices within the dominant structures of representation and not to confront these with another knowledge.

(1987: 43)

12 Much has been made of Said's misappropriation of Foucault. See Ahmad, 1992; Clifford 1988; Young 1990. For a detailed analysis of this, see Ashcroft and Ahluwalia 1999.

3 Modernity and the problem of the nation-state

1 For an excellent review of the debate on the post-colonial state, see Leys 1976. On the need to ground theory and its worldliness, see Ashcroft and Ahluwalia 1999; Said 1983.
2 Beasley-Murray argues that, as long as cultural studies continues to operate under the rubric of hegemony, it will be confined to the logic of populism. He concludes:

> Rather than examining the articulations within the field of civil society – a field that may indeed, one might suggest ... be withering away in a movement that again, perhaps begins in the periphery rather than the metropolis – one might do better to examine the organizational features of culture and state, to re-emphasize their difference rather than their similarity, or rather, to see the *state* as that which has to be explained.
>
> (Beasley-Murray 1998: 212–13)

3 It is important to note that Claude Ake has argued that the assumption that there has been a failure of development is misleading. For Ake, the real problem is that development has never been on the agenda (see Ake 1996).
4 For a scathing critique of NGOs and the foreign aid industry in general, see Maren 1997.
5 The economic hegemony of the IMF and the World Bank and their orthodox economic assumptions have been compared by Susan George and Fabrizio Sabelli (1994) with religious fundamentalism.
6 For an example of how conditionality has been imposed in the Kenyan context, see Ahluwalia 1996a.
7 It is important to recognise that foreign aid comes with strings attached. For a good review of the argument, see Hayter 1971.
8 It is, of course, paradoxical that the World Bank and the IMF have adopted the NGO sector, because it was after all they who had advocated the state-led approach in the 1960s. For liberals in the 1960s it was through the state and 'trickle down' that development was to be effected. For a classical statement on this, see Rostow 1960.
9 There is a considerable literature on the one-party state (see Bayart 1993; Decalo 1985; Hyden 1983; Jackson and Rosberg 1988; Sandbrook 1985; Young 1981; Zolberg 1966).
10 See also Mohiddin 1972 and Saul 1972.
11 For a detailed analysis of the different stages of the villagisation, see Nursey-Bray 1980. See also Mascarenhas 1979; Migot-Adholla 1984.
12 For example, it is surprising that a body of knowledge equivalent to subaltern studies in the African context has not emerged amongst Africanist historians.
13 From a post-colonial perspective such a debate is pointless, given that colonialism alters the very course of history. I will discuss the implications of a post-colonial perspective below.

14 For a report card on the results of the democratisation efforts in the 1990s, see Baker 1998.

15 For Leys, the failure of both Bayart and Davidson is their failure to take into account the logic of capital:

> A central part of any general explanation, however, must be the failure of the colonial regimes to transform the relations of production. To a very large extent, household production of commodities replaced household production for subsistence and local exchange, and that was all. The expansion of output was achieved extensively, not intensively: productivity gains were achieved, but within limits of household production.
>
> (Leys 1994: 45)

16 For Bayart, governmentality is 'a way of governing the actions of individuals or groups' and 'to govern ... is to structure other peoples' possible field of action' (Bayart 1991: 65). On governmentality, see Foucault 1991.

17 It is important to point out that this analysis is riven with ethnocentric biases and downright offensive racist assertions, such as the claim that certain ethnic groups are predisposed to crime. However, so as not to detract from the argument, it is deemed inappropriate to fully engage with these aspects of this book.

18 The independent bureaucracy which is seen to be a cornerstone of the modern state is rapidly shrinking in Africa under the weight of World Bank reforms (see Goldsmith 1999).

19 I have not dealt with the methodological problems of Anderson's assertion when applied to the colonies. As Chatterjee points out, one of the central problems with Anderson's argument is that, if 'nationalisms in the rest of the world have to choose their imagined community from certain "modular" forms already made available to them by Europe and the Americas, what do they have left to imagine? ... Even our imaginations must remain forever colonized' (1993: 5).

20 It is not my intention to engage with Davidson's methodological problems, as these have been taken up by Mahmood Mamdani (see Mamdani 1993).

21 For a detailed analysis of the construction of identity in Rwanda, see Ahluwalia 1997a.

22 In extreme cases in Africa, it is easy to see how such an exercise led to the justification of the one-party state. For an example of how this occurred in Kenya, see Ahluwalia 1996a.

23 For an interesting analysis of national culture and globalisation, see Buell 1994.

24 Although there is some interesting work being done on alternative modernities, as evidenced by a special issue on the topic in *Public Culture* in 1999, there is to date no consideration of this in the case of Africa. For example, see Povinelli 1999.

4 Striving for democratisation: the complexities of civil society and human rights

1 A plethora of literature on democracy in Africa has emerged in recent times. For a sample of this, see Bratton and van de Walle 1997; Diamond 1999; Friedman 1999; Haggard and Kaufman 1995; Hyden *et al.* 2000; Joseph 1999; Mamdani 1996a; Monga 1997; Wiseman 1996.

2 For a report card on the democratic transitions, see Baker 1998; Karatnycky 1999.

3 For a detailed analysis of political instability in Africa, refer to Ake 1973.

4 For an emphasis of different factors and alternative lists, see Callaghy 1986 as well as Zolberg 1968.

5 For a review of the debate from the Western point of view, see Hyden and Bratton 1992.

6 It is important to recognise the role of international capital, which assisted the anti-apartheid movement through disinvestment and the imposition of sanctions.

7 For a detailed discussion of the emergence of the discourse of Africanism, see Ahluwalia 1996a.

8 For Kasfir, the conventional view includes Chazan 1992; Diamond 1997; Hadenius and Uggla 1997; and Schmitter 1997.

9 This view, central to the traditional view which pluralism pushed, has been challenged effectively in mainstream political science but clearly remains important in American African studies.

10 For details on some of the early philosophical statements on human rights, see Locke 1966 [1689]; Paine 1985 [1791] and Rousseau 1960.

11 The distinction between such rights is an important part of the traditional Western thinking on human rights and is articulated best by Maurice Cranston (1979). On the distinction between positive and negative rights, see Berlin 1969.

12 It is important to note that these are caricatures and extreme positions that are being outlined here. There are, of course, many views in between these extremes. For example, there are many radical-liberals who would accept much of the critique that has been mounted against traditional liberals.

13 For an elaboration of the African concept of human rights, see Legesse 1980; Marasinghe 1984; Mojekwu 1980; Pollis and Schwab 1979; Wai 1979.

14 For a detailed analysis of the development argument, see Goodin 1979: 42. Also see A.H. Robertson, who points out that:

> the economic development of underdeveloped countries is necessary for their social well-being and political stability, without which they cannot ensure effectively the civil, political, economic, social, and cultural rights announced in the major international texts and that therefore the 'right to development' is a human right.
>
> (Robertson 1982: 8–9)

15 For an interesting discussion on human rights and democracy, see Arat 1999.

16 This argument is fairly widespread and can be found, for example, in Bayley 1964; Cranston 1973 and Ferguson 1973. For a critique of this position, see Barry 1973.

17 Noam Chomsky has demonstrated the role of the media in ensuring that Western interests are not threatened by simply ignoring such abuses. See Chomsky 1988.

18 On the manner in which these institutions operate on behalf of imperialism, see Barrat Brown 1995; Caulfield 1998; Eze 1990.

19 For a detailed analysis of the Ugandan case, see Ahluwalia and Nursey-Bray 1996.

20 For an excellent account of the manner in which the African Charter was drawn up as well as the rationale behind it, see Mbaye 1993.

21 For a full text of the African Charter of Rights, see International Commission of Jurists 1986.

22 For a detailed discussion of these debates, see Helman and Ratner 1992; Pfaff 1995.

23 It is in this context that Penna and Campbell have recently argued that we need to move beyond universality and relativism and have urged a reconceptualisation of human rights in which both the West and the non-West contribute to a better understanding. See Penna and Campbell 1998.

5 Citizenship, subjectivity and the crisis of modernity

1 For an example of the use of customary law in India, see Mayer 1993.

2 The impact of globalisation is examined in Chapter 6.

3 On the making of citizens into consumers, see Miller 1993, especially Chapter 4.

6 Globalisation and post-colonialism: towards the reconstitution of identity

1 This is a decidedly different position for Ashcroft, who had earlier argued that 'if the African subject re-imagines itself back into the global economy … it imagines itself straight into a position of inescapable subalterneity, a specious universalism in which it is no longer a child of empire but has become a featureless consumer' (1997: 20).

2 For an excellent exposition of the consumption of modernity in the African context, see Paolini 1999.

Works cited

Adotevi, Stanislas (1972) *Négritude et Négrologues*, Paris: Union Générale d'Editions.

Agbese, P.O. (1994) 'The State versus Human Rights Advocates in Africa: The case of Nigeria', in Eileen McCarthy-Arnolds, David Penna, and Joy Cruz Sobrepeña (eds), *Africa, Human Rights and the Global System: The political economy of human rights in a changing world*, Westport CT: Greenwood Press.

Ahluwalia, Pal (1996a) *Post-colonialism and the Politics of Kenya*, New York: Nova Science Publishers.

—— (1996b) 'Founding father presidencies and the rise of authoritarianism – Kenya: a case study', *Africa Quarterly*, vol. 36. no. 4., pp. 45–72.

—— (1997a) 'Post-colonial Dilemmas: Political succession in Kenya', in Pal Ahluwalia and Paul Nursey-Bray (eds), *The Post-colonial Condition: Contemporary politics in Africa*, New York: Nova Science Publishers.

——(1997b) 'The Rwandan genocide: exile and nationalism reconsidered', *Social Identities*, vol. 3, no. 3, pp. 499–518.

Ahluwalia, Pal, and Paul Nursey-Bray (1994) 'The new South Africa: the international arena', *Policy Organisation and Society*, no. 9 , pp. 1–6.

—— (1996) 'Uganda: state and civil society', in Peter Alexander *et al.*, *Africa Today*, Canberra: Humanities Research Centre.

Ahmad, Aijaz (1992) *In theory: Classes, nations, literatures*, London: Verso.

—— (1995a) 'Postcolonialism: what's in a name?', in Roman De La Campa *et al.*, *Late Imperial Culture*, London: Verso.

—— (1995b) 'The politics of literary postcoloniality', *Race and Class*, 36, pp. 1–20.

Ajayi, Omofolabo (1997) 'Negritude, feminism, and the quest for identity: re-reading Mariama Bâ's *So Long a Letter*', *Women's Studies Quarterly*, no. 3–4, pp. 35–52.

Ake, Claude (1973) 'Explaining political instability in new states', *Journal of Modern African Studies*, 11, 3, pp. 347–59.

—— (1996) *Democracy and Development in Africa*, Washington DC: Brookings Institution.

Alavi, Hamza (1971) 'The state in post-colonial societies: Pakistan and Bangladesh', *New Left Review*, 74, July–August, pp. 59–81.

Allen, Chris (1999) 'Warfare, endemic violence and state collapse in Africa', *Review of African Political Economy*, vol. 81, pp. 367–84.

Amnesty International (1991) *Protecting Human Rights*, London: Amnesty International.

Anderson, Benedict (1983, 1991) *Imagined Communities: Reflections on the origin and spread of nationalism*, London: Verso.

—— (1994) 'Exodus', *Critical Inquiry*, 20, Winter, pp. 314–27.

Anyang' Nyong'o, Peter (1995) 'Discourses on democracy in Africa', in Eshetu Chole and Jibrin Ibrahim (eds), *Democratisation Processes in Africa: Problems and Prospects*, Dakar: CODESRIA Books.

Anyinefa, Koffi (1996) 'Hello and goodbye to Négritude: Senghor, Dadié, Dongala, and America', *Research In African Literatures*, Summer, vol. 27, no. 2, pp, 51–69.

Appadurai, Arjun (1990) 'Disjuncture and difference in the global cultural economy', *Public Culture*, vol. 2, no. 2, Spring, pp. 1–24

—— (1996) *Modernity at Large: Cultural dimensions of globalization*, Minneapolis: University of Minnesota Press.

Appiah, Kwame Anthony (1992) *In My Father's House: Africa in the philosophy of culture*, New York: Oxford University Press.

—— (1997) 'Is the "post" in "postcolonial" the "post-" in "postmodern"', in McClintock, Mufti and Shohat (1997).

Arart, Zehra (1999) 'Human rights and democracy: expanding or contracting?', *Polity*, vol. 32, no. 1, pp. 119–44.

Armah, A.K. (1967) 'African socialism: utopian or scientific', *Présence Africaine*, 64, pp. 6–30.

Armstrong, David (1998) 'Globalization and the social state', *Review of International Studies*, vol. 24, pp. 461–78.

Arnold, A. James (1981) *Modernism and Negritude: The poetry and poetics of Aimé Césaire*, Cambridge MA: Harvard University Press.

Ashcroft, Bill (1997) 'Globalism, post-colonialism and African studies', in Pal Ahluwalia and Paul Nursey-Bray (eds), *Post-Colonialism: Culture and identity in Africa*, New York, Nova Science Publishers.

—— (1998) 'Global culture, local identity and post-colonial transformation', unpublished paper presented to the Politics Department, University of Adelaide, pp. 1–21.

Ashcroft, Bill, *et al.* (1998) *Key Concepts in Post-Colonial Theory*, London: Routledge.

Ashcroft, Bill, and Pal Ahluwalia (1999) *Edward Said: The paradox of identity*, London: Routledge.

Ashcroft, Bill, Gareth Griffiths and Helen Tiffin (1989) *The Empire Writes Back: Theory and practice in post-colonial literatures*, London: Routledge.

—— (eds) (1995) *The Post-colonial Studies Reader*, London: Routledge.

Ayittey, George B.N. (1998) *Africa in Chaos*, New York: St Martins Press.

Bâ, Sylvia Washington (1973) *The Concept of Negritude in the Poetry of Léopold Sédar Senghor*, Princeton NJ: Princeton University Press.

Baker, Bruce (1998) 'The class of 1990: How have the autocratic leaders of sub-Saharan Africa fared under democratisation?', *Third World Quarterly*, vol. 19, no. 1, pp. 115–27.

Balibar, Etienne (1991) 'Citizen subject', in Eduardo Cadava, Peter Connor and Jean-Luc Nancy (eds), *Who Comes After The Subject*, London: Routledge.

Baregu, Mwesiga (1995) 'The dynamics of political change and the restructuring of governance in Tanzania', in Frederick Kaijage, *Reflections on the Transition to Democracy in Tanzania*, Dar es Salaam: University of Dar es Salaam Press.

Barrat Brown, Michael (1995) *Africa's Choices: After thirty years of the World Bank*, London: Penguin Books.

Barry, Brian (1973) *The Liberal Theory of Justice*, Oxford: Clarendon Press.

Bayart, Jean-François (1986) 'Civil society in Africa', in Chabal (ed.) (1986).

—— (1991) 'Finishing with the idea of the Third World: the concept of the political trajectory', in James Manor (ed.), *Rethinking Third World Politics*, London: Longman.

—— (1993) *The State in Africa: The Politics of the Belly*, London: Longman.

Bayart, Jean-François, Stephen Ellis and Béatrice Hibou (1999) *The Criminalization of the State in Africa*, London: James Currey.

Bayley, David H. (1964) *Public Liberties in the New States*, Chicago: Rand McNally.

Beasley-Murray, J. (1998) 'Peronism and the secret history of cultural studies: populism and the substitution of culture for state', *Cultural Critique*, vol. 39, pp. 189–217.

Benhabib, Seyla (ed.), (1996) *Democracy and Difference*, Princeton NJ: Princeton University Press.

Berg-Schlosser, Dirk, and Rainer Siegler (1990) *Political Stability and Development: A comparative analysis of Kenya, Tanzania and Uganda*, Boulder CO: Lynne Rienner.

Berlin, Isaiah (1969) *Four Essays on Liberty*, Oxford: Oxford University Press.

Bertens, Hans (1995) *The Idea of the Postmodern*, London: Routledge.

Bhabha, Homi (1986) 'Remembering Fanon: self psyche and the colonial condition', foreword to Frantz Fanon, *Black Skins, White Masks*, London: Pluto Press.

—— (1990) 'Introduction: narrating the nation', in Homi Bhabha (ed.), *Nation and Narration*, London: Routledge.

—— (1994) *The Location of Culture*, London: Routledge.

Birmingham, David (1995) *The decolonization of Africa*, London: UCL Press.

Blackburn, R. (1997) *The Making of New World Slavery: From the baroque to the modern, 1492–1800*, London: Verso.

Blyden, E.W. (1862) *Liberia's Offering*, New York: J.A. Gray.

—— (1967 [1888]) *Christianity, Islam and the Negro Race*, London: Edinburgh University Press.

Boyle, Patrick (1988) 'A view From Zaire', *World Politics*, vol. 40, no. 2, pp. 268–87.

Bratton, Michael, and Nicholas van de Walle (1994) 'Neopatrimonial regimes and political transition in Africa', *World Politics*, XLVI, pp. 453–89.

—— (1997) *Democratic Experiments in Africa: Regime transitions in comparative perspective*, Cambridge: Cambridge University Press.

Brohman, John (1995) 'Universalism, Eurocentrism, and ideological bias in development studies: from modernisation to neoliberalism', *Third World Quarterly*, vol. 16, no. 1., pp. 120–40

Buell, Frederick (1994) *National Culture and the New Global System*, Baltimore MD: Johns Hopkins University Press.

Buergenthal, Thomas (1988) *International Human Rights in a Nutshell*, New York: West Publishing.

Bulhan, Hussein Abdilahi (1985) *Frantz Fanon and the Psychology of Oppression*, New York: Plenum Press.

Cabral, Amilcar (1979) *Unity and Struggle*, New York: Monthly Review Press.

Callaghy, Thomas (1986) 'Politics and vision in Africa: The interplay of domination, equality and liberty', in Chabal (ed.) (1986).

—— (1984) *The State–Society Struggle: Zaire in contemporary perspective*, New York: Columbia University Press.

—— (1987) 'The state as lame leviathan: The patrimonial-administrative state in Africa', in Zaki Ergas (ed.), *African State in Transition*, London: Macmillan.

Caulfield, Catherine (1998) *Masters of Illusion: The World Bank and the poverty of nations*, London: Pan Books.

Caute, D. (1970). *Fanon*, London: Fontana.

de Certeau, M. (1982), *La fable mystique*, Paris: Gallimard.

Césaire, Aimé (1950), *Discours sur le Colonialisme*, Paris: Présence Africaine, 1972.

—— (1968 [1939]) *Return to My Native Land*, Paris: Présence Africaine.

Chabal, Patrick (1996) 'The African crisis: context and interpretation', in Richard Werbner and Terence Ranger, *Postcolonial Identities in Africa*, London: Zed Books.

—— (1998) 'A few considerations on democracy in Africa', *International Affairs*, vol. 74, no. 2, pp. 289–303.

Chabal, Patrick (ed.) (1986) *Political Domination in Africa: Reflections on the limits of power*, Cambridge: Cambridge University Press.

Chabal, P., and J.P. Daloz (1999) *Africa Works: Disorder as political instrument*, London: James Currey.

Chamberlain, M.E. (1985) *Decolonization: The fall of the European empires*, Oxford: Blackwell.

Chatterjee, Partha (1990) 'A response to Taylor's 'Modes of Civil Society'', *Public Culture*, 3, no. 1, pp. 119–32.

—— (1993) *The Nation and its Fragments*, Princeton NJ: Princeton University Press.

—— (1998) 'Beyond the nation? Or within?', *Social Text*, vol. 16, no. 3, 1998, pp. 57–69.

Chazan, Naomi (1992) 'Africa's Democratic Challenge', *World Policy Journal*, vol. 9, no. 2, pp. 249–78.

Chege, Michael (1996) Review of Mamdani (1996) in *African Studies Quarterly*, vol. 1, no. 1, 1996.

Childs, P., and P. Williams (1997) *An Introduction to Post-Colonial Theory*, London: Prentice Hall.

Chinweizu, Onwu-Chekwa Jemie, and Madubuike Mechukwu (1985) *Toward the Decolonization of African Literature: African fiction and poetry and their critics*, London: KPI.

Chole, Eshetu, and Jibrin Ibrahim (eds) (1995) *Democratisation Processes in Africa: Problems and prospects*, Dakar: CODESRIA Books.

Chomsky, Noam (1988) *Manufacturing Consent: The political economy of the mass media*, New York: Pantheon.

Civille, J. (1972) *Tanzania and Nyerere: A study of Ujamaa and nationhood*, New York: Orbis.

Cixous, Hélène (1995) 'Sorties: out and out: attacks/ways out/forays' in D. Tallack (ed.), *Critical Theory: A reader*, London: Harvester Wheatsheaf.

Cliffe, Lionel and Luckham, Robin (1999) 'Complex political emergencies and the state: Failure and the fate of the state', *Third World Quarterly*, vol. 20, no. 1, pp. 27–50.

Clifford, James (1988) 'On orientalism', in *The Predicament of Culture: Twentieth century ethnography, literature and art*, Cambridge MA: Harvard University Press.

—— (1997) *Routes: Travel and translation in the late 20th century*, Cambridge MA: Harvard University Press.

Coleman, James (1954) 'Nationalism in tropical Africa', *American Political Science Review*, XLVIII, no. 2, pp. 404–26.

Condé, Maryse (1994) 'Pan-Africanism, feminism and culture', in Sidney Lemelle and Robin Kelley (eds), *Imagining Home*, London: Verso.

—— (1998) 'O brave new world', *Research in African Literatures*, vol. 29, no. 3, 1998, pp. 1–7.

Connor, Walker (1994) *Ethnonationalism: The quest for understanding*, Princeton NJ: Princeton University Press.

Conover, Pamela Johnston (1995) 'Citizen identities and conceptions of the self', *Journal of Political Philosophy*, vol. 3, no. 2, pp. 133–65.

Cranston, Maurice (1973, 1979) *What Are Human Rights?*, London: Bodley Head; reprinted in Walter Laqueur and Barry Rubin (eds), *The Human Rights Reader*, Philadelphia: Temple University Press.

Crush, Jonathan (1995) 'Introduction: Imagining development' in Jonathan Crush (ed.), *The Power of Development*, London: Routledge.

Dane, Robyn (1994) 'When Mirror Turns Lamp: Frantz Fanon as cultural visionary' *Africa Today*, 2nd quarter, pp. 70–91.

Dash M.J. (1973) 'Marvellous realism – the way out of Négritude', *Caribbean Studies*, 13, pp. 57–70.

Dathorne, O.R. (1981) *Dark Ancestor: The literature of the black man in the Caribbean*, Baton Rouge: Louisiana State University Press.

Davidson, B. (1992) *The Black Man's Burden: Africa and the curse of the nation-state*, London: James Currey.

Dayal, Samir (1996) 'Postcolonialism's possibilities: Subcontinental diasporic intervention', *Cultural Critique*, Spring, pp. 113–49.

Decalo, S. (1985) 'African personal dictatorships', *Journal of Modern African Studies*, vol. 23, no. 2, pp. 209–37

—— (1992) 'The process, prospects and constraints of democratization in Africa', *African Affairs*, vol. 91, no. 362, pp. 7–35.

Derrida, Jacques (1981) *Writing and Difference*, London: Routledge & Kegan Paul.

—— (1982) *Margins of Philosophy*, Brighton: Harvester.

Deutsch, Karl (1966) *Nationalism and Social Communication: An inquiry into the foundations of nationality*, Cambridge MA: MIT Press/Wiley.

Diamond, Larry (1988) 'Introduction: Roots of failure, seeds of hope', in Larry Diamond, Juan Linz, and Seymour Martin Lipset (eds), *Democracy in Developing Countries: Africa*, Boulder CO: Lynne Rienner.

—— (1997) 'Toward Democratic Consolidation' in Larry Diamond *et al.* (eds), *Consolidating the Third Wave Democracies: Themes and perspectives*, Baltimore MD: Johns Hopkins University Press.

—— (1999) 'Introduction' in Larry Diamond and Marc Plattner (eds), *Democratization in Africa*, Baltimore MD: Johns Hopkins University Press.

Diawara, Manthia (1998) 'Toward a regional imaginary in Africa' in Jameson and Miyoshi (eds) (1998).

Dirlik, Arif (1991) 'Culturalism as hegemonic ideology and liberating practice', in Abdul JanMohamed and David Lloyd (eds), *The Nature and Context of Minority Discourse*, New York: Oxford University Press.

—— (1994) 'The postcolonial aura: Third world criticism in the age of global capitalism', *Critical Inquiry*, 20, Winter, pp. 328–56.

—— (1999) 'Is there history after Eurocentrism? Globalism, postcolonialism and the disavowal of history', *Cultural Critique*, vol. 42, pp. 1–34.

Donald, James (1996) 'The citizen and the man about town', in Stuart Hall and Paul du Gay (eds), *Questions of Cultural Identity*, London: Sage.

Donnelley, Jack (1990) 'Human rights and Western liberalism', in A.A. An-Na'im and F. Deng (eds), *Human Rights in Africa: Cross-cultural perspectives*, Washington DC: Brookings Institute.

Drachler, Jacob (1964) 'Introduction: Toward true dialogue with Africa', in Jacob Drachler (ed.), *African Heritage*, New York: Collier.

Dubey, Madhu (1998) 'The "true lie" of the nation: Fanon and Feminism', *differences*, vol. 10, no. 2, pp. 1–29.

Duggan, William, and John Civille (1976) *Tanzania and Nyerere*, New York: Orbis.

Dussel, Enrique (1998) 'Beyond Eurocentrism: The world-system and the limits of modernity' in Jameson and Miyoshi (eds) (1998).

Emerson, Rupert (1975) 'The fate of human rights in the Third World', *World Politics*, vol. 27, no. 2, pp. 201–26.

Escobar, Arturo (1995) *Encountering Development: The making and unmaking of the Third World*, Princeton NJ: Princeton University Press.

Eze, Emmanuel Chukwudi (ed.) (1997) *Post-colonial African Philosophy: A critical reader*, Oxford: Blackwell.

Eze, Osito (1990) 'Human rights issues and violations: The African experience', in George W. Shepard and Mark O.C. Anikpo (eds), *Emerging Human Rights*, New York: Greenwood Press.

Fanon, Frantz (1967) *The Wretched of the Earth*, Harmondsworth: Penguin.

—— (1970) *Toward the African Revolution*. Harmondsworth: Penguin.

—— (1986) *Black Skin, White Masks*, London: Pluto Press. Intro. by Homi Bhabha.

—— (1989) 'Algeria unveiled' in Frantz Fanon *Studies in a Dying Colonialism*, trans. Haakon Chevalier, London: Earthscan.

Ferguson, C.C., Jr (1973) 'Economic development and human rights', *American Journal of International Law*, vol. 65, no. 5, pp. 198–227.

Foucault, Michel (1982) 'The subject and power', trans. Leslie Sawyer, *Critical Inquiry*, vol. 8, no., 4, pp. 777–95.

—— (1991) 'Governmentality,' in Graham Burchell, Colin Gordon and Peter Miller (eds), *The Foucault Effect: Studies in governmentality*, Chicago: University of Chicago Press.

Friedman, Steven (1999) 'Agreeing to Differ: African democracy, its obstacles and prospects', *Social Research*, vol. 66, no. 3, pp. 829–58.

Fuss, Diana (1994) 'Interior Colonies: Frantz Fanon and the politics of identification', *Diacritics*, vol. 24, no. 2–3: 20–42;

Gary, Ian (1996) 'Confrontation, co-operation or co-optation: NGOs and the Ghanaian state during structural adjustment', *Review of Political Economy*, vol. 23, no. 68, pp. 149–68.

Gates, Henry Louis, Jr (1991) 'Critical Fanonism', *Critical Inquiry*, vol. 17, no. 3: 457–70.

—— (1997) 'Harlem on our minds', *Critical Inquiry*, 24, Autumn, pp. 1–12.

Gates, Henry Louis, Jr (ed.) (1984) *Black Literature and Literary Theory*, London: Methuen.

Gendzier, Irene (1973) *Frantz Fanon: A critical study*, New York: Pantheon.

George, Susan, and F. Sabelli (1994) *Faith and Credit: The World Bank's secular empire*, London: Penguin.

Gerassi, J. (ed.) (1969) *Venceremos*, London: Weidenfeld & Nicolson.

Ghandi, Leela (1998) *Postcolonial Theory: A critical introduction*, New York: Columbia University Press.

Gibson, Nigel (1999) 'Thoughts about doing Fanonism in the 1990s', *College Literature*, vol. 26, no. 2, pp. 96–117.

Giddens, Anthony (1990) *The Consequences of Modernity*, Cambridge: Polity Press.

Gifford, P., and W.R. Louis (eds) (1982) *The Transfer of Power in Africa: Decolonization*, New Haven CT: Yale University Press.

Goldsmith, Arthur (1999) 'Africa's overgrown state reconsidered: Bureaucracy and economic growth', *World Politics*, vol. 51, pp. 520–46.

Goodin, Robert E. (1979) 'The development–rights trade-off: Some unwarranted economic and political assumptions', *Universal Human Rights*, vol. 1, no. 2, April–June, pp. 31–42.

Goonatilake, Susantha (1995) 'The self wandering between cultural localization and globalization' in Pieterse and Parekh (eds) (1995).

Gordon, L.R., D.T. Sharpley-Whiting and R.T. White (eds) (1996) *Fanon: A critical reader*, Oxford: Blackwell.

Goulding, Marrack (1999) 'The United Nations and conflict in Africa since the cold war', *African Affairs*, vol. 98, pp. 155–66.

Green, Reginald Herbold (1998) 'A cloth untrue: The evolution of structural adjustment in Sub-Saharan Africa', *Journal of International Affairs*, vol. 52, no. 1, pp. 207–32.

Greenstein, R. (1995) 'History and the production of knowledge', *South African Historical Journal*, vol. 32, pp. 217–32.

Hadenius, Alex, and Frederik Uggla (1997) 'Making civil society work', in Larry Diamond *et al.* (eds), *Consolidating the Third Wave Democracies: Themes and perspectives*, Baltimore MD: Johns Hopkins University Press.

Haggard, Stephan, and Robert R Kaufman (1995) *The Political Economy of Democratic Transitions*, Princeton NJ: Princeton University Press.

Hall, Stuart (1991) 'The local and the global: Globalization and ethnicity', in Anthony King (ed.), *Culture, Globalization and the World System*, London: Macmillan.

—— (1996) 'When was "the post-colonial"? Thinking at the limit', in Iain Chambers and Linda Curti (eds), *The Post-Colonial Question: Common skies, divided horizons*, London: Routledge.

Hannerz, Ulf. (1997) 'The world in creolization', *Africa*, vol. 57, no. 4, pp. 546–59.

Hansen, Emmanuel (1977) *Frantz Fanon: Social and political thought*, Columbus: Ohio State University Press.

Hargreaves, J.D. (1979) *The End of Colonial Rule in West Africa*, London: Macmillan.

Harrison, Nicholas (1998) 'Positioning (Fanon)', *Paragraph*, vol. 21, no. 1, pp. 57–68.

Hayter, Theresa (1971) *Aid as Imperialism*, Harmondsworth: Penguin.

Held, David, and Anthony McGrew (1993) 'Globalization and the liberal democratic state', *Government and Opposition*, vol. 28, no. 2, 1993, pp. 262–3.

Helman G. B., and S. Ratner (1992) 'Saving failed states', *Foreign Policy*, no. 89, pp. 3–20.

Hindess, Barry (1996) *Discourses of Power: From Hobbes to Foucault*, Oxford: Blackwell.

Hirst, Paul, and Grahame Thompson (1996) *Globalization in Question: the international economy and the possibilities of governance*, London: Polity Press.

Hobsbawm, Eric (1994) *Age of Extremes: The short twentieth century*, London: Michael Joseph.

Hoogvelt, Ankie (1997) *Globalisation and Postcolonialism*, London: Macmillan.

Hountondji, Paulin (1996) *African Philosophy: Myth and reality*, Bloomington: Indiana University Press.

Howard, Rhoda (1986a) 'Is there an African concept of human rights?', in R. J. Vincent (ed.), *Foreign Policy and Human Rights*, Cambridge: Cambridge University Press.

—— (1986b) *Human Rights in Commonwealth Africa*, Totowa NJ: Rowman and Littlefield.

——(1996) 'Civil conflict in sub-Saharan Africa: Internally generated causes', *International Journal*, II, pp. 27–53.

Huggins, Nathan (1971) *The Harlem Renaissance*, New York: Oxford University Press.

Hutcheon, Linda (1989) 'Circling the downspout of empire: Post-colonialism and postmodernism, *Ariel*, vol. 20, no. 4, pp. 149–75.

—— (1994) 'The post always rings twice: The postmodern and the postcolonial', *Textual Practice*, vol. 8, no. 2, pp. 205–39.

Hutchful, Eboe (1996) 'The civil society debate in Africa' *International Journal*, II, pp. 54–77.

Hyden, Goran (1980) *Beyond Ujamma in Tanzania*, London: Heinemann.

—— (1983) *No Shortcuts to Progress*, London: Heinemann.

Hyden, G., and M. Bratton (1992) *Governance and Politics in Africa*, Boulder CO: Lynne Rienner.

Hyden, Goran, and B. Karlstrom (1993) 'Structural adjustment as a policy process: The case of Tanzania', *World Development*, vol. 21, no. 9, pp. 1395–1404.

Hyden, Goran, Dele Olowu and Hastings W.O. Okoth-Ogendo (eds) (2000) *African Perspectives on Governance*, Trenton NJ: Africa World Press.

Hymaans, J.L. (1971) *Léopold Sédar Senghor: An intellectual biography*, Edinburgh: Edinburgh University Press.

Ignatieff, Michael (1995a) 'Nationalism and narcissism of minor differences' *Queens Quarterly*, vol. 102, no. 1, Spring, pp. 13–25.

—— (1995b) 'On civil society: Why Eastern Europe's revolutions could succeed', *Foreign Affairs*, March/April, pp. 128–37.

Illife, John (1983) *The Emergence of African Capitalism*, London: Macmillan.

International Commission of Jurists (1986) *African Charter of Rights*, Geneva: International Commission of Jurists.

Irele, Abiola (1971) 'Négritude Revisited', in Paul Nursey-Bray (ed.), *Aspects of Africa's Identity: Five essays*, Kampala: Makerere Institute of Social Research.

—— (1981) *The African Experience in Literature and Ideology*, London: Heinemann.

—— (1996) 'Introduction', in Hountondji (1996).

Jackson, R., and C. Rosberg (1988) 'Why Africa's weak states persist: The empirical and the juridical in statehood', *World Politics*, 35, pp. 1–24

—— (1992) *Personal Rule in Black Africa*, Berkeley: University of California Press.

Jameson, Fredric (1991) *Postmodernism, or, the Cultural Logic of Late Capitalism*, Durham NC: Duke University Press.

Jameson, Fredric, and Masao Miyoshi (eds) (1998) *The Cultures of Globalization*, Durham NC: Duke University Press.

JanMohammed, A. (1983) *Manichean Aesthetics: The politics of literature in colonial Africa*, Amherst: University of Massachusetts Press.

Joseph, Richard (1997) 'Democratization in Africa after 1989: Comparative and theoretical perspectives', *Comparative Politics*, vol. 29, pp. 363–82.

—— (1999) 'Africa, 1990–1997: From *abertura* to closure', in Larry Diamond and Marc Plattner (eds), *Democratization in Africa*, Baltimore MD: Johns Hopkins University Press.

Joseph, Richard (ed.) (1999) *State Conflict and Democracy in Africa*, Boulder CO: Lynne Rienner.

Jules-Rosette, Bennetta (1998) *Black Paris: The African Writers' Landscape*, Chicago: University of Illinois Press.

Kanneh, Kadiatu (1998) *African Identities: Race, nation and culture in ethnography, pan-Africanism and black literatures*, London: Routledge.

Karatnycky, Adrian (1999) 'The Freedom House Survey: The decline of illiberal democracy', *Journal of Democracy*, vol. 10, pp. 112–25.

Kasfir, Nelson (1998a) 'Introduction: The conventional notion of civil society: A critique', *Journal of Commonwealth and Comparative Politics*, vol. 36, no. 2, pp. 1–20.

—— (1998b) 'Civil society, the state and democracy in Africa', *Journal of Commonwealth and Comparative Politics*, vol. 36, no. 2, pp. 123–49.

Keane, John (ed.) (1988) *Civil Society and the State: New European perspectives*, London: Verso.

Kedourie, Elie (1978) *Nationalism*, London: Hutchinson.

Kesteloot, Lilyan (1972) *Intellectual Origins of the African Revolution*, Washington DC: Black Orpheus Press.

Khapoya, Vincent (1998) *The African Experience: An introduction*, Upper Saddle River NJ: Prentice Hall.

King, Anthony (ed.) (1991) *Culture, Globalization and the World System*, London: Macmillan.

Kohn, Hans (1965) *Nationalism: Its meaning and history*, New York: Van Nostrand.

Koshy, Susan (1999) 'From cold war to trade war: Neocolonialism and human rights', *Social Text*, vol. 17, no. 1, pp. 1–32.

Kruks, Sonia. (1996) 'Fanon, Sartre, and identity politics', in Gordon *et al.* (1996).

Laswell, H. D., and A. Kaplan (1952) *Power and Society: A framework for political inquiry*, London: Routledge & Kegan Paul.

Lawrence, Peter (ed.), (1986) *World Recession and the Food Crisis in Africa*, London: James Currey.

Lawson, Letitia (1999) 'External democracy promotion in Africa: Another false start?' *Journal of Commonwealth and Comparative Politics*, vol. 37, no. 1, pp. 1–30.

Lazarus, Neil (1999) *Nationalism and Cultural Practice in the Postcolonial World*, Cambridge: Cambridge University Press.

Legesse, Asmaram (1980) 'Human rights in African political culture', in Kenneth W. Thompson (ed.), *The Moral Imperatives of Human Rights: A world survey*, Washington DC: University Press of America, 1980.

Lemelle, Sidney, and Robin Kelley (eds), (1994) *Imagining Home*, London: Verso.

Leys, Colin (1976) 'The "Overdeveloped" Post Colonial State: A re-evaluation', *Review of African Political Economy*, no. 5, January–April, pp. 39–48.

—— (1994) 'Confronting the African tragedy', *New Left Review*, 204. pp. 33–47.

—— (1996) *The Rise and Fall of Development Theory*, London: James Currey.

Lister, Ruth (1997) *Citizenship: Feminist perspectives*, London: Macmillan.

—— (1998) Citizenship and difference: Towards a differentiated universalism, *European Journal of Social Theory*, vol. 1, no. 1, pp. 71–90.

Lionnet, Françoise (1995) *Postcolonial Representations: Women, literature, identity*, Ithaca NY: Cornell University Press.

Lloyd, David, and Paul Thomas (1998) *Culture and the State*, London: Routledge.

Locke, John (1966 [1689]) *The Second Treatise of Government: An essay concerning the true and original extent and end of civil government*, Oxford: Basil Blackwell and Mott.

Loomba, Ania (1998) *Colonialism/Postcolonialism*, London: Routledge.

Lynch, H.R. (1967) *Edward Wilmot Blyden*, London: Oxford University Press.

Lyotard, Jean-François (1984) *The Postmodern Condition: A report on knowledge*, Manchester: Manchester University Press.

McClintock, Anne (1992) 'The angel of progress: Pitfalls of the term "post-colonialism"', *Social Text*, 31/32, pp. 1–15.

McClintock, Anne, Aamir Mufti and Ella Shohat (1997) *Dangerous Liaisons: Gender, nation and postcolonial perspectives*, Minneapolis: University of Minnesota Press.

McClintock, Anne, and Rob Nixon (1986) 'No names apart: The separation of word and history in Derrida's "Le dernier mot du racisme"' in Henry Louis Gates, Jr (ed.), *Race, Writing and Difference*, Chicago: University of Chicago Press.

McLaren, Peter (1991) 'Postmodernism, post-colonialism and pedagogy', *Education and Society*, vol. 9, no. 1, pp. 3–22.

Madgwick, P.J., D. Steeds and L.J. Williams (1982) *Britain Since 1945*, London: Hutchinson.

Madsen, Richard (1993) 'Global monoculture, multiculture and polyculture', *Social Research*, vol. 60, no. 3, 1993, pp. 493–511.

Mahmud, Sakah Saidu (1993) 'The state and human rights in Africa in the 1990s: Perspectives and prospects', *Human Rights Quarterly*, vol. 15, no. 3, pp. 485–98.

Makumbe, John Mw (1998) 'Is there a civil society in Africa?', *International Affairs*, vol. 74, no. 2, pp. 305–17.

Mamdani, Mahmood (1976) *Politics and Class Formation in Uganda*, New York: Monthly Review.

—— (1993) 'The Sun is not Always Dead at Midnight', *Monthly Review*, vol. 45, no. 3, pp. 27–49.

—— (1995) 'Democratic theory and democratic struggles', in Chole and Ibrahim (eds) (1995).

—— (1996a) *Citizen and Subject: Contemporary Africa and the legacy of late colonialism*, Princeton NJ: Princeton University Press.

—— (1996b) 'Indirect rule, civil society, and ethnicity: The African dilemma', *Social Justice*, Spring, vol. 23, no., 1–2, pp. 145–51.

Manzo, Kate (1991) 'Modernist discourse and the crisis of development theory', *Studies in Comparative International Development*, vol. 26, no. 2, pp. 3–36.

Marasinghe, Lakshman (1984) 'Traditional conceptions of human rights in Africa: The Nigerian experience', in Claude E. Welch and Robert I. Meltzer (eds), *Human Rights and Development in Africa*, New York: State University of New York Press.

Maren, Michael (1997) *The Ravaging Effects of Foreign Aid and International Charity*, New York: Free Press.

Markovitz, I.L. (1969) *Léopold Sédar Senghor and the Politics of Negritude*, London: Heinemann Educational.

—— (1973) *The Concept of Negritude in the Poetry of Léopold Sédar Senghor*, Princeton NJ: Princeton University Press.

—— (1998) 'Uncivil society, capitalism and the state in Africa', *Journal of Commonwealth and Comparative Politics*, vol. 36, no. 2, pp. 21–53.

Marrouchi, Mustapha (1991) 'The critic as dis/placed intelligence: The case of Edward Said', *Diacritics*, vol. 21, no. 1, pp. 63–74.

Marx, Karl (1977) 'The Future Results of British Rule in India', in David McLellan (ed), *Karl Marx: Selected writings*, Oxford: Oxford University Press.

Mascarenhas, A (1979) 'After villagization – what?', in B.U. Mwansasu and C. Pratt (eds), *Towards Socialism in Tanzania*, Toronto: University of Toronto Press.

Masolo, D.A. (1997) 'African philosophy and the postcolonial: Some misleading abstractions about "identity"', in Emmanuel Chukwudi Eze (ed.) (1997).

Mayer, Peter (1993) 'Inventing village tradition: The late 19th century origins of the north Indian "Jajmani system"', *Modern Asian Studies*, vol. 27, part 2, pp. 357–95.

Mazrui, Ali (1967) *On Heroes and Uhuru Worship: Essays on independent Africa*, London: Longman.

—— (1994) 'Development or recolonization?', *New Perspectives Quarterly*, vol. 11, no. 4, Fall: pp. 18–19.

—— (1997) 'The Tutsi-trigger: Redrawing Africa's colonial map', *New Perspectives Quarterly*, vol. 14, no. 1: pp. 48–9.

—— (1999) 'Globalization and cross-cultural values: The politics of identity and judgment', *Arab Studies Quarterly*, vol. 21, no. 3, pp. 96–109.

Mbaye, Keba (1993) *Human Rights in Africa*, Paris: A. Pedone.

Mbembe, Achille (1992) 'Provisional notes on the postcolony', *Africa*, vol. 62, no. 1, pp. 3–37.

Memmi, Albert (1965) *The Coloniser and the Colonised*, New York: Orion Press.

Mezu, S.O. (1973) *The Poetry of Léopold Sédar Senghor*, London: Heinemann.

Michel, Martina (1995) 'Positioning the subject: Locating postcolonial studies', *Ariel*, vol. 26, no. 1, pp. 83–99.

Migdal, Joel (1988) *Strong Societies and Weak States: State–society relations and state capabilities in the Third World*, Princeton NJ: Princeton University Press.

Migot-Adholla, S.E. (1984) 'Rural development policy and equality', in J.D. Barkan (ed.), *Politics and Public Policy in Kenya and Tanzania*, New York: Praeger.

Miller, Christopher (1990) *Theories of Africans: Francophone literature and anthropology in Africa*, Chicago: University of Chicago Press.

Miller, Toby (1993) *The Well-Tempered Self: Citizenship, culture, and the postmodern subject*, Baltimore MD: Johns Hopkins University Press.

Minouge, Martin, and Judith Molloy (1974) *African Aims and Attitudes*, Cambridge: Cambridge University Press.

Mishra, Vijay, and Bob Hodge (1993) 'What is post(-)colonialism?', in J. Frow and M. Morris, *Australian Cultural Studies: A reader*, Sydney: Allen & Unwin.

Miyoshi, Masao (1996) 'A borderless world? From colonialism to transnationalism and the decline of the nation-state', in Wilson and Dissanayake (eds) (1996).

Mohiddin, A. (1972) 'Ujamaa na Kujitegemea', in L. Cliffe and J. Saul, *Socialism in Tanzania: An interdisciplinary reader*, Nairobi: East African Publishing House.

Mojekwu, Chris C. (1980) 'International human rights: The African perspective', in Jack L. Nelson and Vera M. Green (eds), *International Human Rights: Contemporary issues*, New York: Human Rights Publishing Group.

Monga, Celestin (1997) *The Anthropology of Anger: Civil society and democracy in Africa*, London: Frank Cass.

Moore-Gilbert, Bart (1996) 'Frantz Fanon: En-gendering nationalist discourse, *Women: A Cultural Review*, vol. 7, no. 2, pp. 125–35.

—— (1997) *Postcolonial Theory: Contexts, practices, politics*, London: Verso.

Mouffe, Chantal (1993) 'Liberal socialism and pluralism: Which citizenship?', in Judith Squires (ed.), *Principled Positions: Postmodernism and the rediscovery of value*, London: Lawrence & Wishart.

—— (1995) 'Feminism, citizenship and radical democratic politics', in Linda Nicholson and Steven Seidman, *Social Postmodernism: Beyond identity politics*, Cambridge: Cambridge University Press.

Mphahlele, Ezekiel (1974) *The African Image*, London: Faber and Faber.

Mudimbe, V.Y. (1988) *The Invention of Africa*, Bloomington: Indiana University Press.

—— (1994) *The Idea of Africa*, Bloomington: Indiana University Press.

Nandy, Ashis (1983) *The Intimate Enemy: Loss and recovery of self under colonialism*, Delhi: Oxford University Press.

Ngugi wa Thiong'o (1965) *The River Between*, London: Heinemann Educational Books.

—— (1981) *Writers in Politics*, London: Heinemann.

—— (1986) *Decolonising the Mind: The politics of language in African literature*, London: James Currey.

Nkrumah, Kwame (1965) *Neo-Colonialism: The last stage of imperialism*, London: Nelson.

—— (1971) *Ghana*, New York: International Publishers,

Nugent, Paul, and A.I. Asiwaju (eds) (1996) *African Boundaries: Barriers, conduits and opportunities*, London: Pinter.

Nursey-Bray, Paul (1980) 'Tanzania: The development debate', *African Affairs*, vol. 79, no. 314, pp. 65–9.

Nyerere, Julius (1966) *Freedom and Unity*, London: Oxford University Press.

—— (1973a) *Ujamaa – Essays on Socialism*, Dar es Salaam: Oxford University Press.

—— (1973b) *Freedom and Development*, Oxford: Oxford University Press.

O'Callaghan, Marion (1995) 'Continuities in imagination', in Pieterse and Parekh (eds) (1995).

Ogede, O.S. (1993) 'Negritude and Africa: Armah's Account', *Third World Quarterly*, vol. 14, no. 4, pp. 792–801.

Ogot, B.A. and Ochieng, W.R. (eds), (1995) *Decolonization and Independence in Kenya, 1940–93*, London: James Currey.

Oyugi, W.O, Odhiambo, A., Chege, M., Gitonga, A.K. (eds), (1988), *Democratic Theory and Practice in Africa*, Nairobi: Heinemann Educational Books.

Paine, Thomas (1985 [1791]) *Rights of Man*, London: Penguin Books.

Paolini, Albert (1997) 'Globalization' in Philip Darby (ed.), *At the Edge of International Relations: Postcolonialism, Gender, Dependency*, London: Pinter.

—— (1999) *Navigating Modernity: Postcolonialism, Identity and International Relations*, Boulder CO: Lynne Rienner.

Parry, Benita (1987) 'Problems in current theories of colonial discourse', *Oxford Literary Review*, vol. 9, Nos. 1 & 2, pp. 27–58.

—— (1994) 'Resistance Theory/Theorising Resistance or Two Cheers for nativism' in F. Barker, P. Hulme, and M. Iversen (eds) *Colonial Discourse/Postcolonial Theory*, Manchester: Manchester University Press.

Paul, James (1990) 'Participatory Approaches to Human Rights in Sub-Saharan Africa', in A.A. An-Na'im and F. Deng (ed.), *Human Rights in Africa: Cross-Cultural Perspectives*, Washington DC: Brookings Institute.

Penna, David R., and Patricia J. Campbell (1998) 'Human Rights and Culture: Beyond Universality and Relativism', *Third World Quarterly*, vol. 19, no. 1, pp. 7–27.

Pfaff, W. (1995) 'A New Colonialism: Europe Must Go Back into Africa', *Foreign Affairs*, vol. 74, no. 1, pp. 2–6 .

Pieterse, Jan Nederveen (1995) 'Globalization as hybridization' in Mike Featherstone, Scott Lash and Roland Robertson, *Global Modernities*, London: Sage.

Pieterse, Jan Nederveen, and Bhiku Parekh (eds) (1995) *The Decolonization of the Imagination: Culture, knowledge and power*, London: Zed Books.

Pitelis, Christos (1994) 'On the nature of the capitalist state', *Review of Political Economy*, vol. 6, no. 1, pp. 72–105.

Plank, David (1993) 'Aid, debt and the end of sovereignty: Mozambique and its donors', *Journal of Modern African Studies*, vol. 31, no. 3, pp. 407–30.

Pollis, Adamantia, and Peter Schwab (1979) 'Human rights: A Western construct with limited applicability', in A. Pollis and P. Schwab (eds), *Human Rights: Cultural and ideological perspectives*, New York: Praeger.

Potholm, Christian (1979) *The Theory and Practice of African Politics*, Englewood Cliffs NJ: Prentice Hall.

Povinelli, E.A. (1999) 'Settler modernity and the quest for an indigenous tradition', *Public Culture*, vol. 11, no. 1, pp. 19–48.

Prakash, Gyan (1996) 'Who's afraid of postcoloniality?', *Social Text*, vol. 14, no. 4, Winter, pp. 187–203.

Prakash, Gyan (ed.), (1995) *After Colonialism: Imperial histories and postcolonial displacements*, Princeton NJ: Princeton University Press.

Pratt, C. (1976)*The Critical Phase in Tanzania 1945–1968: Nyerere and the emergence of a socialist strategy*, Cambridge: Cambridge University Press.

Pratt, M.L. (1992) *Imperial Eyes: Travel writing and transculturation*, London: Routledge.

Radhakrishnan, R. (1993) 'Edward Said's *Culture and Imperialism*: A Symposium', *Social Text*, 40, pp. 15–20.

Ranger, Terence (1983) 'The invention of tradition in colonial Africa', in E.J. Hobsbawm and Terence Ranger (eds), *The Invention of Tradition*, Cambridge: Cambridge University Press.

—— (1985) *Peasant Consciousness and Guerrilla War in Zimbabwe*, Berkeley: University of California Press.

Rawls, John (1971) *Theory of Justice*, Cambridge MA: Harvard University Press.

Reed, J. and C. Wake (eds) (1965) *Senghor: Prose and Poetry*, London: Oxford University Press.

Reyntjens, Filip (1999) 'Briefing : The second Congo war: More than a remake', *African Affairs*, vol. 98, pp. 241–50.

Reno, William, (1999) *Warlord Politics and African States*, Boulder CO: Lynne Rienner.

Richardson, Michael, and Krzystof Fijalkowski (1996) *Refusal of the Shadow: Surrealism and the Caribbean*, London Verso.

Riddell, Roger (1999) 'The end of foreign aid to Africa? Concerns about donor policies', *African Affairs*, vol. 98, pp. 309–35.

Robertson, A.H. (1982) *Human Rights in the World: An introduction to the study of the international protection of human rights*, New York: St Martins Press.

Robertson, Roland (1987a) 'Globalization and societal modernization: A note on Japan and Japanese religion', *Sociological Analysis*, vol. 47, Spring, pp. 35–43.

—— (1987b) 'Globalization theory and civilizational analysis', *Comparative Civilizations Review*, vol. 17, pp. 20–30.

—— (1991) 'Social Theory, Cultural Relativity and the Problem of Globality', in Anthony King (ed.), *Culture, Globalization and the World System*, London: Macmillan.

—— (1992) *Globalization: Social theory and global culture*, London: Sage.

—— (1995) 'Glocalization: Time-space and homogeneity-heterogeneity', in Mike Featherstone, Scott Lash and Roland Robertson, *Global Modernities*, London: Sage.

Robinson, Ronald (1980) 'Andrew Cohen and the transfer of power in tropical Africa, 1940–1951', in W.H. Morris-Jones and Georges Fischer (eds), *Decolonisation and After: The British and French experience*, London: Frank Cass.

Rodrik, Dani (1997) 'Sense and nonsense in the globalization debate', *Foreign Policy*, Summer, pp. 19–36.

Rostow, W.W. (1960) *The Stages of Economic Growth: A non-communist manifesto*, Cambridge: Cambridge University Press.

Rousseau, Jean-Jacques (1960) 'The social contract' in *The Social Contract: Essays by Locke, Hume and Rousseau*, Oxford: Oxford University Press.

Rush, R., and M. Szeftel (1994) 'States, markets and Africa's crisis', *Review of African Political Economy*, vol. 21, no. 60, pp. 147–56.

Sachikonye, Lloyd (ed.) (1995) *Democracy, Civil Society and the State: Social Movements in southern Africa,*, Harare: Sapes Books.

Said, Edward (1976) 'Vico on the discipline of bodies and texts', *MLN*, October, pp. 817–26.

—— (1978) 'The problem of textuality: Two exemplary positions', *Critical Inquiry*, 4, pp. 673–714.

—— (1979) *Orientalism*. New York: Vintage Books.

—— (1983) *The World, the Text and the Critic*, Cambridge MA: Harvard University Press.

—— (1984) 'The mind of winter: Reflections on life in exile', *Harpers*, 269: 49–55.

—— (1985) 'Orientalism reconsidered', *Race & Class*, vol. 27, no. 2, pp. 1–16.

—— (1986) *After The Last Sky*. New York: Pantheon.

—— (1989) 'Representing the colonized: Anthropology's interlocutors', *Critical Inquiry*, 15, Winter: 224–5.

—— (1991) 'Identity, authority, and freedom: The potentate and the traveller', *Transition*, 54, pp. 4–18.

—— (1992) *The Question of Palestine,*, London: Vintage.

—— (1993a) *Culture and Imperialism*, London: Chatto & Windus.

—— (1993b) 'Nationalism, human rights and interpretation', *Raritan*, vol. 12, no. 3, pp. 26–52.

—— (1994) *Representations of the Intellectual*, London: Vintage.

—— (1995) 'Afterword', in *Orientalism*, New York: Vintage.

San Juan, E. (1998) *Beyond Postcolonial Theory*, New York: St Martin's Press.

Sandbrook, Richard (1985) *The Politics of Africa's Economic Stagnation*, Cambridge: Cambridge University Press.

Sardar, Zia, Ashis Nandy and M.W. Davis (1993) *Barbaric Others: A manifesto on Western racism*, London: Pluto Press.

Sartre, Jean-Paul (1976) *Black Orpheus*, Paris: Présence Africaine.

Saul, J. (1972) 'Nyerere on socialism: A review' in L. Cliffe and J. Saul, *Socialism in Tanzania: An interdisciplinary reader*, Nairobi: East African Publishing House.

de Saussure, Ferdinand (1974) *Course in General Linguistics*, Glasgow: Fontana.

Schmitter, Phillipe (1997) 'Civil society East and West' in Larry Diamond *et al.* (eds), *Consolidating the Third Wave Democracies: Themes and perspectives*, Baltimore MD: Johns Hopkins University Press.

Scott, David (1995) 'Colonial governmentality', *Social Text*, no. 43, pp. 191–220.

—— (1996) 'The aftermaths of sovereignty: Postcolonial criticism and the claims of political modernity', *Social Text*, 48, vol. 14, no. 3, pp. 1–26.

Scott, James (1998) *Seeing Like a State: How certain schemes to improve the human condition have failed*, New Haven CT: Yale University Press.

Sekyi-Otu, Ato (1996) *Fanon's Dialectic of Experience*, Cambridge MA: Harvard University Press.

Sellers, Susan (ed.), (1988) *Writing Differences: Readings from the seminar of Hélène Cixous*, Milton Keynes: Open University Press.

—— (1994) *The Hélène Cixous Reader*, London: Routledge.

Senghor, Léopold Sédar (1962) *Nationhood and the Road to African Socialism*, Paris: Présence Africaine.

—— (1964a) *Liberté I: Négritude et humanisme*, Paris: Présence Africaine.

—— (1964b) *Selected Poems*, London: Oxford University Press.

—— (1965) *Prose and poetry*, selected and trans. by J. Reed and C. Wake, London: Oxford University Press.

—— (1969) *Nocturnes*, London: Heinemann.

—— (1976) *Selected Prose and Poetry*, London: Heinemann.

Seshadri-Crooks, Kalpana (1995) 'At the margins of postcolonial studies', *Ariel*, vol. 26, no. 3, pp. 47–71.

Shivji, I.G. (1989) *The Concept of Human Rights in Africa*, London: CODESRIA.

Shohat, E. (1993) 'Notes on the postcolonial', *Social Text*, 31/32, pp. 99–113.

Shohat, E., and R. Stam (1985) 'The cinema after Babel: Language, difference, power', *Screen*, vol. 26, no. 3–4, pp. 35–58.

Simone AbdouMaliq (1998) 'Urban social fields in Africa', *Social Text*, vol. 16, no. 3, pp. 71–89.

Slater, D. (1993) 'Political meanings of development – New horizons', in F. Schuurman (ed.), *Beyond the Impasse: New directions in development theory*, London: Zed Books.

Soyinka, Wole (1976) *Myth, Literature and the African World*, Cambridge: Cambridge University Press.

Spelth, Janice (1985) *Léopold Sédar Senghor*, Boston: Twayne.

Spivak, Gayatri Chakravorti (1988) 'Can the subaltern speak?', in C. Nelson and L. Grossberg (eds), *Marxism and the Interpretation of Culture*, Basingstoke: Macmillan.

—— (1990) 'The political economy of women as seen by a literary critic', in E. Weed (ed.), *Coming to Terms*, London: Routledge.

—— (1996) 'Poststructuralism, marginality, postcoloniality and value', in P. Mongia (ed.), *Contemporary Postcolonial Theory*, London: Arnold.

Sprinker, Michael (ed.), (1992) *Edward Said: A critical reader*. Oxford: Blackwell.

Steeves, Jeffrey (1997) Re-democratisation in Kenya: "Unbounded Politics" and the political trajectory towards national elections', *Journal of Commonwealth and Comparative Studies*, vol. 35, no. 3, pp. 27–52.

Tagg, John (1991) 'Globalization, totalization and the discursive field', in Anthony King (ed.), *Culture, Globalization and the World System*, London: Macmillan.

Tandon, Yash (1991) 'Political economy of struggles for democracy and human rights in Africa', *Economic and Political Weekly*, vol. 26, no. 25, p. 1495.

—— (1996) 'Reclaiming Africa's Agenda', *West Africa*, July, p. 1101.

Taylor, Charles (1990) 'Modes of civil society', *Public Culture*, 3, no. 1, pp. 102–19.

Thomas, Dominic (1997) 'Constructing national and cultural identities in sub-Saharan Francophone Africa', in Stuart Murray (ed.), *Not on Any Map: Essays on postcoloniality and cultural nationalism*, Exeter: Exeter University Press.

Tordoff, William (1967) *Government and Politics in Tanzania*, Nairobi: East African Publishing House.

Vaillant, J.G. (1990) *Black, French, and African: A life of Léopold Sédar Senghor*, Cambridge MA: Harvard University Press.

Valentine, Gill (1996) 'Angels and devils: Moral landscapes of childhood', *Environment and Planning. D: Society and Space*, vol.14, pp. 581–99.

Viswanathan, G. (1987) *Masks of Conquest: Literary study and British rule in India*, London: Faber.

Wa Mutharika, Bingu (1995) *One Africa, One Destiny: Towards democracy, good governance and development*, Harare: Sapes Books.

Wai, Dunstan (1979) 'Human rights in sub-Saharan Africa', in A. Pollis and P. Schwab (eds), *Human Rights: Cultural and ideological perspectives*, New York: Praeger.

Wallerstein, Immanuel (1979) *The Capitalist World Economy*, Cambridge: Cambridge University Press.

—— (1990) 'Culture as the ideological battleground in the modern world system', in Mike Featherstone (ed.), *Global Culture*, London: Sage.

Waters, Malcolm (1995) *Globalization*, London: Routledge.

Wauthier, Claude (1978) *The Literature and Thought of Modern Africa*, London: Heinemann.

Welch, Claude E. (1992) 'The African Commission on Human and Peoples' Rights', *Human Rights Quarterly*, vol. 14, no. 1, pp. 43–61.

Whitehead, Laurence (1997) 'Bowling in the Bronx: The uncivil interstices between civil and political society', in Robert Fine and Shirin Rai (eds), *Civil Society: Democratic perspectives*, London: Frank Cass.

Williams, Adebayo (1997) 'The postcolonial *flaneur* and other fellow-travellers: Conceits for a narrative of redemption', *Third World Quarterly*, vol. 18, no. 5, pp. 821–41.

Wilson, Rob, and Wimal Dissanayake (eds) (1996) *Global/Local: Cultural production and the transnational imaginary*, Durham NC: Duke University Press.

Wiseman, John (1996) *The New Struggle for Democracy in Africa*, Aldershot: Avebury.

Wood, David, and Robert Bernasconi (eds), (1988) *Derrida and Différance*, Evanston IL: Northwestern University Press.

Wood, Ellen Meiksins (1991) 'The uses and abuses of "civil society"', in Ralph Miliband (ed.), *The Socialist Register, 1990*, New York: Monthly Review Press.

World Bank (1981) *Accelerated Development in Sub-Saharan Africa*, Washington DC: World Bank.

—— (1989) *Sub-Saharan Africa: From crisis to sustainable growth*, Washington DC: World Bank.

—— (1997)*World Development Report 1997: The state in a changing world.*, New York, Oxford University Press.

Xie, Shaobo (1996) 'Writing on boundaries: Homi Bhabha's recent essays', *Ariel*, vol. 27, no. 4, pp. 155–66.

Young, Crawford (1981) *Ideology and Development in Africa*, New Haven CT: Yale University Press.

—— (1994) 'In search of civil society', in J.W. Harbeson, Donald Rothchild and Naomi Chazan (eds), *Civil Society and the State in Africa*, Boulder CO: Lynne Rienner.

Young, Robert (1990) *White Mythologies: Writing History and the West*, London: Routledge.

—— (1991) 'Neocolonial times', *Oxford Literary Review*, vol. 13, no. 2, pp. 2–4.

Zartman, William (ed.) (1995) *Collapsed States: The disintegration and restoration of legitimate authority*, Boulder CO: Lynne Rienner.

Zolberg, A. (1966) *Creating Political Order: The party states of West Africa*, Chicago: Rand McNally.

—— (1968) 'The structure of political conflict in the new states of tropical Africa', *American Political Science Review*, vol. 62, no. 1, pp. 70–87.

Index

abolition 21
absolutism 55–6
Achebe, C. 26, 33, 132
active globalisation 128–30
Adotevi, S. 28
Africa: African crises/tragedy 53–4, 133–4; post-colonialism and 8–14
African Charter of Human and Peoples' Rights 92–5
African Commission on Human and Peoples' Rights 94
African National Congress (ANC) 38, 70, 71, 103–4
African socialism 26–7, 57–9
African state *see* state
Africanisation 100
Afro-pessimism 133
Agbese, P.O. 90–1
Agency for International Development 90
Ahluwalia, P. 2, 6, 16, 38, 75, 84, 104, 109, 111, 132–3
Ahmad, A. 2–3, 5, 52
Ajayi, O. 31
Ake, C. 55–6
Alavi, H. 52
Algeria 25, 39
Amnesty International 93, 94
Anderson, B. 45, 67–8, 80, 103, 110, 122
anthropology 28–9
anti-colonial nationalism 80–1
anti-racist racism 24–5, 26
Anyang' Nyong'o, P. 77
Anyinefa, K. 30
Appadurai, A. 122–3
Appiah, K.A. 8–9, 114, 118, 124–5, 128
arbitrariness 55–6
Arendt, H. 45

Armah, A.K. 30
Armstrong, D. 115–16
Arnold, A.J. 28, 29
Arusha Declaration 57–9
Asad, T. 52
Asante state 61
Ashcroft, B. 2, 4, 6, 10, 31, 92, 109; concept of 'Africa' 12–13; meaning of post-colonialism 91; transformation 124; T-shirt 129
Asiwaju, A.I. 69
Associated States 38
Australia 5, 10
authoritarian rule 74–5
Ayittey, G. 132

Bâ, S.W. 24
Balibar, E. 105
Banda, H. 75
Baregu, M. 16, 59
Bayart, J.-F. 62–4, 65, 82–3
Beasley-Murray, J. 52–3
Berg report 54
Berg-Schlosser, D. 59
Bhabha, H. 13–14, 35–6, 71–2, 128
binaries 40; citizen and subject 98–102; human rights 91–2
Birmingham, D. 38
black consciousness 32–3
black man's burden 60–2
Black Renaissance movement 23
Blyden, E. 21–2
borders 69
Bratton, M. 60, 73
Britain 34, 36
Buell, F. 118
Buergenthal, T. 94

Bulhan, H.A. 39
Burchell, S.C. 34

Cabral, A. 35
capitalism 15; civil society 79–81, 82, 85;
    globalisation 114, 125–6; print-
    capitalism 67–8, 78
Carter, P. 5
Catholic Church 127
Certeau, M. de 20
Césaire, A. 18, 21, 22, 23, 26, 27–9, 32
Chabal, P. 64–5, 74, 82, 133
Chamberlain, M.E. 36, 38
Chatterjee, P. 68, 70, 78–81, 123
chiefs 100–1
Childs, P. 15
Chinweizu, O. 51
Chole, E. 77
Christopher, W. 73
cities 128–9
citizenship 19, 97–112; complexities of
    105–8; Mamdani on citizen and subject
    98–102; post-colonial reflections on
    citizenship and subjectivity 108–12;
    problems with the Mamdani thesis 102–5
civil society 18–19, 73–96; in Africa 82–6;
    centrality of 77–86; 'good governance'
    76–7
Civille, J. 58
Cixous, H. 91–2
Clifford, J. 124, 129–30
Coleman, J. 36
collapsed states 53
colonialism 7, 14; Césaire 26, 27, 29;
    French 22, 37–8
colonisation 4–5, 21, 34; oppressed
    consciousness 39–42
commodification of culture 8–9
communication technologies 128–9
communism 29
communitarians 98
community 45; citizenship and
    subjectivity 110–11; civil society 79–81;
    petrol stations and local communities
    126–7
competing ethnicities 10, 68–9
compression of the world 119
Condé, M. 27–8, 130
Connor, W. 68
Conover, P.J. 105–6

Conrad, J. 44
consciousness: black 32–3; critical 43–4;
    global 119; oppressed 39–42; social
    48–9
consumption 114, 125–6
contact zones 17, 128
co-operation 58
corruption 126
creolisation 21, 127, 128
criminalisation of the state 65
crisis of modernity 97–112
critical consciousness 43–4
Crowder, M. 37
cultural rights 87
cultural specificity 87–8
culture 29, 30; commodification 8–9;
    cultural studies 52–3; decolonisation
    40–2, 50–1; and globalisation 117–22;
    hybridity 11–12, 21, 45–6, 66–7, 128;
    national 41–2, 71; transculturation 17–
    18, 66–7, 123–30
customary law 100–1

Daloz, J.-P. 64–5
Damas, L. 22
Dane, R. 39, 49
'Dark Continent' 12–13
Dathorne, O.R. 23
Davidson, B. 21, 38, 60–2, 68, 97
Davies, I. 113
Dayal, S. 7
De Gaulle, C. 38
debt crisis 117–18
Decalo, S. 90
'decentralized despotism' 101, 102, 103,
    104
*Declaration of the Rights of Man and of the
    Citizen* (1789) 105
decolonisation 14, 18, 34–51; Fanon 18,
    35, 38, 39–42, 48–9, 49–50, 71; Said
    18, 35, 42, 43–50
delegitimation 8
democracy 36
democratisation 18–19, 62, 73–96; African
    Charter of Rights 92–5; African
    perspectives on 'good governance' 76–7;
    centrality of civil society 77–86; human
    rights in Africa 86–92; rise of
    authoritarian rule 74–5
Depestre, R. 28, 29

deracialisation 101–2
Derrida, J. 73, 82
despotism 101, 102, 103, 104
detribalisation 101–2
development 11, 101–2; failure of 53–4,
    60–2; and human rights 89–91
developmentalist state 110–11; nationalism
    and 67–71
Diamond, L. 73, 74
Diawara, M. 125–6
difference: between ethnic groups 68–9;
    citizenship and 108
direct rule 99–100
Dirlik, A. 2, 5, 15, 71
discourse of Africa 13
disorder 64–5
Disraeli, B. 52
Dissanayake, W. 121
Donald, J. 107
Donnelly, J. 87
Drachler, J. 32
Dussel, E. 114–15

Eastern Europe 77
economic reform 54–5, 66, 77
economic rights 87
education, political 42
education minute 35–6
Ellis, S. 65
Ellison, R. 20
Emerson, R. 93
emotion 24
Enlightenment project 16–17
epistemological revolution 48
equality, promotion of 58
essential negritude 24
essentialism 28–9, 30; strategic 26
ethnic groups, competing 10, 68–9
ethnoscapes 122–3
Etudiant noir, L' (*The Black Student*) 22, 23
Eurocentric theories 134
Europe 20
European modernity 7–8
extraversion 63–4
Eze, E.C. 17

Fanon, F. 29, 88, 92, 109; decolonisation
    18, 35, 38, 39–42, 48–9, 49–50, 71;
    negritude 25–6, 30
financescapes 122–3

Foucault, M. 2, 43, 44, 63, 106, 110; state
    and civil society 69–70
'founding fathers' 75
France 22, 23, 34, 37–8
Franco-African union 26
French Communist Party 29
French Community 38
French Union 38
Friedman, S. 81, 85
Frobenius, L. 28

Gandhi, M. 20, 21, 36
Gary, I. 55
Gates, H.L. 39, 42
genocide 132
Ghana 36–7, 56–7
Ghandi, L. 6–7, 67, 124
Ghosh, A. 129–30
global consciousness 119
global–local interactions 12, 123–4, 126–7
global mass culture 119
global monoculture 121
globalisation 5–6, 19, 113–31; culture and
    117–22; and inflections 124–30; post-
    colonialism and 122–4; theories of
    113–16
'glocalization' 120–1
'good governance' 11; African perspectives
    on 76–7
Goonatilake, S. 120
governance 38, 54–5; good 11, 76–7
governmentality 63, 69, 106
Gramsci, A. 2
Green, R.H. 90
Greenstein, R. 28

Hall, S. 6, 119
Hannerz, U. 127
Hegel, G.W.F. 79
Held, D. 114, 115
heroes 75
Hibou, B. 65
Hindess, B. 105, 106–7
Hirst, P. 116
historical negritude 24
historicity 62–4
Hobsbawm, E. 82
Hodge, B. 3
Hoogvelt, A. 117–18
hooks, b. 97

Hountondji, P. 28–9
Howard, R. 87
Hughes, R. 5
human rights 19, 86–96; in Africa 86–92; African Charter of Rights 92–5; politics of 88–91; post-colonial theory and 91–2; universal rights vs cultural specificity 87–8
Hutcheon, L. 2, 3
Hutchful, E. 83
Hutu 68
hybridity 11–12, 21, 45–6, 66–7, 128
Hyden, G. 59, 60, 76, 104

Ibrahim, J. 77
identity 109; globalisation 19; multiple identities 11–12, 14, 45–6, 120; national liberation and 45–7; nationalism and 68–9; negritude and nativism 18, 20–33
ideoscapes 122–3
Ignatieff, M. 68, 77–8
Illife, J. 130
independence 34–5, 38, 50, 70; *see also* decolonisation
India 9–10, 35–6, 104
Indian Opinion 36
indirect rule 35, 99–101, 104
inflections 17–18; globalisation and 124–30
Inkatha Freedom Party (IFP) 103–4
institutions, crisis of 61–2
integral state 60, 84
intellectual traditions 9–10
intellectuals 109–10
interdisciplinarity 15
International Commission of Jurists 93
International Monetary Fund (IMF) 11, 83; SAPs 54–5, 59, 86, 90–1, 118
international society 116
Irele, A. 22, 23, 24, 28, 33

Jacoby, R. 15
Jameson, F. 2
Janmohamed, A. 40
Japan 61
Joseph, R. 74

Kaplan, A. 106
Karlstrom, B. 59
Kasfir, N. 83–5

Kaunda, K. 75
Keane, J. 85
Kenya 16, 37, 84, 111
Kenyatta, J. 75
King, A. 118–19
Kiswahili 128
knowledge 43
Koshy, S. 87
Kruks, S. 25

Lacan, J. 35
language 20, 21
Laswell, H.D. 106
law: customary 100–1; national 94
Lawrence, P. 54
Lazarus, N. 41
Leys, C. 53, 61, 62, 64
liberalisation 54–5, 66, 77
liberation, national *see* national liberation
likeness/similarity 28
Lionnet, F. 17
Lister, R. 108
Lloyd, D. 53
local–global interactions 12, 123–4, 126–7
localisation 119–22
Locke, J. 78–9
longue-durée 62–4
Loomba, A. 4, 7
Lukacs, G. 48, 49

Macaulay, T. 35
McClintock, A. 3, 5, 82
McGrew, A. 114, 115
McLaren, P. 2
Macmillan, H. 37
Madsen, R. 121
Mahmud, S. 88
Makumbe, J.M. 83
Mamdani, M. 19, 60, 70, 77, 97–105; citizen and subject 98–102; problems with the Mamdani thesis 102–5
Mandela, N. 38, 75
Manzo, K. 133–4
market-places 125–6
Markovitz, I.L. 26, 85
Marrouchi, M. 47
Marx, K. 39, 80
Marxism 6, 29
Masolo, D.A. 14
mass culture, global 119

Mazrui, A. 75, 121
Mbembe, A. 135
media 125
mediascapes 122–3
Mezu, S.O. 32–3
Michel, M. 108–9
Migdal, J. 85
Miller, T. 107–8, 110
mimicry 35–6
mind, decolonisation of 38, 39–42
Minouge, M. 89
Mishra, V. 3
Miyoshi, M. 124
modernisation 11, 97; nation-building 68
modernists 98
modernity 2, 121; crisis of 97–112;
    European 7–8; and the nation-state 18,
    52–72; post-colonialism, African state
    and 66–71; world system and limitations
    of 114–15
Moi, D.A. 84
Molloy, J. 89
monoculture, global 121
Montesquieu, C. de S. 78–9
'Mother Africa' 31
Mouffe, C. 107
Mphahlele, E. 20, 29, 30, 31
Mudimbe, V.Y. 22, 127, 133
multi-party elections 74
multiple identities 11–12, 14, 45–6, 120

Nandy, A. 38, 111
narcissism 68–9
nation-state: globalisation and 122–3;
    modernity and 18, 52–72; *see also* state
national culture 41–2, 71
national law 94
national liberation 18, 34–51; Fanon and
    oppressed consciousness 39–42; Said
    and resistance 43–8; strategy towards
    49–50
nationalism: anti-colonial 80–1; and the
    post-colonial developmentalist state 67–
    71
Native Authorities 101, 103
nativism 31–2, 123
negritude 18, 20–33; Césaire 18, 21, 22,
    23, 26, 27–9, 32; critiques of 30–2;
    Senghor 18, 21, 22, 23–7, 28–9, 33
neo-colonialism 7, 9, 38

'new' Africans 21–2
new internationalism 12–13
Ngugi wa Thiong'o 44
Nixon, R. 82
Nkosi, L. 30
Nkrumah, K. 37, 38, 56–7, 75, 88
non-governmental organisations (NGOs) 55
novels 8
Nugent, P. 69
Nursey-Bray, P. 104
Nyerere, J. 75, 104; African socialism 16,
    57–9; and human rights 88–9, 89–90

Ochieng, W.R. 37
Ogede, O.S. 31
Ogot, B.A. 37
one-party state 56–7, 83, 111
oppressed consciousness 39–42
Organisation of African Unity (OAU) 69;
    African Charter of Rights 92–3, 94
Other, self and 44–7

Pan Africanism 36, 137
Paolini, A. 114, 121
parastatal organizations 58, 59
Parekh, B. 50
Paris 22, 130
Parry, B. 25, 32, 109
particularism 120
partition 69
passive globalisation 128–30
patrimonial state 60, 64
Paul, J. 93
peoples' rights 92–5
personal rule 74–5
petrol stations 126–7
Pieterse, J.N. 50, 117
planning 70
political education 42
politics: 'of the belly' 63–4; disorder as a
    political instrument 64–5; post-
    colonialism's lack of engagement with
    15–17
post-colonialism 1–19, 132–5; and Africa
    8–14; beyond literary studies 14–18;
    citizenship and subjectivity 108–12; and
    globalisation 122–4; human rights 91–2;
    modernity and the African state 66–71;
    post-structuralism, postmodernism and
    1–8

postmodernism 1–8
post-structuralism 1–8
Potholm, C. 56–7
power 43, 69, 72
Prakash, G. 5–6, 81, 114
Pratt, M.L. 17, 21, 66, 128
Présence Africaine 23
print-capitalism 67–8, 78
public opinion 78

racism: anti-racist 24–5, 26; colonial state
    100
Radhakrishnan, R. 5
Ranger, T. 118
Rawls, J. 89
reason 24
redistribution 100
Reed, J. 24
regionalism 76
Reno, W. 66
resistance 34, 109; Said and 43–9; *see also*
    decolonisation
Rhodes, C. 132
Richburg, K. 132
rights: human *see* human rights; peoples'
    92–5; subjective 78–9
Robertson, R. 114, 119, 120–1
Rodrik, D. 116
rural–urban division 102
Rwanda 68, 132

Sachikonye, L. 76
Said, E. 1–2, 7, 11, 67, 72, 111, 123, 131;
    Australia 5; decolonisation 18, 35, 42,
    43–50; imperialism 10; intellectuals
    109–10; location of theory in the world
    6; nativism 31–2; and resistance 43–9;
    worldliness 17
Salih, T. 44
Sandbrook, R. 53
Sardar, Z. 20
Sartre, J.-P. 23, 24–5, 46–7
Saussure, F. de 91
Scott, D. 15–16, 69, 70
Scott, J. 59
'scramble for Africa' 14, 21, 34
Sekyi-Otu, A. 39, 42
self: and other 44–7; universal 49
self-determination 36
self-governance 110

self-reliance 58
Senegal 26, 33
Senghor, L.S. 75; negritude 18, 21, 22, 23–
    7, 28–9, 33
Seshadri-Crooks, K. 8
shared responsibility 134
Shivji, I.G. 91
Shohat, E. 4, 50
Siegler, R. 59
sign value 129
similarity 28
Simone, A. 129
Slater, D. 134
slavery 21
social consciousness 48–9
social movements 76
social rights 87
socialism 15–16; African 26–7, 57–9
society-centrism 98
South Africa 38, 70, 71, 100, 103–4
sovereignty, state 54–5, 115–16
Soviet Union 16, 121
Soyinka, W. 26, 30–1
space, global 114
Spivak, G.C. 7, 8, 26
Sprinker, M. 49–50
Stam, R. 50
state 18, 52–72; African socialism 57–9;
    African studies and conceptualisation of
    the African state 55–66; black man's
    burden 60–2; and civil society 76–81;
    criminalisation of the state 65; crisis of
    the African state 53–5;
    developmentalist state 67–71, 110–11;
    disorder as a political instrument 64–5;
    integral state 60, 84; *longue durée* 62–4;
    one-party state 56–7, 83, 111;
    patrimonial state 60, 64; post-
    colonialism, modernity and African
    state 66–71; sovereignty 54–5, 115–16;
    warlord state 65–6
state-centrism 98
strategic essentialism 26
strong state 62
Structural Adjustment Programmes (SAPs)
    54–5, 59, 86, 90–1, 118
subjective rights 78–9
subjectivity 19, 97–112; citizen and subject
    98–102; complexities of 105–8; post-
    colonial reflections on citizenship and

108–12; problems with the Mamdani thesis 102–5
symbiosis 26
syncretism 51

Tagg, J. 117
Tandon, Y. 55, 90
Tanzania 16, 57–9, 89, 104, 111
Tanzania African National Union (TANU) 57, 58, 89, 104
Taylor, C. 78, 79
technoscapes 122–3
Tempest, The (Shakespeare) 44–5
Thomas, D. 86
Thomas, P. 53
Thompson, G. 116
Touré, S. 75
towns 40
traditionalism 76
transculturation 17–18, 66–7, 123–30
transformation 124–30
tribalism 101–2
Truman, H.S. 11
T-shirts 129
Tutsi 68
Tutu, D. 34

Uganda 91
Ujamaa 58
United States (US) 11, 90
Universal Declaration of Human Rights (1948) 87, 88, 93
universal rights 87–8
universal self 49
universalism 120
urban–rural division 102

Vaillant, J.G. 25, 27

van de Walle, N. 60, 73
Vico, G. 48
villagisation 58–9
violence 37, 48–9
'voyage in' 45, 47–8, 49

Wa Mutharika, B. 76
Wake, C. 24
Wallerstein, I. 117
warlord state 65–6
Waters, M. 114
Wauthier, C. 30
weak state 62, 66
Welch, C.E. 94
Whitehead, L. 84
Williams, A. 6–7, 9–10
Williams, P. 15
Wilson, R. 121
Wolin, S. 73
women 31
Wood, E.M. 85
World Bank 11, 77, 83; SAPS 54–5, 59, 86, 90–1, 118
world systems theory 117–18
worldliness 17
writing back 45, 47–8, 49

Xie, S. 6

Yeats, W.B. 31–2
Yoruba Man with a Bicycle 124–5
Young, C. 60, 84
Young, R. 3–4, 10, 134

Zambia 89
Zartman, W. 53
Zimbabwe 38
Zulu migrant workers 103